Archduke of Sarajevo

The Romance and Tragedy of Franz Ferdinand of Austria

Archduke of Sarajevo

The Romance and Tragedy of Franz Ferdinand of Austria

GORDON BROOK-SHEPHERD

LITTLE, BROWN AND COMPANY · BOSTON · TORONTO

LIBRARY OF CONGRESS CATALOGUE NUMBER 84-81201

FIRST AMERICAN EDITION

Maps by Brian Elkins

MV

PRINTED IN THE UNITED STATES OF AMERICA

Contents

List of Illustrations

Between pages 64 and 65

Franz Ferdinand's father, Archduke Karl Ludwig,
    and his mother, Maria Annunziata.
Emperor Franz Joseph towards the end of his reign.
Archduke Franz Ferdinand surrounded by the gamekeepers and
    beaters who had provided him with a 'slaughter' of chamois.
Franz Ferdinand's first tiger, shot in 1893 in India.
Countess Sophie Nostitz.
Sophie in demure attendance.
Franz Ferdinand and Sophie on the tennis court at Pressburg.
A coded postcard sent by the Archduke to Sophie.

Between pages 128 and 129

An artist's impression of the renunciation ceremony held
    in the Hofburg.
The wedding in Reichstadt.
Married bliss: the honeymoon.
The 'official' picture of the newly-married pair.
Franz Ferdinand with his first child, named Sophie after her mother.
Part of the famous rose gardens at Konopischt.
Janaczek, the former gamekeeper who rose to be the head of
    the Archduke's household.

Between pages 224 and 225

The family: Franz Ferdinand, Sophie and the three children.
Emperor William of Germany on one of his many shooting visits
    to Konopischt.
Emperor William being greeted by the Archduke's children on
    what was to be his last visit to Konopischt.
The last message the Archduke sent to his daughter from Sarajevo.
The Archduke and Sophie walking down the steps of Sarajevo
    Town Hall minutes before their assassination.
The sarcophagi of Franz Ferdinand and Sophie in the crypt at
    Artstetten.
Artstetten Castle.   vii

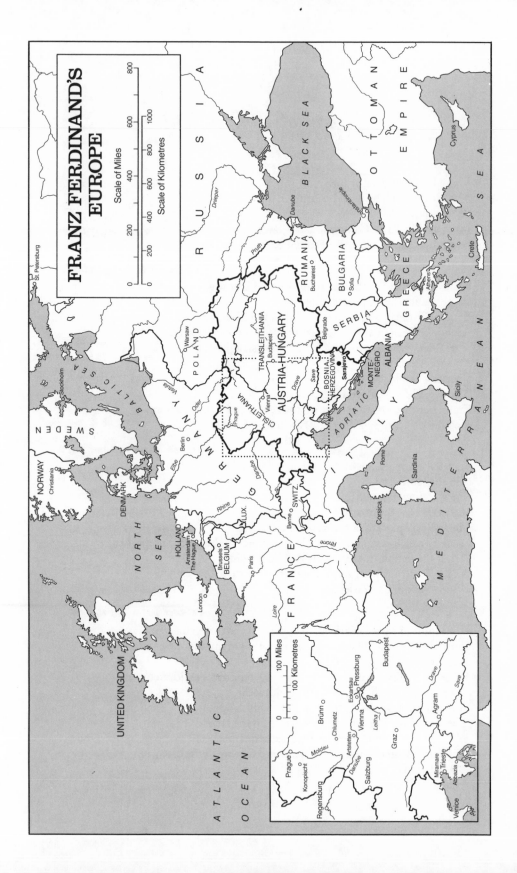

THE HOUSE OF HABSBURG-LOTHRINGEN

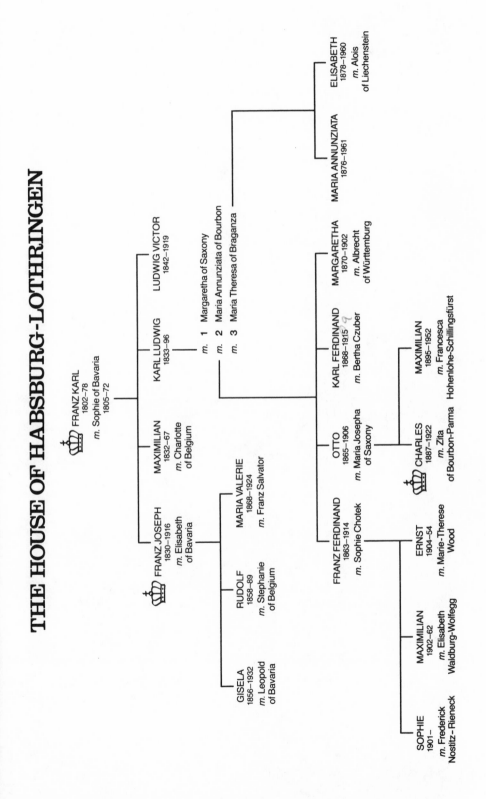

Foreword

LOOKING BACK, it seems always to have been on the cards that I
would one day tackle an English biography of Archduke Franz
Ferdinand. In post-war Vienna, where I lived for nearly fifteen
years, first as an army officer and then as a foreign correspondent, I met his two sons, Duke Max and Prince Ernst Hohenberg,
both of whom had seen the inside of Hitler's concentration
camps. The town apartment where I lived was almost opposite
the Archduke's Belvedere Palace, whose park was one of my
favourite post-luncheon strolls. At one time or another I have
visited nearly all the other castles and shooting lodges Franz
Ferdinand and his morganatic wife Sophie once lived in, and
have indeed had the good fortune to shoot over some of the same
ground. It was, I think, his grandson, Georg, the present head of
the family, who first put into my head the idea of writing about
the Archduke, with the remark (which must have been made
over twenty years ago) that so much of the inaccurate nonsense
one read about his grandfather could easily be put right if
someone objective would only take the trouble to consult the
family archives, the family friends and above all his daughter
Sophie, the one child of that controversial marriage who was
then, and still is, alive. (Prince Ernst had died in 1954 and Duke
Max in 1962.)

Half a dozen other books, some of them on Austrian themes,
have got in the way since; but when I finally took up the project
it was these family sources – strangely neglected by Franz
Ferdinand's Austrian biographers – which I concentrated on,

alongside the substantial amount of official documentation. As a result it has been possible to find, even after a gap of nearly three generations, a few new insights into his political thinking and much new material about Franz Ferdinand the man – above all, Franz Ferdinand the passionate wooer against all the odds, and devoted husband once he had won his prize.

I have to thank first and foremost his daughter, the present Countess Sophie Nostitz (who was an alert and intelligent thirteen-year-old when the disastrous news from Sarajevo was broken to her) for many hours of enjoyable conversation during several visits to her peaceful Salzburg villa. They provided not only a detailed picture of Franz Ferdinand as a father and family man and much new material on the famous romance, but also a few unpublished documents and letters of a political nature.

I had the lucky advantage over previous biographers that while my own book was being researched and written, the Hohenbergs were putting together their own 'Franz Ferdinand Museum' at Artstetten, the family castle near the Danube in Lower Austria where the Archduke and his wife lie buried. I have to thank Count Romeè d'Harambure (husband of Princess Anna Hohenberg) and his wife for their help and hospitality on my several visits there; also Count Vladimir Aichelburg (descendant of one of the Archduke's tutors) who has done much of the work on the museum exhibits and in doing so has unearthed some new facets of the Archduke's life and times. The Archduke's official papers are deposited as restricted documents in the Vienna Haus Hof und Staatsarchiv as the 'Nachlass Franz Ferdinand', and I am grateful to the present Duke of Hohenberg (the same man who first interested me in his grandfather) for permission to see them. It was a long business to go through them and make one's own selection of material and I could never have completed it in time without the sterling assistance of Frau Annelise Schulz, my long-time research assistant in Vienna.

To all this I have added many enquiries among my own Austrian friends whose families were closely linked with the Archduke. Often, nothing of any interest could be produced – either because nothing was ever put on paper or, more often alas, because everything was destroyed. But there were a few interesting finds. Thus, Count Karl Draskovich produced the personal diary and other contemporary writings of his uncle, Count Adalbert Sternberg. Though 'Monchi', as he was universally known, was not the most level-headed of witnesses, he was for years on close terms with the Archduke and has some interesting anecdotes, both private and political, to contribute. Another old friend, 'Goldy' Mathé, is the grand-daughter of Prince Montenuovo, Court Chamberlain to the Emperor Franz Joseph and the Archduke's implacable protocol adversary in the struggle for his beloved wife's status in society. From what little escaped the destruction of her grandfather's papers, Frau Mathé has unearthed a hitherto unknown document bearing on that struggle, namely evidence of Sophie's first official appearance at the Viennese Court.

Countess Maria Fedrigotti, whose father, Count van der Straten, was one of the Archduke's aides, has found a number of old game-book records showing the Archduke's prowess as a marksman at various shoots in the Austrian Monarchy and in England, on his one sporting visit to this country in November of 1913. I am, in this connection, also grateful to the Duke of Portland for providing me with the account his ancestor wrote of the Archduke's stay at Welbeck Abbey during that visit.

The Royal Archives at Windsor contain, in the diaries and letters of King George V and Queen Mary, much interesting comment on the four days which the Archduke and his wife spent at Windsor Castle earlier that same month – an invitation which marked the crowning triumph of Franz Ferdinand's campaign to win for Sophie due recognition abroad. Barely six months later, Queen Mary was writing touching letters about their deaths. The Windsor archives also provide much of interest about official preparations for the Archduke's progress around India during his world tour of 1892–3, preparations which were not without controversy. By gracious permission of Her Majesty the Queen, I have been given access to all these papers. I must also thank Sir Robin Mackworth-Young and Miss Jane Langton for the unfailing courtesy and efficiency they displayed on this as on all previous occasions when I have asked the Royal Archives for their assistance.

As for the Archduke's own court, there is, happily, one survivor of that long-vanished world of the Hofburg, Schönbrunn and Belvedere. When, on 21 October 1911, the nineteen-year-old Princess Zita of Bourbon-Parma married Archduke Charles of Austria, she acquired the Emperor Franz Joseph as great-uncle and Franz Ferdinand – to whom her husband was next in line for the throne – as her 'Uncle Franzi'. From then until Sarajevo, this vivacious and highly intelligent Princess saw at first hand the closing years of Franz Ferdinand's life – all his domestic problems as well as political ones and the endless question marks they raised – not as a half-informed courtier, but as a member of the ruling family itself.

Ever since researching, twenty years ago, a biography of her late husband, the Emperor Charles (as he duly became in November 1916, in the middle of the Great War), I have been paying fairly regular annual visits to the ex-Empress Zita and, inevitably, Franz Ferdinand figured large in our conversations long before I embarked on this present book. Could he, as sovereign, have 'saved' his empire (which meant, in practice, delaying its dissolution)? Could he have preserved the peace, not just by avoiding his own murder, but by helping to change European alignments? What were the keys to his enigmatic character? What were he and Sophie like as people, as viewed by someone who spent countless hours in their company, both under the chandeliers of Vienna and in the seclusion of remote shooting-boxes? The answers are sprinkled through this book and give some insights that even the Archduke's own contemporaries were probably unaware of, so small and closely-sealed was the Habsburg family circle. I will always be grateful to this last representative of the old European ruling order, who has become a very cherished figure in my own life, for all the memorable days spent with her.

Hungary was the Archduke's *bête-noire*. He saw the proud and assertive Magyar nation, partners with the Austrians in the Dual Monarchy, not as a twin pillar of the empire, but as a destructive force underneath it which, unless controlled, would bring the whole structure crashing down with its chauvinism and resistance to democratic reform. Much has been written on this theme by German-language historians but I wanted a view from Budapest, even today's Communist Budapest, which is, incidentally, rediscovering so much of the old Magyar national pride. My old friend there, Dr Istvan Gàl, undertook to help and supplied me with a stream of ideas and papers on Franz Ferdinand's time. Last year, a few days after sending yet another epistle on the subject, he died, a victim of arthritis and, even more perhaps, of the sufferings he went through during the Stalinist persecutions. He was a great intellectual presence, a great Hungarian patriot, and a great friend of this country.

Finally, though he may look a little odd in this distinguished company, I must mention Sam, the black, semi-wild farm cat who adopted me just before I started on the Archduke and stayed with me in my Chilterns hide-out until nearly the end. Though of little formal education, Sam took to the literary scene with gusto. He would nestle in a pile of books at the far end of the large refectory table where I write and would then purr for hours on end, until announcing, with a sudden wail, that the moment had come for both of us to have a drink. His sense of timing on these occasions was always immaculate, as was the manner of his departure. As the book was nearing completion, he slept it out quietly, without fuss or nuisance, on his favourite patch of dawn sunshine in the gardens over which he had presided for so long. He now has his place there, and he deserves it also here, for he was the perfect, and quite irreplaceable, author's familiar. I am rather glad that he never lived to learn, from those final chapters, that the very last thing the Archduke shot in his insatiable sportsman's life tally of 272,511 head of game was, of all things, a wild cat, spotted on a Sunday morning stroll around his Bohemian estates.

GORDON BROOK-SHEPHERD
Hughs, Hambleden
Oxon.

CHAPTER ONE

---- ✖ ----

War Museum

UNDER A LONG RECTANGULAR VITRINE in Vienna's Museum of Military History, the uniform is spread out for inspection like a crumpled butterfly. From one side, grey sunshine filters in through crepe curtains draped around iron-barred windows. Directly overhead, a pale yellow light shines down from a crystal chandelier; a closer look reveals that the top section is shaped like a hollow crown. The colours in the vitrine stand out under this blend of drab illuminations: the bright green plumes of the Archduke's hat, the blue cloth of the coat with the three gold stars of a Cavalry General mounted in triangles on either side of the collar band. So too do the dried bloodstains, scattered between the buttons like red dust, and the slashes in the tunic itself. The biggest of these are the two diagonal cuts across the chest and up the left arm, meeting in a jagged V at the shoulder. They were the first to be made by the doctors who rushed to the murder scene and who assumed, from the flow of blood, that the wound lay somewhere near the heart. The third and smaller cut is down the back of the collar, which they split open when they realized that it was an artery in the neck which the bullet had severed.

Roped off along the wall opposite the windows stands the borrowed automobile which suddenly became a hearse – Count Harrach's *Graef und Stift*, a so-called '*Doppel Phaeton*' or open tourer, with its huge outside handbrakes, thin studded tyres and the dented number plate, A111-118. From the running board at the front, the black and yellow Habsburg standard is still folded limply against the perpendicular windscreen. Behind the chauffeur's seat a hole is ringed in white in the passenger door. This marks the path of the other bullet which fatally wounded in the stomach the Cavalry General's morganatic wife, Duchess Sophie Hohenberg, and so brought to an end – among many other things – one of the most extraordinary royal love stories which the twentieth century would witness.

If that one white-ringed bullet hole symbolizes the tragedy of the Archduke's personal life, a portrait of him on a stand next to the motorcar sums up the frustrations of his political existence. It is an oil painting, executed by one Wilhelm Vita, which shows the sitter resplendent in the uniform and orders which he would have worn, and could only have worn, as Austrian Emperor. The Archduke looks across at Count Harrach's open tourer with that calm, enigmatic gaze of his and just the trace of a resigned smile, as though admitting that he was tempting providence perhaps a bit too much by giving Mr Vita that commission.

Along the opposite side wall, under the windows, the glass cases include mementos of what never took place on that 28 June 1914: an invitation, for example, to the Archduke's nine-course dinner, which was to have wound up the formal part of his stay in Sarajevo. As so often in their married life (though here with every justification, for it was basically a military function), Sophie's name is not included. But the music programme alongside the seating plan hints that someone may have had the charming idea of suggesting her presence. Among the rousing march numbers to be played was a very unmilitary waltz by Chladek called '*Ohne Lieb' kein Leben*', which means 'No life without love'.

Suddenly, the hush of the Sarajevo chamber is broken by a fast-approaching wave of sound, a babel of young Austrian voices. A group of some sixty schoolchildren aged between fourteen and sixteen crowd into the room, accompanied by two of their class teachers and one of the official museum guides. The children flock around the long vitrine under the chandelier and point down excitedly at the bloodstained blue uniform. It makes

2

an odd contrast to their own T-shirts – with motifs ranging from the faces of pop stars to the names of mass holiday resorts on the Italian Adriatic – which are reflected in the glass case as they bend over it.

The chattering stops as the guide runs quickly through his usual routine (even to the extent of starting with 'Ladies and Gentlemen'). He explains about the cuts in the uniform and the bullet hole in the car. Then, as he winds up, he turns to the two teachers and, at a signal, the three of them intone, 'And this was the start of the . . .?' They wait for the children to chime in with the required response, '. . . the First World War'.

Satisfied, the guide leads them on with the words, 'Good, and now I will show you the biggest gun which was used in that war.' And off they go, along a narrow corridor to an artillery hall in the centre of which a huge Austrian thirty-eight centimetre Howitzer ('Firing Capacity: one shot of seven hundred and forty kilograms every five minutes, with range of fifteen thousand metres') points its snub nose upwards to the window and the blue Vienna summer sky.

Inevitably, there were many things the guide had to leave out from his brisk Sarajevo commentary. There would have been little point, as well as too little time, in going more deeply into the tragedy. To the children this was, after all, the remote affair of their grandparents – linked to them, yet apart from them, just as the single-headed eagle of their neutral little Republic stands linked yet apart from the double-headed eagle of the sprawling empire which those two bullets were ultimately to tear apart.

But there was at least one historical irony which the guide himself may not have grasped. That narrow corridor down which he hurried his charges is a gallery of paintings from the 1914–18 war, with the collective title 'From Hurrah! to the field of corpses'. The first of the 'Hurrah' pictures shows a very handsome Austrian officer on horseback, sword upraised, eyes shining, leading his troops into battle – seemingly the very embodiment of the happy soldier-patriot, confident, as they all were in all armies, of early victory. The caption identifies him as Colonel Alexander Brosch von Aarenau, commander of the 2nd

Regiment of the élite *Tiroler Kaiserjaeger*.

What the caption did not add was that for more than five years before the war that same officer had headed the so-called 'Military Chancery' of the murdered Archduke, which was in fact the Heir-Apparent's Shadow Cabinet, planning the form and style of the empire he was waiting impatiently to rule and trying to influence its course in the meantime. What perhaps even the guide could not have added was that the gleam in the officer's eyes, as bright as his upraised sword, betokened not so much the glory of battle as a desperate wish for death. Colonel Brosch's comrades-in-arms swore that he deliberately sought his end on the Galician front, and duly met it at Rawa Ruska on 6 September 1914 when the war was barely a month old. And the reason, they said, that he wanted to die was his conviction that without his late master the Habsburg empire had lost its own last chance to live.

Could the murdered Archduke have preserved, even for a generation, that rickety multinational state which Sarajevo did indeed doom to destruction, along with two other great European empires? Had he survived the wound, even badly injured, could he have helped to prevent the war and the rain of bullets which went on to kill or maim some twenty million others? And had he reigned, and reigned in peacetime, what would have happened to his beloved 'Sopherl' and, above all, to the two sons she bore him?

These questions can never be answered. Yet they will always be asked; and the sum of the clues to the answers lies in a story we can tell, the romantic tragedy which was his truncated life.

CHAPTER TWO

---◁▷---

A Strange Young Habsburg

CONSIDERING WHAT the world had in store for him, and he for the world, the entry into it of the infant Franz Ferdinand was remarkably inconspicuous. Indeed, outside the gilded stockade of Habsburg court society, few took any note at all of the birth. It was a great event only in the family itself. His father, the Archduke Karl Ludwig, younger brother of the reigning Emperor Franz Joseph, had already suffered a tragic first marriage with a Saxon Princess, Margaretha, who had died in 1858, within two years of the wedding and without bearing him a child. Karl Ludwig's second choice for a bride, after a proper interval of mourning and a careful study of the eligible ladies, had been Princess Maria Annunziata of the Bourbon house of Sicily, whom he married in Venice four years later. Yet his new wife was extremely frail in health, so frail indeed that the couple decided to spend the first year of their married life at Gorizia in the mild air of the south before risking the relatively raw climate of Graz, the provincial capital of Styria, where they rented the Herberstein Palace in the Sackgasse. It was here, at 7.15 a.m. on 18 December 1863, that Maria Annunziata was delivered of their first-born, who not only seemed a healthy infant in every respect but was a boy into the bargain: a veritable Christmas present for the father.

The infant was christened Franz Ferdinand Karl Ludwig Joseph Maria, the first name, a good Habsburg one, no doubt partly in homage to the Emperor. The second was certainly in memory of his maternal grandfather, Ferdinand II of Sicily, the

5

famous 'Re Bomba', so-called because, in the revolutionary year 1848, he had not hesitated to bombard both his principal cities of Messina and Naples to cling on to his threatened throne. (As will be seen, the infant was to inherit more than the name from that Sicilian volcano.) Beginning with Bourbon and Habsburg, the noblest Catholic blood of all Europe flowed through the baby's veins. A genealogist[1] later traced for him no fewer than 2047 reigning or princely ancestors going back through eleven generations: they included seventy-one German or German-Austrian, twenty Polish, eight French, seven Italian and six miscellaneous.

Not, of course, that there was anything particularly remarkable about that in a Europe where royal cousin was constantly obliged to marry royal cousin just to keep the reigning blood blue, however thin this blood might be turning in the process. And in any case, during his early life, no lineage could have been distinguished enough to put Franz Ferdinand in the limelight, if only because his own father had deliberately withdrawn from it. Karl Ludwig's sole experience of public office had been his appointment as Governor of Tyrol in 1855, when aged only twenty-two. He was not disappointed when, just six years later, constitutional changes barred him, as an Archduke, from state service; the new anti-clerical, anti-monarchist spirit surging up south of the Brenner Pass was anyway anathema to his ultra-conservative, ultra-religious soul. Since then, he had lived the life of an imperial country squire, patronizing charities, opening exhibitions and living above all for the family that had now, at last, started to grow around him. A second son, Otto, was born, also in Graz, on 21 April 1865; a third, Ferdinand Karl, on 27 December 1868 in Vienna, where the father had bought a large town mansion in the Favoritenstrasse; and a fourth child and first daughter, Margarethe, on 13 May 1870 at Artstetten, a castle nestling just north of the Danube in a sleepy corner of Lower Austria which was one of Karl Ludwig's country properties.

It is at Artstetten that, among many other mementos, the best portrayal of Karl Ludwig, a contemporary oil painting, still hangs today. It shows him looking rather like a benevolent walrus with his narrow forehead, piercing blue eyes and long white moustache drooping downwards to two ragged points. But the essence of the man as he sits there puffing contentedly at his pipe, with row upon row of relatives' photographs lined up on the desk behind him, is of the family man *par excellence*, the man for whom, in the end, carpet slippers would always feel better on his feet than polished boots.

He had to struggle, nonetheless, to keep his married bliss going. A year after giving birth to their fourth child, Maria Annunziata's frail health – the illness was consumption – claimed her at last. Saddened but undaunted, Karl Ludwig for the third time scoured the European horizons for a suitable royal bride, and his choice now fell on Maria Theresa of the Portuguese house of Braganza, who was more than twenty years his junior. This Portuguese princess (who was to bear him two more children, both of them daughters) was not only the prettiest of his three wives, she was also by far the most remarkable, a gentle creature of such transparent goodness that she could walk unscathed across the burning coals of Viennese court intrigues, winning, as she did so, the increasing respect and affection of the Emperor himself. As for Karl Ludwig's four bereaved children, they had found a stepmother who quickly became a true mother to all of them, so that Franz Ferdinand, who was at the sensitive age of nine-and-a-half years when his father remarried, never suffered from the slightest lack of affection.

This family background needs to be painted in precisely because nothing in it (not even, as yet, grandfather 'Re Bomba') explains the strange character which the boy developed. His parents had all the time and all the devotion in the world for their children. Moreover, the family routine might have been designed for boyhood happiness, the weeks in Vienna being usually outnumbered by months spent in the countryside, either at Artstetten, or at the nearby Danube castle of Persenbeug, or at Wartholz, at the foot of the Rax mountains, where, in 1872, Archduke Karl Ludwig had built himself a large but unpreten-

7

tious shooting lodge surrounded by lush green forests. Nor does there seem to have been any friction or jealousy between the three brothers and their sister and half-sisters. Indeed, as children, the brothers themselves got on famously – though it was to be another story later on as most of them went through agonizing traumas in their own personal lives. Yet despite this near-idyllic existence, Franz Ferdinand became a child apart, introspective sometimes to the point of brooding, and always bottling up those feelings to which the others gave free rein. They all grew to wondering where on earth 'Franzi', or 'Franzl' as he was known in the family, could have got it from.

He also seems to have been mentally a late developer. The grown man was to show a rapacious appetite for knowledge of all sorts and for art in particular. Even more pronounced was his incisive mind and natural gift for words (albeit many of them laced with biting sarcasm) which, to that degree, was rare in any Habsburg archduke. Yet even when turned fourteen and already entered on the rolls as a lieutenant in the imperial army, the scores of letters which he wrote to his adored stepmother look more like jottings from the nursery. Almost every item of news is told in flat, unrelated perspective, so that receiving the Order of the Golden Fleece, the Monarchy's highest decoration, reserved exclusively for Catholic princes, reads much the same as donning his first pair of long trousers, an excitement in the life of all youths of all classes. There is however a jumbled passage in one of these letters, dated 24 April 1878, which points to the man of the future. Describing a visit just paid to the Villa Wartholz he writes:

> Things are blooming quite well in the glasshouses and some canary chicks are hatching out there while the others are already in the woods. There is a whole bush of blossoming roses near the *volière*, and among them one which is completely green. The roebuck has an odd set of antlers. One side is quite regular but the other is much shorter as the top part has been thrust back by three of the points . . .[2]

Hunting and gardening – and especially the shooting of stag and deer and the cultivation of roses – were to become two of the greatest passions of Franz Ferdinand's life.

It is quite likely that, as with many another royal princeling throughout Europe sweating out his early education with a series of private tutors, the young Archduke was put off learning by the sheer weight of books piled on him and by the fact that he was expected to master them without the stimulus of a school classroom. Of his many instructors (who included, over the years, six counts and one baron), two stand out. The first was Professor Onno Klopp, who taught him history with a conservative Catholic fanaticism which only such a convert from Protestantism and a refugee from the Hanoverian court could muster. The second and totally contrasting influence was that of Prelate Godfried Marshall, a genial, liberal and worldly priest well known in the salons of Vienna, who looms up as a sort of Friar Tuck alongside the passionately earnest professor.

One very unusual – indeed almost unheard of – event broke the predictable pattern of this archducal childhood. On 20 November 1875, when Franz Ferdinand was not quite twelve years old, he acquired both a great fortune and a new name on the death of a distant kinsman, Franz V, Duke of Modena, Massu, Carrara and Guastella. The full background, hitherto unrelated,[3] is as strange as the event itself. A year or so before his death, the Duke, whose line was dying out for lack of any male heir, had approached Karl Ludwig with a startling request. He would bequeath his entire fortune to any one of the Archduke's three sons on two conditions: first, that the child concerned took the Modena family name of Este (one of the oldest in Europe) and second, that he acquired a working knowledge of Italian within twelve months.

Otto, the only other candidate really old enough to be asked, turned the offer down flat because of the extra academic drudgery involved – a foretaste of a life that was to be devoted, with tragic single-mindedness, to the pursuit of pleasure. His more thoughtful elder brother jumped at the chance, and though, then as always, a miserable linguist, he managed to scrape enough Italian together within the prescribed period to qualify. One suspects the test was not too severe and certainly

9

bore no relation to the prize, one of the richest in Europe.

Providence was, however, to exact another more ironic price for the bargain. This first (and last) of the Habsburg-Estes was to develop a political and personal hatred for everything Italian. So virulent was this feeling that though Franz Ferdinand squeezed all he could out of the inheritance (and despite his later grumbles about running costs, the gain was considerable, both in cash and in art treasures) he never enjoyed, and in some cases never even visited, his Este properties. Franz V, Duke of Modena, would not have been amused.

Franz Ferdinand's Este inheritance – involving, as it did, that rarest of happenings, a change of name for a member of the reigning house – was a matter which had to be personally approved by the Emperor himself. Probably for the first time, this meant that Franz Joseph had to take a closer look at the character and attributes of his brother's eldest son, while the boy was made especially aware of the head of the Habsburg family. Thus began that curious relationship between uncle and nephew which was to grow steadily more fateful for the Monarchy, and steadily more uncomfortable for the two men themselves as time passed.

For the twelve-year-old Archduke, his sovereign, then in the prime of life, was the unclouded sun around which the dynasty and the whole universe of Austria–Hungary steadily revolved. Apart from the awesomeness of his uncle's position, there was, for the boy, a personal radiance about him. The drama of Franz Joseph's accession had, after all, been a traumatic chapter in the centuries-old imperial saga.

In 1848, when revolutionary turmoil shook continental Europe, it had looked at times as though even the ancient Habsburg crown might be toppled into the streets. Twice in that terrible year, the weak and ailing Emperor Ferdinand I was forced by the mob to flee with his court from Vienna to the provinces. The crown seemed only precariously secure when, at the end of the year, the army finally restored order in the capital; to make it safe, it would have to be placed, through abdication, on another head. But whose? By rights, the succession passed to the Emperor's brother, Franz Karl. Yet even his own wife, the formidable Sophie (a princess of Bavaria known in Vienna as 'the only man in the family'), realized that her husband was too closely identified with the old regime of oppression to be acceptable to the people. What was needed was a fresh, untainted face, and preferably a young one, pointing towards a brighter future rather than recalling a troubled past. And so, with the approval of powerful king-makers like Prince Felix Schwarzenberg, Franz Karl was persuaded to step aside and, on 2 December 1848, the crown was passed instead to his eighteen-year-old son, Franz Joseph.

The young prince who entered that day upon a reign that was to last for sixty-eight years looked as though he had been sculpted for his symbolic role. He was a tall, slender and gracious young man with blond hair, clear, wide-set blue eyes, and a well-shaped mouth and chin in which only traces of the pendulous Habsburg lower lip and heavy jowl were discernible. He did all the things a Habsburg should do, like riding and shooting, and did them uncommonly well. The men at court admired him for his brave bearing when serving briefly in the 1848 campaigns against Italian nationalists in Lombardy. The women at court were ravished by his good looks and his quite exceptional talents as a dancer. Most of these qualities the people could appreciate as well.

Though at first under the tutelage of Schwarzenberg and his own strong-willed mother, the young sovereign soon showed that he also had a mind of his own – a mind moulded from the start by a determination never again to allow the reigns of power to slip from the palace to the pavements. But what had preserved Franz Joseph as a romantic figure long after the dramas of 1848 had faded in the popular mind was the story of his marriage. This seemed to come straight out of the fairy tale books, complete with a touch of royal Cinderella. For the Emperor's twenty-third birthday, two Bavarian princesses – the nineteen-year-old Hélène with her sixteen-year-old sister Sisi – had been invited to the imperial villa at Bad Ischl, amidst the lakes and mountains of the Salzkammergut. Their mother, Princess

Louise, was Archduchess Sophie's sister, and the two ladies had decided between them that it was time to tie yet another marriage bond between the Austrian house of Habsburg and the Bavarian house of Wittelsbach, and that the grown-up Princess Hélène was the obvious bridal candidate.

Yet from the moment the young Emperor saw the two sisters, he had eyes only for Sisi. She was scarcely out of childhood, but her budding beauty was already captivating; so was her spontaneous, quicksilver gaiety, which delighted Franz Joseph – so bored with all the formal, well-rehearsed princesses presented to him thus far – as much as her physical looks. It was an imperial *coup de foudre*. His decision was tacitly announced the following evening when at a select ball in the villa (which was too small even for the ninety guests invited) he not only chose Sisi to partner him at the final *cotillon* but even handed her his whole collection of bouquets which, by rights, ought to have been distributed among his earlier dancing partners. Three days later, on 19 August 1853, the day after his own birthday, the engagement was made official. First the little town of Bad Ischl, then the Salzkammergut and then the whole empire around exploded with delight. From end to end of the Monarchy, church bells rang, bonfires were lit on mountain peaks, soldiers cheered and waved their caps on parade grounds and priests went down on their knees to pray for divine blessing and a plentiful progeny.

Until the dark tragedy of her death forty-five years later, Franz Joseph's devotion endured, undimmed and untainted. What made it doubly moving was that after rapidly presenting him with two daughters and a Crown Prince, their paths as life companions separated as the vivacity in Sisi turned slowly into a morbid and self-absorbed fever of restlessness. Eventually, the Empress was everywhere except in Vienna at her husband's side: in Gödöllö, her favourite castle near Budapest among her favourite Magyar subjects; in Paris or Cap Martin on the French Riviera; in Miramare, the Habsburgs' marble castle on the Adriatic; in Egypt and the Arab deserts; in Corfu, where she had her own villa; in Ireland and the hunting shires of England, where her wonderful horsemanship became a legend even among a society which lived in the saddle. She was constantly on the move, followed everywhere by his anxious, affectionate letters in which the loneliness was only occasionally tinged with courtly reproach. The beautiful bride of Bad Ischl had turned into a beautiful seagull. For his part, the husband was no man to take to mistresses; he took to his work-desk instead. Such was the middle-aged sovereign whom the young Franz Ferdinand, like the rest of the great Habsburg clan, had come to revere rather than love.

The inheritance of 1875 had made the boy a very special sort of Habsburg, but it had not thrust him to the centre of the Emperor's dynastic calculations. True, eight years before, in 1867, the pathetic career of Franz Joseph's eldest brother Maximilian as Emperor of Mexico had ended before a revolutionary firing-squad. That removed any possibility that Maximilian might renege on the pledge extracted from him before he assumed his Mexican crown, namely renunciation of all his rights to the Habsburg succession. But Franz Joseph had a son by his lovely if unbalanced Bavarian wife, and Rudolf, seventeen years old in 1875, seemed healthy, vigorous, intelligent enough and altogether far removed from the terrible shadows which were to close in on him later. He, surely, would marry and have sons, and the succession in direct line would be assured. And so even after the illustrious Este inheritance, Franz Ferdinand's life continued to be guided along the fixed tramlines laid down for any other archduke of the reigning branch. That meant above all service in the army, with as many different regiments and as many different garrisons as possible being worked into the sequence, to provide living contact with the eleven-nation Habsburg Monarchy.

His first attachment in 1878, as that fourteen-year-old subaltern writing childlike letters to his stepmother, had been highly appropriate: it was to the 32nd Infantry Regiment, which had long borne the name 'Este' he now carried himself. But this was a posting on paper only (he continued his studies at home) and it was only in the autumn of 1883, when he was transferred to the 4th Dragoons, that the apron strings were finally cut and he began an independent existence of his own. The regiment was stationed at Enns, halfway to Salzburg, a delightful part of Austria and a convenient distance from the suffocating attention of the Vienna court.

Five years the young Archduke spent there, and they must have been the happiest of his early adult life. As yet untroubled by any of the political entanglements, the alarming bouts of illness and the personal dilemmas which were soon to crowd in on him, he could enjoy to the full the delectable routine of the princeling-officer in this Indian summer of the empire. If contemporary accounts are anything to go by, it was far from exhausting. The hunting rifle and shotgun were certainly fired far more often than the army pistol at target practice; the horses mounted more often for racing than cavalry manoeuvres; while pictures of him at costume balls and carnivals suggest that he had temporarily shaken off his introspection, though without ceasing to be something of a loner, even in the social whirl.

He had by now grown into an attractive young man. Though certainly not as handsome as his brother Otto, who could have passed in a later age for a film star, he was good-looking enough, with a tall, slim figure and, in those days, light brown hair. Yet he was never – not even in physical appearance – the conventionally elegant Habsburg prince. The eyes – his most striking feature throughout his life – reflected a dual personality. The irises were a piercing light blue with, inside them, two large pupils that seemed to be equally strong dark blue. It was as though two sets of eyes and two different people were looking out at the world, very searchingly, from inside him.

Apart from his own brother Otto, Crown Prince Rudolf probably stood closer than anyone else to Franz Ferdinand at this time and it is Rudolf's letters[4] which confirm that the young lieutenant of the 4th Dragoons was not taking his duties too seriously. True, a brief note of congratulation from the Crown Prince sent on 18 December 1883 to mark his cousin's twentieth birthday does urge him to 'enjoy his life to the full, though always with moderation and common sense' (the last word sounding odd indeed coming from this particular writer, who was himself uncontrolled in almost every passion). But a year later, in November 1884, Rudolf sent a dire warning to Enns, singling out that ultra-conservative Habsburg veteran, Field-Marshal Archduke Albrecht, who was Inspector General of the imperial army, as their most dangerous common enemy:

> I regard it as my duty as a friend to let you know that there is an agitation making itself felt here in high military circles – and above all, unfortunately, at the very highest level – against your too frequent leaves of absence and visits to Vienna ... I have gone through similar and many other even worse experiences in my own military career to date and can only advise you to be really cautious ... Uncle Albrecht is still here at the moment and when he is around, you can prepare yourself for all sorts of unpleasantness ... You must at all costs avoid having your name being brought up before the Emperor and torn to shreds: it could produce a lot of trouble for you ... So be careful.

And it is, incidentally, from the other end of this correspondence between the royal cousins that we get the clearest proof that Franz Ferdinand savoured lovely young women as well as fine old stags. The actress Mizzi Caspar was the *grande cocotte* of the eighties who, like her counterpart and contemporary Lily Langtry in Victorian England, had worked her way up into the favour, and the bed, of the heir to the throne. She would occasionally visit army garrisons, with or without him, and one such trip, in 1886, took her to the 4th Dragoons in Enns. How close she got physically to the most illustrious officer of that regiment can never be established; but there is no doubt that she made an overwhelming impression on him. In a letter to the Crown Prince after her visit, Franz Ferdinand describes her as 'a superbly beautiful woman', and the German adjective *wunderschön* is underlined no less than three times, as though the writer were still quivering under Mizzi's impact.[5]*

---

* Her photographs, by themselves, make it a little difficult today to understand her devastating success. She appears as a plump, almost fat young woman, already with the beginnings of a double chin; but the eyes and long dark hair coiled on top of her head are very fine.

Any young archduke – especially if he was both rich and personable – had women from all social classes flung at him by the score; and indeed, the further up the ladder one went, the more persistent did the pressure become. But at the higher levels chaperoning was fierce and despite flirtatious advances and hopeful maternal intrigues a young daughter's reputation was still held more precious than her tiara. So the princelings usually learned the practical facts of life from actress-courtesans like Mizzi Caspar. Franz Ferdinand seems to have been no exception. By now, he had his own bachelor quarters in the Modenapalais (long since demolished) of Vienna's fashionable Third District, and in one of the adjoining houses belonging to the property there lived, rent free, a fair-haired young woman named Mila Kugler who was naturally assumed to be his mistress.

The fact of the matter was that with his cousin Rudolf and his brother Otto constantly at his elbow in Vienna he never had to look far for feminine distractions. Otto, in particular, was fast becoming the talk of the capital – indeed of the Empire – for his nocturnal orgies and unbridled sexual appetite. Whether it is truth or varnished half-truth that he once pranced out of a *chambre séparée* in the famous Sacher's Hotel stark naked but for a sabre slung around his loins, only to run into the scandalized presence of the British ambassadress, the story perfectly fits the man. The problem was aggravated, with both cousin and brother, by marriages which were dynastically suitable but personally disastrous.

In May 1881 the Crown Prince had been wedded, at the age of twenty-two, to Princess Stephanie of Belgium, then only sixteen years old. But the tender age of this tragic creature was her greatest physical attribute. Even the most flattering court photographs and the most beautiful gowns and jewels can do little to embellish the somewhat scrawny frame, the receding chin, the overlarge nose and ungenerous eyes. Rudolf, who would have needed a tigress to hold him, had been tied instead to a chicken. Even on the wedding portrait the ill-matched couple stand stiffly apart, and soon after the birth of their one and only child (a daughter, christened Elisabeth after the Empress) they started to live apart. Rudolf's ideal of a royal lady was said, incidentally, to be his own aunt by marriage and Franz Ferdinand's stepmother, the gentle but very womanly young Archduchess Maria Theresa, to whom Rudolf was warmly attentive at every occasion. But this was one potential scandal that was never given the slightest chance of developing.

Otto's case was even worse. Unlike the Crown Prince, who was a keenly intelligent man, interested and up to his neck in the political maelstrom of a troubled empire, Otto lived only for the pleasures of the flesh. It was clear that after his marriage to the distinctly plain and dowdy Maria Josepha of Saxony he would never find those pleasures at home. Indeed, in one of his cruel and drunken moods he is said to have burst into her bedroom one night just to point out to his drinking companions how unattractive she was. These lessons, coming from the bosom of his own family, were not to be lost on Franz Ferdinand. It was Rudolf, of all people, who drew his attention to them. Writing to his cousin in July of 1886 about Otto's engagement, he had expressed scepticism whether 'the Saxon' would be able to keep her husband's undivided attentions for long.[6] By now, the Crown Prince could speak with some authority on the subject.

The eighties, though they had begun happily enough, were far from being untroubled years for Franz Ferdinand. To begin with, in the middle of his carefree days at Enns, the first signs appeared that he had inherited the dangerously weak lungs of his Portuguese mother. To help him get fit again his uncle the Emperor relieved him from garrison duty during the winter and spring of 1885 so that he could spend the months from February to May on a convalescent sightseeing tour of Alexandria, the Holy Land, Syria, Athens and finally Corfu, the Empress Elisabeth's beloved island of retreat. In June he returned to his regiment bronzed and seemingly restored; but the illness had been dampened down, not extinguished.

Then, as the decade wore on and the Crown Prince became totally estranged from his Belgian wife, it became more and more probable that their daughter, always known in the family as

'Erzi', would be their only child. That would mean no grandsons for the Emperor and no direct male heirs, and this in turn meant that after Rudolf's own presumed reign the succession would pass to one of Karl Ludwig's descendants, the eldest of whom was Franz Ferdinand. No-one could guess whether he would outlive the Crown Prince or not; but he was, after all, five years younger, and the threat of consumption to him still seemed less than the threat of dissolute living to his cousin. Accordingly, by 1887, we find a marked increase in official concern both over his health and over his sense of dynastic responsibility. Occasionally, his own father sounds a reproving note in their correspondence, but the sternest mentor of all remained his great uncle and military chief Field-Marshal Albrecht, who in addition to his legendary reputation as a soldier* was also the oldest of all the Habsburg archdukes and spoke with a crushing authority only surpassed by that of the Emperor himself.

This grizzled paladin, with the shrewdest of eyes and the thickest of Habsburg lower lips, took his great nephew severely to task in three long letters penned between 2 February and 8 August 1887.[7] The young officer (by now promoted Rittmeister, or Captain, and panting for further advancement) was told to avoid 'excesses of any sort whatever'. He was also warned about being too pleasure-seeking – travelling around aimlessly and, above all, his passion for hunting being singled out as especially dangerous distractions. (Franz Ferdinand was already acquiring the reputation of only standing still when he had a shotgun or a sporting rifle in his hands.) The old Field-Marshal then held the crown of the double-headed eagle over his great-nephew's head as though it were the Holy Grail itself: 'Think of your sacred family duty in the cause of Austria's future, for this depends, almost totally, on the worth of the dynasty, both as a whole and in its branches.' This valiant old keeper of the Habsburg conscience added a piece of more homely advice: Franz Ferdinand should also soon set about marrying and founding a family, which would be a good example to others. The Field-

* Archduke Albrecht had commanded the Austro-Hungarian forces in the victorious battle of Custoza against the Italians in 1866.

Marshal's wishes in this respect were to suffer a very rude shock.

As the decade drew to an end, therefore, Franz Ferdinand felt the carefree start to his life fast slipping away with his youth. The idyllic existence at Enns and Salzburg with the 4th Dragoons had already been wound up in October of 1888, when he was promoted to major and transferred as a staff officer to the 102nd Infantry Regiment in Prague. It was symbolic, not simply of his promotion but also of his growing stature within the imperial family itself, that his new quarters were a splendid suite of rooms in the mighty Hradschin Castle. He had barely settled into them than the blow fell which shook the house of Habsburg to its foundations, as well as transforming overnight his own position in it.

Soon before dawn on 30 January 1889, in his bedroom at the little hunting lodge of Mayerling in the Vienna woods, Crown Prince Rudolf put a bullet through the pretty head of his latest and most devoted mistress, the seventeen-year-old Marie Vetsera, and then, with a second bullet from temple to temple, blew his own brains out. Even after nearly a century has passed the death pact at Mayerling (assuming that such indeed it was)* lies veiled in a half-light cast by destroyed evidence, manipulated testimony, evasiveness and misleading or contradictory versions put about by actors in the drama who were anxious either to conceal or to exaggerate the part they had played.

The romantic scenario of a Wagnerian *Liebestod* presented in so many films and historical novels is almost certainly false. It is true that, for her part, the little Baroness was determined to die with her irresistibly tragic Archduke, like a white moth drawn to, and consumed by, a dying flame. But there is not a scrap of evidence that he put an end to his own life because he could not share it with her. The political scenario – that he killed himself out of fearful frustration at his father's stodgily traditional policies, which he actively opposed both in domestic and foreign affairs – probably comes closer to the truth, though without embracing it entirely.

---

* There have been periodic but never very convincing attempts to suggest that the couple were murdered for political motives.

The fact of the matter is that, with or without the little Vetsera, and with or without politics, Rudolf was born and bred for suicide as sparks fly upwards. His own mother had much of the congenital instability of the Bavarian Wittelsbachs in her blood, and what the son did not inherit he had himself induced. Long before he put a bullet through it, his brain as well as his body was being gnawed at by the syphilis that the likes of Mizzi Caspar had bestowed on him, and as early as 1887 he had begun constantly talking of suicide to her, among many others. Marie Vetsera was simply the last memento of life he took with him, as a pharoah might take a golden bauble in his funeral casket to comfort him on the final journey.

Even in the immediate aftermath of Mayerling, the motives seemed far less important than the outcome. The Crown Prince of the Austro-Hungarian monarchy was suddenly gone. Idle now to speculate whether he might eventually remember his dynastic duty and produce a son or, if not, outlive others in the succession line. Now, the Archduke Karl Ludwig was technically next in that line as the Emperor's eldest surviving brother. But the man who, nearly thirty years before, had found even a provincial government too much to cope with was hardly fitted in this crisis to be groomed as Heir-Presumptive to the whole empire; in any case, he was nearly as old as the Emperor himself, and, of the two, it was the Emperor who appeared to be in rather better health. So, on 30 January 1889, the mantle fell on Karl Ludwig's eldest son, the twenty-six-year-old Franz Ferdinand of Habsburg-Este.

CHAPTER THREE

Globe-Trotter with a Rifle

FRANZ FERDINAND SOON FELT the freshening wind in his face. For one thing, his persistent mentor, Archduke Albrecht, now redoubled his efforts to keep his great-nephew on the straight and narrow but rather boring path of conscience. In a letter written during the summer after the Crown Prince's death, the old Field-Marshal warned Franz Ferdinand (who had been raising eyebrows by joining in a few rowdy escapades with his fellow officers) that, 'now, even more than before, you should not behave like a raw young lieutenant'.[1] Meanwhile, Franz Ferdinand's military career – in essence a political training – took a significant new turn. In April 1890 the Emperor promoted him to full Colonel and transferred him to command the 9th Regiment of Hungarian Hussars at Ödenburg, a move designed to bring the twenty-seven-year-old Archduke face to face with the most virulent force in the whole empire – Magyar nationalism.

What the young Colonel experienced during his two years with a Hungarian regiment was to fashion his constitutional views as heir to the throne until the end of his days: officers stubbornly resisting regulations which laid down that, as in all regiments of the imperial army, their language of command should be German, and issuing even the simplest orders in Hungarian instead. The furious Archduke wrote to Vienna, 'The officers spoke in Hungarian even in front of me and the simplest German question produced the answer "*nem tudom*" ("I don't understand"). Military terms were translated into long-winded Hungarian phrases. In short, throughout the regiment, not a word of that German language so detested by the Hussars.'[2]

As the unity of the empire was almost synonymous with the unity of the army, the moral was clear, and ominous, enough. The warning signal came through even more strongly when the royal Colonel put aside his uniform and travelled incognito around the villages of the neighbouring countryside. One who accompanied him on these trips wrote, 'Whether priest, peasant or swine-herd, everyone talked politics ... All the pulpits preached the concept of the Hungarian state and the peasants complained that their children were no longer even taught to pray in German.'[3]

The Emperor had expressly forbidden his nephew to give voice to any misgivings he might feel during his army service in Ödenburg. The misgivings were accurately predicted, but not the strength of the reaction. Franz Ferdinand's temper, which always walked at his side like a red demon, broke through in public for the first time when his bitter criticisms of Magyar chauvinism were picked up and published in the Budapest newspapers. Once again, Archduke Albrecht swung wearily into action, warning Franz Ferdinand against offending these 'vain and sensitive' Hungarians and reminding him once again that, in his new position, he must keep the trust of everybody 'and so avoid even the appearance of a rift in the family'.[4]

That new position was by now clearly reflected in Franz Ferdinand's status in the world outside his regiment and his empire. Already in June of 1889, only five months after Mayerling, he had been sent to Stuttgart, in the place of the dead Crown Prince, to convey congratulations to the King of Württemberg on the twenty-fifth anniversary of his reign. In August of that year, the Emperor took his nephew with him when he went to Berlin to greet William II, Emperor of Germany since the previous year, and Franz Ferdinand had his first official look at this bombastic young sovereign with whom he was to develop an ambivalent friendship. Finally, in the winter of 1891, he was sent on his first major independent mission, to St Petersburg, on a special goodwill visit to Tsar Alexander III. Though he took time off to shoot a few bears, this was high politics of the old dynastic style between the two doomed empires. Behind the exchanges of decorations, the toasts at banquets, the military parades and the court balls lay an Austrian attempt to stop Russia sliding into the waiting arms of France and revive instead the old 'Three Emperors' League' of 1872 between Austria, Germany and Russia. The bid failed, then as later; but Franz Ferdinand always cherished the dream which that visit to the Winter Palace had evoked.

All seemed to be going swimmingly, however, as 1892 came round. Then his health started to play him up again, not, as yet, seriously, but enough to cause concern. Clearly, before another winter began he would have to get away to the sun once more, but the prospect of another convalescent journey around the Mediterranean seemed too humiliating to contemplate. Fortunately, an exciting alternative had already presented itself: the new battle-cruiser *Kaiserin Elisabeth*, one of the few showpieces of the still modest and outmoded Austrian fleet, was due to sail to east Asia to train her crew and show the flag in far-off waters. This was a very different proposition. No Habsburg prince before him had ever been able to make such a journey; moreover, instead of being shunted like an anonymous tourist from hotel to hotel, he would sail the world as Heir-Presumptive and ambassador of his empire, aboard a floating steel fragment of that empire. The Emperor, whose permission was, of course, needed, proved hard to persuade. He had already sat forty-four years on his throne and was, by now, reluctant to agree on principle to anything unconventional in any of those great family and political spheres which revolved around him. Moreover, he had little personal rapport with his nephew; rather less with his own navy; and less still with Asia. But, between them, the Empress Elisabeth, Franz Ferdinand's sister Margaretha, and his stepmother the Archduchess Maria Theresa (now, as ever, the Archduke's good fairy) managed to talk the Emperor round. So, on 15 December 1892, in the harbour of Trieste, the adventure of a lifetime began.

It had an embarrassing and thoroughly undignified pro-
logue. On the evening of the eighth, as the august traveller was
preparing to leave Vienna, Mila Kugler, his little actress from
the nearby house in the Beatrixgasse, burst into the apartment of
one of Franz Ferdinand's academic friends and mentors* and
declared that she would raise the scandal of all scandals unless
the Archduke took her with him. She even produced a very
recent historical parallel, none the less emotive for being
inaccurate. Only three years before, an archduke from the non-
reigning branch of the family, Johann Salvator, had renounced
his title and his prerogatives, assumed the name Johann Orth,
and married a comely young girl of the people called Lori
Stubel. What made the whole affair doubly romantic was that he
had then sailed away with her round the world on his yacht, on
board which he was believed to have perished in 1891 in a
storm in the south Atlantic. The real-life story became a legend
which, ever since, had titillated the imagination of every
Austrian *Fräulein* who had climbed into an archducal bed. Mila
Kugler tearfully drew on it now, as though there were the
remotest chance of the Heir-Presumptive turning himself, for
her sake, into a sort of Habsburgian Flying Dutchman, roaming
the oceans in self-banishment on one of the Emperor's
battleships.

The professor politely saw the actress to the door with
assurances that he would do his best and, first thing the next
morning, put the whole matter in the lap of the Archduke's chief
equerry, Count Leopold Wurmbrandt-Stuppach. The Count, a
lean and down-to-earth bachelor, took the news calmly while
still shaving, and commented that what Fraulein Kugler needed
was either bribing or arresting. And that was probably the end of
that. True, there were rumours that the actress, disguised as a
sailor, had been smuggled on board the *Kaiserin Elisabeth* and
had completed the first stage of the voyage; but the rumours
seem based on nothing much more substantial than an item in
the theatrical columns of a Vienna newspaper that Christmas.

* Professor Müller-Guttenbrunn, the anonymous author of the gossipy but, in parts,
well-informed *Franz Ferdinand's Lebensroman* (Stuttgart, 1919).

This reported that Mila Kugler was returning from Port Said 'after a short holiday in Egypt' to resume her engagements in the Austrian capital.[5]

Even without the importunate actress, the Archduke's suite contained some interesting names. Apart from Count Wurm-brandt (recently promoted to Major-General) these included Count Heinrich Clam-Martinic who, despite his background as a feudal nobleman from Bohemia, held some remarkably progressive ideas, having pioneered agricultural co-operatives, for example. Then there was Dr Ludwig Ritter von Liburnau from the Natural History Museum in Vienna, and one Eduard Hodak, a taxidermist. These men, between them, were to select and prepare wild life specimens from all the countries visited; like many passionate hunters, the Archduke was an almost equally passionate collector. A certain Julius Pronáy von Tót-Próna also deserves special mention – less for who he was than for what he represented, namely the army officers and landed gentry of Hungary. His name was not on the Archduke's original list. Franz Ferdinand had to be persuaded that the Magyar-dominated half of the empire would take it badly if the newspaper photographs of the illustrious party, which would soon be turning up from all over the globe, did not include the face and uniform of even one dashing lieutenant from the Hungarian Hussars. Heading the list of the servants came the name of Franz Janaczek, described as 'personal gamekeeper'. The good Janaczek, one of the most remarkable figures in Franz Ferdinand's life, was destined to become a great deal more than that. Finally, there was another Archduke on board, the young Leopold Ferdinand, who was there not as a member of the suite but as a junior officer of the ship's company. He soon brought both suite and ship nothing but shame.

From the send-off he was given as the battle-cruiser weighed anchor on the stroke of 2 p.m., one might have thought that Franz Ferdinand really was some latter-day Johann Orth, setting out on a journey from which there would be no return. His whole family had travelled down to Trieste to bid him goodbye and, not content with a day of leave-taking, they boarded a smaller warship, the *Greif*, and steamed out to sea as far as Pirano with the battleship before turning back. On board the *Kaiserin Elisabeth* the ship's band, echoed by other vessels in the harbour, burst forth with the strains of the national anthem and that marvellous military tune, the Radetsky March, which was almost an anthem in itself, especially for the soldiers of the Monarchy. When the *Greif* finally put about, the family signalled one last message: 'Happy journey; farewell and good hunting.'

The Archduke began straightaway to make notes for what eventually emerged as a huge two-volume journal of his travels. The very first entry, penned as the *Greif* disappeared from sight, is revealing: 'Deep inside me came the sinking feeling of an infinite longing for the homeland . . . it was homesickness, which I had never known before.'[6]

This was an outburst of typical Austrian sentimentality, not least because it came when he was still so near home. That most typical of songs of native longing, 'Vienna, city of my dreams', was written when the composer, so far from being exiled at the other end of the earth, was merely spending a weekend in the mountains only fifty miles away from his beloved capital.

The Archduke records that he subdued his own wave of melancholy by busily spreading family photographs around the spacious cabin allotted to him, and by unpacking and inspecting the considerable armoury of shotguns and rifles he had brought along. 'Good hunting' was what the *Greif* had wished him, and good hunting he was determined to have, whenever the sightseeing and the representational functions allowed. His suite had certainly caught their master's mood, for when, three days out to sea, his twenty-ninth birthday was celebrated, they staged for the occasion a procession of dummy lions, elephants and other animals which he hoped to have in his sights for real during the months ahead.

The Archduke lived up to all expectations. True, on his first day on dry land, at Port Said, the quarry was merely flamingo on the Menzaleh Lake – which, after a few misses, he managed to down in flight with a rifle bullet at three hundred yards. But at

Ceylon, which they reached on 7 January 1893, he duly encountered the biggest game of all when the party embarked on a five-day elephant shooting expedition into the interior. Again, he missed the first time by firing excitedly from too far (a range of only ten yards, he was told, was the ideal distance, provided the nerves would stand it); but he eventually killed the second animal and was nearly trampled to death by the charge of a third. All in all, it was a well-rounded hunter's trip, especially when the many cormorants and two large monkeys shot on the shores of a nearby lake were added to the bag.

From Colombo, the *Kaiserin Elisabeth* set sail for Bombay, the gate to the British Raj. Before he lands there, it is worth looking at the earnest deliberations which had been going on in Victorian London between the Court of St James and the India Office as to how, precisely, the Archduke should be treated on arrival. The matter was opened by Edward, Prince of Wales, who got his secretary to write to the Queen's secretary to settle a point 'concerning which he knows the Austrians are very sensitive' – namely, the Archduke's precedence.[7] Recalling the offence given during the recent visit of the Russian Tsarevich, who was placed below the Governors of Bombay and Madras, the Prince suggests that though the Viceroy, Lord Landsdowne, being the Queen's direct representative, 'could not resign his position in favour of anyone but a sovereign', why should not the Governors of the two Presidencies give the Archduke precedence?

One reason why 'Bertie', as the Prince of Wales was affectionately known, should have raised the issue was that he was already acknowledged as the master of European protocol and arbiter of public form, a mastery due in large measure to the fact that he had nothing more substantial to get his teeth into. This suggests a second and rather more personal interest in the matter. As Heir-Apparent himself, and nearly a generation older than the Austrian Heir-Presumptive, he well knew what frustrations and pricks of protocol afflicted those who sat waiting on the steps of a throne. Franz Ferdinand was, to him, a fellow-sufferer who needed all the help he could get.

It was not all plain sailing, however. Lord Kimberley at the India Office joined forces with Lord Rosebery at the Foreign Office in bridling at the Prince's proposal. Though the two Governors should meet the Archduke in uniform and place him on their right in the carriage, surely, it was argued, it would be otherwise proper if they maintained their position as representatives of the sovereign? Each minister added a departmental argument of his own. The India Office suggested that any other arrangement 'might have a prejudicial effect on the minds of the Indian population'. The Foreign Office wondered whether the Russians might not be offended if another imperial heir were given better treatment than their own. But Queen Victoria came down firmly on her son's side, commenting, through her secretary, 'There is no need of fearing that the native population will misunderstand our act of civility as they are themselves so courteous.' Indeed the Queen went one further by ruling in her own handwriting that even the Viceroy, 'in *private*, in his own house', should give the Archduke precedence.[8] All this, of course, was made known to Vienna nearly two months before the Archduke set out, and the Emperor had expressed 'his great satisfaction' to the Queen for her decision.[9] It all made a complete nonsense of reports that Franz Ferdinand would be travelling incognito. Only the elephants in the jungle could fail to know who he was, and for them it was irrelevant.

As a result of the Queen's decision, the Viceroy, in a circular of 8 December 1892, laid down details of the full ceremonial treatment to be accorded to their visitor. Accordingly, when the Archduke stepped ashore at Bombay on 17 January 1893, he found himself greeted by the Commander-in-Chief of India, General Lord Roberts; a salute of twenty-one guns; a guard of honour of one hundred rank and file with band and colour; and all the other accoutrements of protocol. His hosts had laid down in advance the procedure for toasts at the official banquets – six bars of their national anthem to be played when the Archduke proposed the health of the Queen-Empress and the whole of the Austrian national hymn when the Governor replied by toasting the Emperor Franz Joseph. This sequence seems to have astounded Franz Ferdinand, who was used to the continental system where the sovereign of the honoured guest was toasted first. Here, he had no option but to follow the customs of England and the Victorian Raj, where even the good Lord himself might have experienced difficulty being put above the Queen.

Another problem also presented itself on his first major ceremonial occasion, the dinner of the Governor of Bombay, Lord Harris, and this was to persist throughout the entire world tour. Franz Ferdinand spoke very little English* and had hitherto relied on his reasonably fluent French for any foreign excursions. But Englishmen who spoke French in the India of the nineties were rare birds indeed and so conversation, except on the subject of hunting, tended to be somewhat stilted. Lord Harris, in his report to Queen Victoria on the four-day Bombay visit, made no bones about this two-way language handicap; but, despite it, he assured his sovereign, 'H.H.'s amiability and consideration have so impressed that to everyone it has been a pleasure to meet H.H.'s wishes in every way.'[10] And the following month the Viceroy himself sent home an even more glowing testimonial, which also reads more spontaneously: 'His Imperial Highness has left a very good impression: he has excellent manners but is perfectly natural and unaffected and was very friendly and considerate in his demeanour towards all, whether European or native ...'

It was interesting evidence, from a people well-known for their own reserve, that, whenever he was obliged to, or whenever the mood took him, Franz Ferdinand could throw off all his natural introspection and exude that one quality that foreigners expected above all from an Austrian – charm.

The banquets were important but relatively rare events in the less taxing routine of sightseeing and shooting. The former included, of course, a visit to Agra and the Taj Mahal, about which the Archduke writes in his journal with deeply expressive

---

* 'Why can't he talk a word of English?' Queen Victoria demanded when meeting the Archduke for the first time, and refused to accept the explanation that he had been too preoccupied learning the various tongues of his own empire.

feeling, almost as though he already sensed what a symbol this monument to the love of one single woman was to be for him.

As for the shooting, that embraced just about everything the subcontinent had to offer, from the Himalayas downwards. After Bombay came an elaborate tiger shoot at Tandur in Hyderabad, where a town of tents had been erected in the jungle for five hundred guests. But despite an army of elephants (this time as tame mounts) and the efforts of four hundred beaters, no tigers appeared. Then at Gwalior the Archduke had his first taste (and his first success) at boar-hunting Indian style – on horseback and with a lance. When the pig-sticking flagged, he returned to his rifle to pick off a few vultures who were unwisely circling around at what they had hitherto imagined to be a safe distance.

Though he seems to have got on very well with his various hosts, there were times when their ideas of what was sporting differed sharply from his own. Writing after an expedition to Alwar, for example, he attacks the English for hunting the panther with lances, as though it were a pig: 'If the panther had fallen to my bullet, at least the kill would have given me a sportsman's satisfaction; as it was I could only deplore the ruination of the lovely skin by lance thrusts.'[11]

On the other hand, the following month at Jaipur, he was himself taken politely but firmly to task for picking off a wild boar with that deadly bullet of his. 'Please don't,' he was urged, 'it's as bad as shooting fox.' As the Archduke had never ridden to hounds but had despatched fox by the score back home, as a menace to both livestock and pheasants, one wonders how he reacted to the reproof.

However, in between these two episodes, he managed, during a seven-day shoot at Siriska (the most elaborate of all with 1793 men, 25 elephants, 148 horses, 39 dogs plus 40 Indian cavalrymen for communications and 72 infantrymen as camp guards!) to kill his first tiger. 'I cannot describe my joy,' he wrote. And that, despite a final hunting trip to Nepal, was probably the high point of his enjoyment as an archducal Nimrod. At the end of March, after six weeks in India, he embarked on the *Kaiserin Elisabeth* again at Calcutta, and they set sail, via Singapore and Java, to a very different part of the British Empire – Australia.

One difference he noted immediately on landing at Sydney was the pretty girls. How nice it was, he observed in his dairy, to see white faces again after all those Asian physiognomies, 'not exactly attractive to our tastes'.[12] But, for the rest, the next few weeks might have been Nimrod back in India again, except that the quarries were different, and even more exotic. Within twenty-four hours of arriving in Sydney, we find him out in the bush, shooting kangaroos, emus, bustards, wallabies, the Australian bear and – a great rarity – a duckbill. All the good specimens were stuffed by the industrious taxidermist, Herr Hodak, while the zoologist of the party, Dr von Liburnau, was also constantly at work, here as throughout the journey, in selecting and cataloguing flora and fauna to add to this one-man collection. Franz Ferdinand, in his own words, 'suffered from museum mania', and one institution that was to derive permanent benefit from his travels was the Natural History Museum of his native Vienna.

It was at Sydney that Franz Ferdinand had to take a very unpleasant decision over a very unpleasant matter. His kinsman Archduke Leopold had already started defying all codes of naval discipline before the battleship was clear of the Mediterranean and, as the cruise proceeded eastwards, the young lieutenant's behaviour became unbearable. As Franz Ferdinand now reported to the Emperor, Leopold was refusing even to eat with his fellow officers and was spending all his time instead with the cadets of the ship's company – and with one especially, giving rise to much talk that he was conducting a homosexual affair. He shirked all his duties and, when reprimanded, retorted that he prayed every day the wretched ship would sink. What this misfit was doing in a naval uniform in the first place is a mystery. What was clear was that could no longer be tolerated on board the *Kaiserin Elisabeth*. He was accordingly sent packing in disgrace by Franz Ferdinand and told to make his own way home from Australia. (Leopold duly ran the whole course of a Rake's

Progress. A few months later, he wrote to Vienna from Brussels renouncing all his titles and privileges. He was last heard of in the Berlin of the twenties – called himself Leopold Wolfling and earning his living as a singer in nightclubs.) Though bad enough, this was the only shadow over the whole cruise.

After final expeditions into Asian jungles in the Solomon Islands, New Guinea and Dutch Amboyna, Franz Ferdinand had to put away his guns for a long spell of receptions and sightseeing: at Singapore and Hongkong, where he again admired the comfortable style of British colonial life; at Canton and Macao; and finally in Japan. It is here that he gives us another glimpse of that fountain of highly emotional patriotism which always flowed inside him.

When he left Japan, on 25 August 1893, to sail the Pacific, he had to transfer from his warship to the Canadian liner *Empress of China*. One would almost have thought, when he bade farewell to the *Kaiserin Elisabeth*, that he was taking leave of life itself. Describing the moment when he left the vessel which had been his 'floating piece of homeland' for the past eight months, with the Austrian national hymn thundering out from the ship's band, he writes, 'I am not ashamed to admit that tears streamed down my cheeks.' He soon found a lot else besides nostalgia to make him regret the change. What began on the *Empress of China* was to continue, at a steadily accelerating pace throughout the remaining weeks of his journey: an uncomprehending aversion to the New World and almost everything it contained and represented.

It began straightaway when he looked around him: 'Instead of our own agile sailors, we see sulky Americans, stiff Englishmen and slant-eyed Chinese.' Another complaint was that the warship's band, which used to play familiar Austrian airs, had been replaced by 'a furious Wagnerian torturing a poor piano from dawn to midnight'.[13] The only consolation he found was playing mixed doubles at deck tennis with 'a charming little American girl'. But she was a notable exception. His other fellow-passengers seem to have filled him with unrelieved distaste, and he even complained that the ship's dance was a fiasco because only a few American couples had ventured on to the floor, adding the interesting comment, 'If all the ladies of the New World will only dance with their husbands, how boring the balls must be on this continent.'[14]

A lot of this sourness may well have been due to the abrupt – and, to him, totally novel – drop in dignity he had just experienced. Instead of the heir to the throne lording it on one of those imperial warships he fully expected one day to be his own, he was now just another commercial, if very distinguished, passenger, not even allowed to go on the bridge, let alone give commands to the captain. But part of the reason for his attitude went deeper, and shows us a little more of the character of the man: an inability to adapt easily and, with it, a suspicion of the unfamiliar and an intolerance of the unwelcome. In this, of course, he was merely an archducal version of the thousands of conservative nineteenth-century travellers from the old world visiting the new and finding its brashness unappetizing and its energy frightening.* However, this particular traveller hoped one day to rule a great empire whose horizons could not possibly, in the century to come, be confined to Europe. Moreover both the brashness and the energy went to make up an enemy he would have to come face to face with – republican democracy.

Franz Ferdinand had developed these prejudices while still crossing the ocean and with only his fellow-passengers to go on as specimens of American culture. But he found his misgivings doubly justified when, on 19 September, he crossed from Canada into the United States. From that day on, the journal is peppered with hostile irony. Chicago, the first major city he saw, was disliked for its huge buildings 'with not a trace of ornament or anything to beautify them'. In New York, where he stayed at one such building, the Hotel Windsor, he let fly against the entire national character. The Americans, he concluded, had become obsessed with the drive to exaggerate and to have the

---

* A small symbol of this had been the speed and force with which they played tennis, a favourite sport of Franz Ferdinand's. He writes (*Tagebuch* II, p. 432) of a visit to the Vancouver Tennis Club: 'How much I would have liked to join in, but my courage failed me, looking at the expertise displayed.'

biggest of everything, 'but they struck me as cold people and seemed to lack both kindliness in their heart and charm in their temperament'. What a contrast to that heir to another European throne, the Prince of Wales, who, on his one and only tour of America forty years before, had been captivated by the easy-going friendliness of the people as well as by their vitality. But 'Bertie' was, after all, an unashamed extrovert, for whom human beings of all sorts and classes were a never-ending source of delight.

On 18 October, after a return journey via Le Havre, Paris and Stuttgart, the Archduke's train crossed the borders of his empire, and he records an immense surge of joy as he saw again the frontier posts in his black and yellow Habsburg colours. The family, who had seen him off at Trieste, were now waiting at St Pölten to make the last short stage to Vienna with him. The traveller had been away for ten months and had covered, by land and sea, nearly fifty thousand miles. To mark the occasion, the Emperor decorated him with the Grand Order of St Stephen (St Hubert or St Christopher would have been more appropriate saints, but neither figured in the Austrian list of decorations). In addition, a special 'Ocean Journey Commemorative Coin, 1892–3' was struck. Such were the ephemera. What were the more lasting results?

One is the Archduke's massive journal of some thousand printed pages, still preserved in the libraries of museums and geographical societies all over the world. It is necessary to stress that it was indeed his own creation. Nothing infuriated him more at the time than suggestions that it had all been ghostwritten for him, to use the phrase of later generations. ('People simply believe that every archduke just has to be a nincompoop,' was one characteristic explosion of his on this sore subject.) The basic statistics of each country visited had obviously been researched on his behalf, and so too had much of the scientific material. It is also known that one of his most trusted friends and tutors, Dr Max Beck, helped him to edit his notes into the final text. Yet these original diary notes, covering many handwritten volumes, survive today in the family castle at Artstetten as proof that the book – complete with its poetic and sentimental passages and all its flashes of sarcasm – was essentially his own creation.

Indeed, a comparison of the unedited manuscript with the published text shows that, if anything, Dr Beck's role had been to water down, rather than touch up, the strength of the original. For example, in his original entry for 17 January 1893, the Archduke derides the procedure he had just been introduced to at the Governor's banquet in Bombay – toasting the sovereign of the host *before* that of the guest of honour – as being against the practice 'of all civilized countries'. He criticizes the arrogant English habit of 'obliging everyone to follow their customs in every respect', and later goes on to describe with relish the occasions on which he had refused to fall into line:

> I believe that I may have come in for some criticism on their part during the trip by, for example, refusing to follow this absurd business of putting on evening dress and white tie in a tent in the middle of a wilderness or a jungle where one is anyway only together with other men. Instead, I appeared in a sort of hunting garb. In the same way I ordered my meals in camp for six or seven and not for nine o'clock, which I consider very bad for hygienic [sic] reasons. Even if the astonished company laid an English curse on me for it, I don't care. I and the gentlemen of my suite were very happy with the arrangement.

This is rather a different person from that perfect guest 'friendly and considerate in his demeanour towards all' who was so to impress the Viceroy. But the jungle was not Viceregal Lodge and it was typical of the Archduke, who hated undue pomposity, to ram home the difference.

If further proof of authenticity in the diaries were needed it is provided by comparision with his other writings and utterances. '*Le style, c'est l'homme.*' Franz Ferdinand's emotionally acerbic style was unmistakable, as was the keen intelligence which set him apart from almost the entire imperial family. His travel journal is the clearest as well as the most substantial surviving testimony to that intelligence.

More important, however, are the impressions which this

journey round the world had left on that lively mind. There are probably only two people left alive today who heard Franz Ferdinand discuss the journey in later years: his daughter, now Countess Nostitz, and the Archduchess Zita, later Empress of Austria-Hungary. Both have stressed that the impact was political as well as personal.[15,16] The Archduke now realized what might and strength existed outside the confines of his own European homeland and how, in the case of the British empire, that strength rested upon a powerful navy. There was no question of Austria needing a navy of that size, for the horizons of her oceans were modest by comparison. But there was one sea, the Adriatic, where she did need more warships, to counter Italy, whom Franz Ferdinand had already come to regard, somewhat unrealistically, as the arch-enemy. Quite apart from that, he had seen – in Hongkong, in Sydney, in Singapore, in Bombay – how the ubiquitous British navy was, by its very presence, a political factor. If the Habsburg Monarchy was not to appear too weak alongside its ally, the German empire, then the Austrian fleet surely must not look too absurd alongside the fast-expanding navy of the Emperor William. This particular doctrine was one of the few that the Archduke was able to translate into practice during his lifetime. Though he was never to travel the great oceans of the world again, their lessons were to be applied vigorously on his own narrow shores.

The Order of St Stephen and the commemorative medal were not the only favours bestowed on him after his return. Franz Ferdinand had requested a military transfer from the Hussars in Hungary to a command in Bohemia, either the brigade of cavalry at Pardubice or the brigade of infantry at Budweis. (As he now held the rank of Major-General, either appointment was feasible.) He had sent in his request through official channels, which meant an application to the War Office in Vienna; but it was, of course, the Emperor himself who decided such matters and, in April of 1894, Franz Ferdinand found his wish granted with a posting to the 38th Infantry Brigade at Budweis.

It was the first such specific request the Archduke had made, and the Emperor may well have been persuaded to grant it by the reasons which his nephew gave.[17] He had cited, first of all, the need to establish himself in the two big properties he had already acquired in Bohemia (the castles of Konopischt and Chlumetz, about which much more will be heard later). The Archduke's second reason, though just as natural, was much more intriguing. Having settled into his new estates, he wrote, he would then like to marry. If Franz Joseph had known what he was letting himself in for by accommodating that last request he would have posted his nephew to a garrison stationed as far away from Budweis as the imperial army stretched. Franz Ferdinand had already met, and was soon to fall passionately in love with, a Bohemian lady who, despite her noble birth, was deemed totally unsuitable as the consort of a future Emperor. Almost simultaneously, the question arose as to whether he would be healthy enough to marry at all. The most agonising period of his life was about to begin.

CHAPTER FOUR

Sophie

BEFORE HE LOST HIS HEART to his dynastically unsuitable lady, Franz Ferdinand's name had been linked, with varying degrees of plausibility, to three royal princesses. The first and most feasible had been Princess Mathilde of Saxony, the German Catholic kingdom which over the centuries had provided brides for so many Habsburg archdukes (including, of course, his own father). Mathilde was intelligent and sweet-natured but she was also very plain: so much so, in fact, that despite the examples of his ancestors, Franz Ferdinand, after one look, had backed out hastily. King George of Saxony had been much offended by the refusal and the Emperor Franz Joseph had had to work hard to mend this unusual rift between the two closely-linked courts of Vienna and Dresden.[1] Part of the mending had been the wedding, in 1886, between Otto, Franz Ferdinand's handsome younger brother, and Mathilde's own younger sister Maria Josepha, who was almost as plain as herself. The disastrous outcome of this marriage we have already seen.

The next name which cropped up was none other than Stephanie, the Belgian-born widow of the ill-fated Crown Prince. Though it was not uncommon in European royal and noble houses for bereaved fiancées or widows to be taken on, as an act of pious loyalty, by a brother or close relative of the dead man, this particular salvage operation does not seem to have been taken very seriously, least of all by Franz Ferdinand. He remained on the best of terms with Stephanie (and indeed, common agonies over their respective wedding problems in the

years ahead were to provide a very special bond between them);
but he clearly never thought of her as a bride. To begin with, she
suffered, though to a lesser degree, from the same physical
drawbacks as the unfortunate Mathilde of Saxony (who was
never to find a husband). Moreover, her experiences with Rudolf
cannot have endeared her to the prospect of another dynastic
marriage of convenience.

The third bridal candidate was said to be a daughter of the
heir to the throne of England, Edward, Prince of Wales, though
this rests on nothing more than one speculative report circulated
years later by the Archduke's aide-de-camp, Baron Albert
Margutti. In one of his books of memoirs, he recalls seeing a
letter written on royal notepaper from Sandringham which was
received by the Archduke while he was stationed at Budweis.
Did this, the inquisitive aide-de-camp enquired, indicate that an
unprecedented royal match was in the offing between the
Protestant throne of England and the Catholic throne of
Austria? Margutti has a habit of ruining his imperial anecdotes
by the ponderously artificial language he puts in the mouths of
his august speakers, and this is no exception. 'It really would be
high time', the Archduke is said to have replied, 'that we also
started thinking again about raising the prestige of the imperial
house through suitable marriages and so saving the Monarchy.
But such a marriage – even if at all possible, which I do not know
and cannot know – lies so far in the future that one is well advised
not to concern oneself with it at the moment.'

If ever Franz Ferdinand did utter these tortuous and
confusing words (which are totally unlike his normal crisp style)
he could scarcely have been thinking about himself: as he had
already turned thirty, it was not time to be talking of marriage
possibilities which still stretched many years ahead. More to the
point is that no descendant of the Vienna court circle of the
nineties can be found who ever heard the English link being
discussed, even as a rumour, in their families. Still more to the
point, there is no trace of such a Sandringham letter in the
copious collection of Franz Ferdinand's correspondence with
foreign royalty. Finally, and probably conclusively, there is no

reference of any sort to the subject in the Royal Archives at Windsor.

In any case, the Archduke, encouraged by the Empress Elisabeth, had already developed very rebellious ideas himself about the hallowed traditions of dynastic intermarriage, at least as practised hitherto by the house of Habsburg. He once burst out to his private doctor, 'When one of us finds someone he likes, they always discover some triviality in the family tree which forbids the match and so it happens that, with us, man and wife are related to each other twenty times over. The result is that half of the children are either epileptics or idiots!'[2] It was a highly revealing remark, the significance of which escaped the good doctor, who strikes one nonetheless as a much more faithful recorder than the aide-de-camp. That explosion is vintage Franz Ferdinand.

Only once before the secret came out did Franz Ferdinand unburden himself on paper on the subject of royal marriages, and that was in a letter written to a great confidante of his, Countess Nora Fugger, who had suggested that it was surely time for him to settle down. He replied:

> You are so right in telling me, urging me, to marry and I am gradually coming to the same conclusion myself, as I already long for peace, for a cosy home and family. But now I must put to you the big question: whom then should I marry? There is nobody there. You say, Countess, that I should take a wife who is kind, clever, beautiful and good. All right, but tell me where can such a woman be found! Sadly, there is nobody to choose from among the marriageable princesses; they are all children, chicks [*Piperl*] of seventeen and eighteen, one uglier than the other. And I am too old and have neither the time nor the inclination to see to the education of my own wife. I can readily imagine the ideal woman as I would like her and with whom I could also be happy. She should be not too young, and her character and views should be fully developed. I know of no such princess . . .[3]

By the time he wrote those lines, the great deception had in fact begun, for Franz Ferdinand had already found that ideal woman and, having lost his heart, had even begun to agonize over whether he would have to lose his crown as well. The lady's name was Countess Sophie Chotek, a lady-in-waiting to the Archduchess Isabella, and she met the requirements on every point save one. Born on 1 March 1868, she would have been about twenty-seven when the Archduke finally made up his mind that he simply could not live without her, and by nineteenth-century marriage standards twenty-seven was certainly 'not too young'. As for her physical attractions – which, as we have seen, played a big role in Franz Ferdinand's life – Sophie, though not a classical beauty, was handsome, wholesome, womanly, yet strikingly dignified. A family oil portrait (which the Archduke himself always found a bit too fussy) shows why she would stand out in any room: huge dark brown eyes set under a coiled mass of matching dark brown hair whose brilliant colour was set off by a perfect complexion. The eyes suggested both an obvious intelligence ('character and views fully developed') and a hidden fire: it was a powerful combination. A full century later, a diary of one of Franz Ferdinand's friends, Count Sternberg, has come to light which shows the effect which Sophie had on the Archduke, as witnessed by contemporaries. Describing a social meeting between the couple at Abbazia, when Franz Ferdinand's interest in the lady-in-waiting was already aroused, Sternberg writes:

> In true Christian humility in the Archduke's presence, she lowered her heavy lids over the glowing dark eyes. That fascinated him and spurred him on to the attack. What their Highnesses love above all else is the unreachable, or at any rate that which shows fight and doesn't allow itself just to be served up on a salver. Countess 'Sopherl' met his approaches with the firmest resistance. And thus she aroused in him that relentless urge which proves stronger than any force set against it, and worth any sacrifice in order to achieve.[4]

The single drawback of this alluring paragon was what the Archduke had contemptuously described to his doctor as 'some triviality in the family tree'. But, inclined though he always was by taste and temperament to an unorthodox marriage, Franz Ferdinand was well aware that the problem in Sophie's case was far from trivial. The Choteks of Chotkova and Wognin, to give them their full title, were undeniably an old family: Bohemian Barons since 1556; Counts of Bohemia since 1723 and Counts of the empire since 1745. Without ever rising to the top of the political or social tree, they had given, through many generations, loyal service to the Monarchy. Sophie's own father, Count Bohuslav, had served, for example, as Austro-Hungarian Minister to the court at Brussels (when he had helped to arrange the luckless marriage of Princess Stephanie to Crown Prince Rudolf) and had ended his diplomatic career as Minister in Dresden, where he had chosen to live after retirement. Her mother, who had died in 1886, was a Kinsky, which made the lineage more impressive still. The Kinskys were among the most distinguished names of the empire, with several country estates and a delightful baroque palace in Vienna which is still owned by a member of the family to this day. They were also more cosmopolitan than the Choteks. In 1883, a Count Kinsky had, after all, won the Grand National steeplechase in England and that put the family on a roll of honour that was to continue unfolding long after the books had been closed on the Habsburg Monarchy.

Yet not even this combination of parents could bring Sophie within the pale of imperial eligibility. This may appear odd indeed to readers a hundred years later. They, after all, have witnessed an American woman being a serious candidate for the King of England's hand (and being ruled out more because she was a divorcée than because she was a plain Mrs); and later, another Prince of Wales actually marrying the equivalent of his Countess Sophie amid a universal chorus of approval and rejoicing. But the Habsburg court of Franz Ferdinand's time – and particularly its ruling branch, in which he himself had come to figure so prominently – lay a universe as well as a century apart from these events. Even leaving aside the Olympian figure of the Emperor himself, the gap between archdukes and ordinary nobility was in some ways as great as the gap between nobility and the *grande bourgeoisie*. (The nobility, well aware of this, consoled themselves by exaggerating their own importance: 'Life begins from count upwards' was their lofty motto, which betrayed that vulnerability which is at the root of much loftiness.)

Nor, so far as the Habsburgs were concerned, was the situation defined only by mottoes. It had been formally set out in 1825 when the ruling houses of Prussia, Austria, Bavaria, Hanover, Württemberg, Baden and Hesse (all the Germanic ones still in place after Napoleon had completed his ravages) agreed on schedules of nobility who were formally declared eligible for marriage into their august circle. The list, as published on 7 October 1825 for Austria[5], included fourteen 'princely houses domiciled in the Monarchy' and six old families headed by mere counts who were included for special historical or genealogical reasons. But neither the Choteks nor even the Kinskys – and indeed some names still more illustrious – had got on that list; and once drawn up, the magic circle was defended to the death by those inside it.

The love of the Archduke and his Bohemian Countess was the purest of all that varied procession of romantic tragedies which the Habsburg dynasty unfolded in its dying years. There had been, for example, precious little true romance about the over-sentimentalized death pact of Mayerling, itself but a sordid puppet show compared with the fateful tragedy of Sarajevo. Yet though that last orgy of self-pity in Crown Prince Rudolf's life has been described in minute (if often contradictory) detail by literally dozens of figures who flitted about on the wings of the Mayerling stage, much of Franz Ferdinand's love-story, like the man himself, remains veiled. Even his one surviving child cannot remember ever being told (and never seems to have asked) when and where her father and mother first met. Professor Adam Mueller-Guttenbrunn,* who was certainly very close to the Archduke at this stage in his life, writes of a ball attended by Franz Ferdinand at Prague – no year given – at which he, the Professor, saw Sophie for the first time. But though he describes how she was constantly seeking the Archduke out with those

---

* The anonymous author of *Ein Lebensroman*.

large brown eyes of hers, he makes it plain that the royal guest of honour may not have noticed these attentions, let alone responded to them, so preoccupied was he throughout the evening with other people.[6] This has not stopped later writers building a whole wedding-cake fantasy upon this one reference, with the Archduke advancing on the curtsying Countess and sweeping her away for a waltz under the chandeliers, followed by a long and animated conversation with her alone on the sofa of an adjoining salon. In fact it has now become quite clear that this Prague ball was by no means the first occasion that the Archduke had caught a glimpse of Countess Chotek.

The earliest tangible evidence of the couple together is a photograph, produced by the Windisch-Graetz family nearly a century after these events, of a shooting party held at Halbthurn near what is now the Hungarian border, in the winter of 1893. Halbthurn was one of the many properties of Archduke Frederick, husband of the Archduchess Isabella in whose household Sophie was engaged as lady-in-waiting, and the picture seems to portray the relationships as well as the features of the people in it. In the centre, the Heir-Presumptive, in the most jovial of moods at resuming his beloved sport in his beloved homeland after his world travels, embraces his host and cousin for the benefit of the camera. Archduke Frederick himself, agreeable though far from handsome, cuts a distinctly unimpressive figure compared with his wife. Isabella looks (and was) a formidable lady indeed: a short and bulky stature which seems compressed with energy and the steady gaze of a highly-capable and highly-motivated matriarch. As befits her position, Countess Sophie stands on the outside of the group. She looks demure, but by no means downtrodden.

Ironically, the lives of both women, the lady-in-waiting as well as her Archduchess employer, were dominated by the same problem – too large a family. Sophie was one of eight children which Wilhelmine had borne to Count Bohuslav before her death, and five of these were daughters. As the Count relied largely on his salary and then his pension, any of the girls who reached marriageable age without marrying sought to take themselves off his hands by finding employment: and for a young lady of noble birth in Franz Joseph's Monarchy this meant, in turn, becoming either a lady-in-waiting or a nun. (One of Sophie's elder sisters, Zdenka, in fact did both – starting off in the service of Crown Prince Rudolf's widow before eventually taking holy orders.) And so it was that in the summer of 1888, Sophie, the fourth of Count Bohuslav's daughters, took up her post with the Archduchess Isabella.

There were certainly no financial difficulties in her employer's household. Isabella was born a Princess Cröy (one of the foreign families within that small magic circle of nobility deemed eligible for marriage to royalty*) and was not without means of her own. But when, on 8 October 1878, at the age of twenty-two, she married the Archduke Frederick at Hermitage Castle, her Belgian family home, she joined hands with one of the richest of all the Habsburgs. In the smoking room of a secluded house in the Styrian mountains, one of the grandchildren from that marriage still possesses a five-panelled rosewood screen which has, on the top of the five panels, a painting of the five principal properties her grandfather possessed. The most magnificent is the Albertina in Vienna, long since converted, with many of its original treasures, into one of the principal art museums of the Austrian republic. But the most delightful of the five is certainly the castle at Pressburg in Bohemia – an eighteenth-century gem of that greatest of baroque architects, Fischer von Erlach. The beautifully proportioned wings, parapets and windows are perfectly set off over the centre by a large copper dome whose green colouring blends in turn with the yellow of the façade below. It was a castle almost fashioned for romance.

But if the Archduchess Isabella had no shortage of money, she suffered, to an even greater degree than Count Bohuslav Chotek, from a worrisome surplus of daughters. Between November 1879 and January 1893, she bore her husband six in a

---

* Prince and Princess were not royal titles in Austria. All members of the royal house of Habsburg were archdukes and archduchesses and everything else was aristocracy, in which the highest rank was duke and duchess, followed by prince and princess, etc.

row who were to survive to marriageable age, before finally, in June of 1897, presenting him with Albrecht, a son and heir.

Isabella clearly made herself many enemies, as someone of her great wealth and strong personality was bound to do in the intrigue-ridden, incestuous court society of the day. But even those critics who claimed that her husband's great fortune had completely gone to her head could not deny that she managed that fortune – and the numerous great households it sustained – far better than a gentler and less energetic wife could have done. The charge against her of overweening social ambition is even less generous. Of princely birth herself, she had married into the ruling branch of the Habsburg family (her husband, who was also Duke of Teschen, was descended from a brother of the Emperor's grandfather). With six daughters to wed, all of such pedigree and wealth, she could only set her sights high, as indeed any mother would. And the highest catch in the empire was Franz Ferdinand, who in addition to being Heir-Presumptive to the throne was the only other Archduke whose private fortune rivalled that of her own husband. What a match that would make! By the time the Archduke was transferred in 1894 to Budweis, so conveniently close to Pressburg, Isabella's eldest daughter, Maria Christina, was fifteen years old. Very young perhaps for this thirty-one-year-old man: but the mother was not to know that, in his private letters, he was dismissing such teenagers as raw chicks who were not worth the labour of turning into proper women. If the Archduke remained, as was normal, two to three years with his Bohemian brigade, that would surely give time enough for attraction and affection to develop between the two.

Isabella's own letters to the Archduke have survived. They give a lively picture of his first year at Budweis when, according to another witness,[7] he usually found time – despite his military duties, his preoccupations with his own Bohemian estates, and the obligatory trips to Vienna – to visit Pressburg twice a week. They are cosy, chatty letters always beginning with his nickname, 'Dear Franzi', and ending in the intimate *Du* style of address, 'Your dear cousin'. This intimacy she was fully entitled to employ as the wife of another member of the senior branch of the Habsburg tree. Yet all the time one senses that she is relishing not simply having joined his august family herself but the thought of welcoming him back into her own. It is the future mother-in-law rather than the cousin by marriage who wields the pen.

Fortunately, they shared the same passion for shooting and these early letters, sent in the autumn of 1894,[8] are full of invitations for him to shoot stag or roebuck with them or effusive thanks for return visits which they had paid to his own shooting lodge at Hahnenhort in Lower Austria ('We look back with the greatest joy to those cosy and merry days ...'). The daughters are rarely mentioned by name and the principal candidate, Maria Christina, never. But as the eldest she would usually accompany her parents; and the camera, all the rage and busily employed on these occasions, acted as a silent reminder of her presence. In one letter, sent the following May, she suggests that he should come to Pressburg just to collect some photographs and 'enjoy a good game of tennis'. Next to holding a gun in his hand, Franz Ferdinand enjoyed wielding a racquet. Little could he have dreamt what that tennis court at Pressburg held in store for him.

We are now into the year, 1895, when, as the Archduke himself was later to tell Archduchess Stephanie, he had fallen secretly in love with Sophie Chotek. Suddenly, a dark shadow falls across what must have been for him this happy, exciting scene. In the first week of August he writes to Pressburg with the sad message that his health is failing again, so that he must now hand over command of his brigade at Budweis (which he was to have led in the great summer manoeuvres) and seek instead rest and a complete change of air to cure his lungs. The effect of this message can be imagined. Isabella's reply begins, 'I cannot tell you how depressed I was with your news and how this preoccupies me ...'[9] But she is made of too stern stuff just to lament. She goes on to give him her 'grandmotherly advice' to follow the doctor's orders. Everything will surely be well in the end. And she assures him that even as 'a wretched cripple' (evidently his phrase to her) he will always be welcome in her home.

For the next part of the story we must turn in the main to the account given by Victor Eisenmenger, the young Viennese doctor who that summer, to his surprise and delight, found himself provisionally appointed the Archduke's personal physician, and was to remain so throughout the period of convalescence. At first, the patient refused point-blank to travel abroad – having just acquired another and quite overpowering reason for staying close to home. Indeed, it needed an order from the Emperor, no less firm for being couched in the style of kindly advice, to settle the matter: the Archduke could begin his cure in the mountains but should then move south for the winter.[10] Count Wurmbrandt, who would be travelling with his master, had no illusions over the difficulty of enforcing a regime of complete rest on the patient. He warned the doctor, 'The Archduke's accustomed lifestyle is the exact opposite of what you are demanding of him. Rarely ever does he stay in the same place for more than a day. For the last fortnight, I haven't slept once in a proper bed, always in a railway carriage.'[11]

He was not exaggerating Franz Ferdinand's restlessness, which was now more acute than ever. The first stage of the cure was spent at a hotel on the Mendel Pass above Bozen in what was then the Austrian South Tyrol. The Archduke soon got bored with lying on a bed or deck chair in the garden and admiring the lovely panorama of the Etsch and Eisack valleys below. One distraction he promptly hit upon was to shoot with a small air rifle at the tiny branches of a pine tree some thirty yards away. He knocked off hundreds of them, and so cleanly that the tree finally looked as though it had been trimmed by a gardener's shears.

Thus could he at least keep in touch with his oldest passion. To maintain contact with his newest passion, he had to rely on letters. The doctor soon noticed with what impatience the Archduke awaited the post each day, and how his spirits went up or down according to what it brought. Wurmbrandt grumbled that there must be a woman of some sort behind the mystery and even muttered that he knew who she was.[12] That is far from certain. Though the gruff Count may have had his suspicions, the only person in the Archduke's household who was certainly privy to the secret at this time was that indispensable private factotum, Franz Janaczek. Indeed, he had already begun his five-year stint in the additional role of Cupid's messenger between the Archduke and his Countess, posting letters or smuggling secret messages between the two. Little wonder that this archducal Leperello should eventually rise to become master of Franz Ferdinand's household.

The patient could not even last out in the South Tyrol for three weeks. After a family council held on the spot, Egypt was decided on for the winter's convalescence and the Adriatic island of Lussin (close to the great Austrian naval base of Pola) was chosen as a staging post for the autumn months. That meant that the Archduke, on his journey south, could pass through Vienna, and there he lingered until the last possible moment, doubtless giving the good Janaczek plenty to do in every respect.

The setting at Lussin was idyllic for anyone seeking relaxation and a complete escape from the world. The Archduke was quartered in the small pension of Dr Veth, well known for its excellent food, and he spent most of his days – when he was well enough and the rough Bora wind was not blowing – on the beach of a tiny isolated bay enclosed by an olive orchard. The trouble was, first, that Franz Ferdinand could never relax and, second, that, now more than ever, he was itching to get back into the world rather than turn his back on it. His Bohemian Countess was not the only reason for his restlessness. The dreadful thought had now begun to nag at him that back at court in Vienna they might already be writing him off as a doomed man and looking around for his replacement on the dynastic ladder.

Count Sternberg's unpublished diary gives a graphic description of the patient's mood at this time. Sternberg had the happiest memories of the Archduke from a trip around the Mediterranean they had made together that March in the chartered yacht *Flavio Giova*. It had been a merry journey, with Franz Ferdinand sometimes 'laughing until the tears rolled down his cheeks', and haunting the casino ('playing passionately at roulette, though with very low stakes') when they put in at Monte Carlo.[13] Then, on a visit to Vienna in November, Sternberg learned that his royal travelling companion of the summer was now lying gravely ill with tuberculosis on an Adriatic island. He set off at once, arrived at Lussin on 20 November 1895, and hurried straight to the Archduke, whom he found 'altered beyond recognition'.

'What do you say to this?' was the greeting. 'I suddenly wake up one day ill and now they have given me up. I feel so weak and I can hardly walk. For me, it's now only a question of time.'[14]

During the next few days, the jovial Sternberg – who, one feels, could have brightened up a batch of funeral mutes with his company – did his level best to pump cheerfulness and confidence into the sick man. But his jokes seem to have fallen as flat as the plentiful doses of their favourite Agale champagne. The Archduke only sparked once, and that was when the copy reached him of a tasteless article in the Budapest paper *Magyar Hirlap*, expressing great satisfaction that the star of this notoriously anti-Hungarian Habsburg was sinking fast. Sternberg was asked to draft a peppery reply, and the Archduke wrote a furious letter of complaint himself to the Emperor. Next to a reunion with the woman he loved and a reassertion of his position as Heir-Presumptive, confounding the Magyars was the next best incentive for regaining his health. But nothing seemed to be helping when Sternberg (after sailing around in the bay without the Archduke in a yacht prophetically called *Sofie*) took an emotional leave of the patient. 'When you get home, greet my beloved Vienna for me, for I shall never see it again,' was the Archduke's lachrymose farewell.

Someone who was very naturally concerned that he should see not only Vienna, but also Pressburg again was the Arch-duchess Isabella. Throughout that autumn, she sent the sick man long, cheerful letters, full of shooting gossip (who had bagged or missed the best stags, and where) as well as advice on which country and which spa might be best for the next stage in his cure. The Archduke had written one letter to Pressburg especially for one of the youngest daughters, the seven-year-old, nicknamed 'Isi'. The child was about to reply and enclose her picture, wrote her mother, adding archly, 'It seems to me the flirtation is going along very nicely.' But to make sure that her eldest daughter was also not forgotten, she sent him a photograph of all six of them together, mounted on horseback. Whatever her underlying motives, this was just the sort of medicine that any morbidly sick man can do with.

By the end of his time at Lussin, he was indeed improving: the temperature down, the coughing stopped, and the body weight at last increasing. Winter in Egypt was intended to carry on the good work, and so it did, once Eisenmenger and the now indispensable Janaczek (Count Wurmbrandt had been dropped from the party) could get the patient away from Cairo. One pest in this respect was the Austrian Ambassador there, Baron Heidler, whose social ambitions could not resist the temptations of having the Heir-Presumptive in his capital. Heidler had been expressly warned in advance that the Archduke wanted to have no formalities or festivities whatever; indeed, not even a speech of welcome. The patient himself was sceptical about the outcome. 'Our ambassadors are almost all useless at their work and only bother about giving dinners and getting grand crosses bestowed on them. Nothing else concerns them and if you want to get anything done, you must turn to the German embassy,' he burst out to his doctor.

The Archduke's scepticism was justified. He had barely entered the foyer of his hotel on Gezireh island when he glimpsed the unctuous figure of the Austrian envoy bearing down upon him. On that occasion, Franz Ferdinand escaped by simply bolting up the staircase to his rooms, a snub which was soon going the rounds of Cairo society. But in March of the following year, after a long sightseeing cruise by chartered steamer down the Nile to Luxor and Aswan (where his parents and two sisters joined him to ease his growing boredom) the Archduke had to return to Cairo and its social maelstrom again. This time Heidler, who had been complaining, bitterly and successfully, to Vienna about his treatment, got his satisfaction.

He was able to organize a full-blown mass in Cairo's Catholic church with a high chair covered in gold-trimmed velvet for the fuming Archduke to sit on in front of the whole congregation. There followed official dinners and courtesy calls on the Khedive, who complained, as he did to all sympathetic visitors, that he was virtually ignored by the British civil and military leaders, who were the real overlords of his land. Franz Ferdinand's ears proved particularly sympathetic as the Khedive had been partly educated at Vienna's Theresianum and could pour out his reproaches in fluent German.

More than once during his travels round India four years before, the Archduke had bridled against what struck him as the imperial arrogance of the English; now, he fairly bristled with indignation. The result was one of the very few political letters of Franz Ferdinand's to the Emperor which have survived – a four-page philippic levelled against the Austrian envoy and the British authorities in equal proportions. The former, he advised his uncle, 'should be transferred as soon as possible to Brazil or North America, where his tactless behaviour would cause less damage than in Egypt, a country which had shown hospitality to so many Austrians, including members of the royal family'. As for the British, the 'dreadful ruthlessness' of their behaviour caused general indignation: 'Each day one sees how they grasp every opportunity, through bribery and other means ... to deprive the Khedive of his last shreds of power and ultimately take his whole country from him, which is the prime aim of their policy of lies and deception.'[15]

Franz Ferdinand was himself a man who, once in power, would have ridden roughshod over any opposition to achieve a worthwhile aim, and the British were preoccupied in Egypt at that time with an aim they considered especially worthwhile – the despatching of an army southwards into the Sudan to take revenge upon the Mahdi and put down the dervish insurrection. How much the Archduke's words reflected pure moral indignation and how much a frustrated envy against the seemingly effortless exercise of imperial might must therefore remain uncertain.

53

But whatever state his temper was in, his health was steadily improving as he left Egypt and made his way home by slow and pleasant stages. His route took him via the Riviera, Spain and Lake Geneva (where he visited the Empress Elisabeth, always just as restless to get away from Vienna as he was to return to it). It was there that, on 17 May 1896, a message reached him that his father was dangerously ill. From Aswan, the Archduke Karl Ludwig had made a pilgrimage to the Holy Land, and there, ignoring the pleas of his doctor and putting piety before hygiene, he had drunk the waters of the sacred but very polluted Jordan river. The result was typhoid, in those days all too often a lethal disease.

So it proved now. His father died while Franz Ferdinand was hurrying back by special train from Switzerland to be at the bedside. It was his younger brother Otto who broke the news as the train pulled in at St Pölten, which is the last main stopping-point before the capital. A week later, the thrice-married Archduke was buried amidst the untidy jumble of Habsburg tombs in the vault of the Capuchin church in Vienna. A resolute *pater familias* even from beyond the grave, the dead man in his will expressed the desire that all his children should make dynastically suitable marriages, and even enjoined the Emperor to see to it personally that this was done. It was an ironic last wish, especially in view of the presence of Countess Sophie Chotek in the back row of the funeral service.

Franz Ferdinand was now Heir-Apparent to the throne; but appearances, as he rapidly discovered, could be very deceptive. Some of the outward trappings were forthcoming: he was provisionally quartered in Schönbrunn Palace and allotted a new Chamberlain – Count Franz Thun, who, as the Archduke immediately suspected, was to prove far too grand and politically ambitious a choice for the post.[16] But no formal announcement of Franz Ferdinand's status was ever made and this, coupled with his absence from Vienna throughout most of that summer, meant that the change simply passed the general public by. He spent the next few months at his great Bohemian estate of Konopischt; at Lölling (a small and far more intimate country house in Carinthia); and finally at Eckartsau, an eighteenth-century jewel of a castle some fifty miles north of Vienna which he promptly set about rescuing from its dilapidated condition.

All three venues were excellent for shooting (indeed they had been built largely or wholly with that in mind); and all gave possibilities for meetings with Sophie, formal or otherwise, at houses of relatives or mutual friends in the neighbourhood. But all kept him rusticated and away from the capital. This suited his enemies in the government or at court who wanted a more amenable as well as a healthier Habsburg prince to be groomed for the succession. The most powerful among the former was the Foreign Minister of the day, Count Agenor Goluchowski who, as a Pole, hated Russia and therefore fought tooth and nail the pro-Russian line that Franz Ferdinand had always favoured. The Archduke had demonstrated these sympathies in dramatic fashion as recently as September of that year when he had turned up – uninvited and totally unexpected – at the festivities to welcome the young Tsar Nicholas II on his first visit as sovereign to Vienna. Goluchowski was to get his revenge, however, when he persuaded the Emperor to take Archduke Otto, and not Franz Ferdinand, with him on the return visit to St Petersburg.

Otto was indeed the natural choice of those who preferred an heir to the throne with a weaker will as well as a seemingly stronger body. Goluchowski's chief ally with the Emperor in all this was the Court Chamberlain himself, Prince Alfred Montenuovo, a stiff and humourless martinet of a man whose passion for protocol concealed certain family complexes of his own.* Montenuovo was to prove a thorn in Franz Ferdinand's side until the Archduke's death, and did not abandon his pursuit even then. In 1896, presuming that the Archduke was a doomed man anyway, he was trying to kill him off politically. In this neither Goluchowski nor Montenuovo, nor any other of the imperial circle who now began, with them, to turn their faces

---

* He was descended from the morganatic marriage which Napoleon's widow, the former Austrian Archduchess Marie Louise, had entered into with Count Neipperg – of which the name Montenuovo is, of course, an Italianized version.

towards the 'new sun', seems to have realized that Otto as Emperor would most probably have meant not added radiance for the dynasty, but its total eclipse. Charming but utterly feckless and dedicated only to the pursuit of women, wine and song (in that order of priority and with quite a gap between the first and second) he was already – had his backers only realized it – in the process of driving his own body into a much earlier and far less honourable grave than the one destiny had marked out for his elder brother.

Seemingly blind to all this, the 'Otto lobby' set to work with renewed energy when Franz Ferdinand, his health improved though still not restored, left again, with the onset of autumn, for the South Tyrol, then Corsica and finally Algiers. It was Otto who now suddenly became archducal patron of all manner of societies and charities (none of which, given his hectic lifestyle, can have derived much direct benefit from the honour). It was Otto who was installed in the Augarten Palace, close to Schönbrunn itself, and with a far grander establishment of servants and livery than anything the real Heir-Apparent could boast of in Vienna. Most wounding of all, it was Otto who, more and more, was called on to represent the Emperor at formal functions both at home and abroad.

Though affection between the brothers was not yet soured by all this (that was to come soon over an issue just as close to Franz Ferdinand's heart) this winter of 1896–7 plumbed the depths of the sick man's angry despair. It comes pouring out in another long letter he wrote to his confidante, Countess Fugger, this time sent from Algiers. The torrent is touched off when he talks of seeing her again in Vienna:

> But you will realize that, in the pathetic and humiliating situation which I find myself forced into – an heir to the throne placed, so to speak, on paid leave of absence – I don't want to show myself in Vienna and have nothing to look for there. It is unbelievable what Goluchowski, who believes he is some sort of god, and his followers think up just to annoy me and alienate me, and simply kill me off morally ...
>
> Believe me, I'm not speaking out of envy. I don't begrudge

good old Otto – who is always fearfully begging my forgiveness – all this and more; I speak out because of my feelings for justice and also because of the light all this puts me in. For, if you please, I'm always being asked in letters from abroad: what have I done wrong . . . ? If only they at least had the tact to ask me whether this or that might be taken over by my brother so that I don't over-exert myself during my convalescence; but no, everything is simply decreed behind my back, and over my dead body . . .[17]

But in fact that letter, and that February of 1897, marked the beginning of the climb back up, as well as the low point of Franz Ferdinand's fortunes. The following month, he met the Emperor in Cannes, and though the Archduke got nowhere with a renewed campaign to strengthen the ties between Vienna and St Petersburg (Franz Joseph was not keen on conducting grand diplomacy from the Riviera), uncle and nephew parted on cordial terms. Indeed, the Archduke succeeded in making a real impression with a written plea to be consulted more often and not cut off entirely from the various affairs of state which especially concerned him. A few weeks later, in April of 1897, the Emperor wrote in reply one of the most heartening, if one of the bluntest, letters the Archduke was to receive from that undemonstrative sovereign:

Just like yourself, I have long felt the need to talk over with you all the questions which you touch on in your letter, and much else besides. I have only refrained from doing so thus far for fear of damaging your frail condition, for our discussion will be lively and not altogether agreeable; hopefully however it will lead to an understanding and convince you that I am guided by what is best for you, though I must also keep in mind my duty towards the Monarchy and the good of our family . . .[18]

The Emperor had also assured his troubled nephew that, once his health was restored, he would be given 'all the rights and duties appropriate to his station', and these now began to trickle in. He was allowed to take over from his late father, for example, the laborious work of examining and deciding upon appeals for clemency addressed to the Emperor; he was also made Colonel-in-Chief of the 7th Regiment of Uhlans, a military honour to add to his earlier promotion to the rank of Lieutenant Field-Marshal.

By that summer the Archduke, back in Austria again, already looked a healthier man. But to make sure there was no relapse he had to endure another winter's convalescence at home before the doctors would officially pronounce him a cured man. The end of the long ordeal, and the end of the Otto lobby, was an imperial edict of 29 March 1898 which appointed Franz Ferdinand to undertake broad supervisory duties on behalf of the High Command, in order to acquaint himself better 'with all aspects of the armed forces on land and sea'. He was in fact being made an unofficial Inspector-General. The formal rank would have suited him better, but he was nonetheless delighted with what he had got, for with the new post came the tiny nucleus for a Military Chancery of his own, with access to all relevant official papers.

That was the rehabilitation at home. Its equivalent to the outside world had come already in June of 1897 when it was Franz Ferdinand, once again the Emperor's Heir-Apparent, who was sent to London to represent the monarchy at the Jubilee celebrations for the sixty years of Queen Victoria's reign. His friend Count Sternberg, determined not to miss the event himself, was walking along the London pavements when he suddenly glimpsed the Archduke driving slowly by in his carriage and elbowed a way through the crowd to greet him. This time the reunion was a happy one.

The lungs were indeed healed, and for good. But where the scar remained for life was in the mind. Franz Ferdinand's temperament had always been introspective, despite his bursts of gaiety and his impish humour. On top of that introspection there was now superimposed a thick layer of suspicion. It was not simply that he never forgave those individuals who had intrigued against him. He also never forgot the side of human nature they had displayed and he tended, ever afterwards, to regard that darker side as being the whole of man.

At all events, he was now to face similar intrigue and opposition from an entirely different angle. The battle for his health was over; but the battle for his heart's desire was only just beginning.

CHAPTER FIVE

Scandal

THE GREAT SECRET of Franz Ferdinand's private life was so
closely guarded by him, and cloaked in such discretion by the
handful of people in the know, that not even his own descendants
can today fix the time when the scandal broke. The cardboard
boxes of his personal correspondence can, however, bring us
quite close to the answer. Vague references can be found dotted
about in several places; but the firmest clues are contained in
that stream of letters which he received, from the mid-nineties
onwards, from the Archduchess Isabella (and also, in this
particular context, those sent to him by her husband, Archduke
Frederick). Thus it is the would-be parents-in-law who establish
the date when their hopes were dashed.

Isabella's letters to her 'Dear Franzi' continue throughout
1898, the year of his final recovery and rehabilitation, in
precisely the same intimate and affectionate style as before. Only
one shows signs of being written under severe emotional stress;
but the cause, on this occasion, had nothing to do with Franz
Ferdinand. On the morning of 10 August 1898, the Empress
Elisabeth was stabbed to death by a deranged Italian anarchist as
she was walking from her favourite Geneva hotel, the Beau
Rivage, to the lake steamer station opposite. It was, surely, one
of the most senseless as well as the most unpredictable of all royal
assassinations. The murderer, Luigi Luccheni, had really come
to Geneva to kill the Duke of Orleans, who was due there that
day; the Duke did not turn up so Luccheni killed the Austrian
Empress as a substitute. Whether first or second choice,

however, the terrible deed was done, and the shock wave in Vienna was commensurate. The following day, Isabella scribbled an almost hysterical note in pencil to Franz Ferdinand about the murder, asking if they could possibly meet and talk the whole tragedy over.[1] But that moment of stress soon passed, and her correspondence for the rest of the year (during which the Archduke received her and her family, and also, presumably, her lady-in-waiting, as his shooting guest at Konopischt) is back in the normal vein.

Christmas greetings follow, and throughout the first seven months of the following year, Archduke Frederick continues such a friendly and chatty correspondence with Franz Ferdinand (including frequent references to the shoots they have had or expect to have together) that it is difficult to believe anything out of the ordinary had happened to disturb the familiar pattern. One of the last such letters, for example, written from Pressburg, is all about gun dogs: will 'Franzi' lend him one of the marvellous animals he has trained?[2] But the very last of such letters from anyone at Pressburg is dated the final week of July 1899. From then on, there is total silence. In Isabella's case, the silence is only broken by a telegram, sent to Franz Ferdinand in her son's name a full fifteen years later, and only one month before his assassination. Her husband, who was an infantry general, broke the silence after eight years, but only in a formal note from one military man to another concerning arrangements for the forthcoming Jubilee celebrations to mark the Emperor's fifty years on the throne.[3] Clearly, therefore, the scandal over Sophie must have erupted during June or July of 1899.

We are better served with descriptions of where and how it broke; indeed, almost too well served. All manner of fanciful reports were spread about afterwards. According to one version, the Archduke's secret passion for Countess Chotek came to Isabella's eyes and ears in Abbazia, when the Archduke, after a violent scene, is supposed to have ended the discussion with the ringing words 'Sophie is my bride.' As we have seen from Count Sternberg's diary, the Archduke and Sophie had indeed met during the springtime in previous years at Abbazia. But Franz

Ferdinand never visited that resort in midsummer; and we know from other evidence that, during that particular July and August of 1899, he was, as usual, on his estates at home.

It is the fateful incident after the tennis party at Pressburg itself that must be accepted as the true story. This not merely because it was fully described in 1925 by the Archduke's own private secretary,[4] but also because it has been confirmed long afterwards to the present writer both by Franz Ferdinand's daughter and by the grandchildren of the aggrieved Isabella. As so often on the Archduke's summer visits to Pressburg, there had been a tennis party on the court in the castle park and, at the end of the day, Franz Ferdinand had departed with the usual affectionate leave-taking and plans for the next reunion. Then a servant, clearing up in the changing-room, found something which the Archduke had left behind, and took it in to Archduchess Isabella. It was a heavy gold watch, made even heavier by the so-called *breloques* attached to it: seals, cigar-cutters and other small trinkets which the owner had collected over the years. One of these was a flat round medallion with a closed lid. It clearly contained someone's miniature portrait or photograph. Could that someone possibly be the eldest daughter of the house, on whom all hopes rested? The mother could not resist opening this very private possession, and, for her pains, promptly suffered a similar fate to those eavesdroppers who seldom hear good of themselves. Gazing out of the medallion were not the features of her own Maria Christina, then nearly twenty years old, but of her own lady-in-waiting, the thirty-one-year-old Countess Chotek.

It was probably the greatest shock and the greatest disappointment which the forceful Isabella, who was so used to getting her own way, had ever experienced. Mixed with it went a certain sense of betrayal, for ladies-in-waiting in private houses, though obviously not servants and certainly above governesses, were still members of the household and lived in a strange and awkward limbo between family and staff. A heated confrontation followed. Sophie, after initially trying to shield the Archduke, confessed to the relationship, and was ultimately, and inevitably, told that she could not continue in the Archduchess's service. But again, the accepted version of events, repeated in every book on the subject whether scholarly or academic, needs correcting. The distraught Countess was not thrown out on the spot as though she were some disgraced scullery maid. Her mistress may have had an iron will and a lively temper but she remained a *grande dame* for all that. Sophie had a fortnight's holiday due to her and she left Pressburg technically 'on leave'. While away she offered her resignation in writing from Vienna, and this was accepted. The proprieties had been observed.*

Another detail needs to be interjected here which also only came to light years later. Shortly before 1914, when Franz Ferdinand was a happily married man, already with three children, he invited his nephew Archduke Charles (who was to become the last of the Habsburg emperors) to visit him at Hahnenhort, a favourite shooting lodge of his in Lower Austria. With Charles went the vivacious Bourbon Princess he had married in 1911, the future Empress Zita. With a wry smile, Franz Ferdinand showed them a telegram which had been sent to him by the Archduchess Isabella some fifteen years before, inviting him to a shoot. It ended with the telltale sentence, 'Countess Chotek will be there.' Archduchess Isabella never dreamt that the heir to the throne would actually marry her lady-in-waiting (who could have imagined such a thing in *fin-de-siècle* Austrian society?), but she *had* realized that the Archduke was greatly attracted to Sophie, and had tried to turn this to advantage. Franz Ferdinand had had the telegram specially framed and hung up on the wall of his inner sanctum.[5] He can be pardoned for such mischievous satisfaction: he had carried away the bait whole, while avoiding the hook.

But back to Pressburg in midsummer of 1899. What was to happen now? Let us look to begin with at Sophie's plight, and the first thing to be said is that she now found herself not only exposed but compromised. Daughters of good families were not

---

* The fact that this information was supplied by Sophie's namesake, her own daughter – who certainly had no motive to defend the Archduchess Isabella – is good enough testimony to its accuracy.

The home-loving Archduke Karl Ludwig and the second of his three brides, the Sicilian Bourbon princess, Maria Annunziata, who died of consumption when Franz Ferdinand was seven years old.

The legendary Emperor towards the end of his ixty-eight-year reign. He is pictured at the desk, a lain field-army table, where he often spent up to urteen hours a day.

The Archduke surrounded by the army of gamekeepers and beaters who had provided him with a 'slaughter' of chamois. In fact, bags of this size were not unusual for the sportsmen of his day.

His first tiger, shot in 1893 on a six-week trip to India during his world tour. 'I cannot describe my joy,' he wrote.

The thirty-year-old lady-in-waiting he fell in love with. 'Apart from her striking looks . . . it was her air of quiet calm he found so irresistible.'

Sophie in demure attendance as her mistress, the formidable Archduchess Isabella, entertains the German Emperor, William II (left) and Emperor Franz Joseph (right).

Franz Ferdinand and Sophie – their love still a secret – on the castle tennis court at Pressburg where the scandal broke in 1899.

A postcard message sent by the Archduke to Sophie in their own 'lovers' code' while he was fighting for permission to marry her.

expected to indulge in secret romances and this applied with redoubled force to ladies-in-waiting, who were considered to be especially taboo for any predators – almost as though they were the secular equivalents of the vestal virgins. We know that Sophie, for her part, had confided in her own brothers and sisters (her father had followed her mother to the grave in 1896) when the Archduke first declared his love for her. They, contrary to popular belief, were more anxious than ecstatic over the extraordinary news. They shared the general philosophy of the time: an Archduke of the reigning branch, and above all one who was expected to reign himself, could never marry outside the small closed circle of eligible princesses; so where, they asked themselves, would this whole affair end for their sister – surely only in tears and shame? This was doubtless one reason why, on their side too, the secret had been so jealously guarded; now their worst fears seemed realized. Nobody as yet, not even, perhaps, Sophie, knew the depths of Franz Ferdinand's love and the price he was prepared to pay for it.

Sophie herself could do nothing but cling to his pledge and, in the meantime, had nowhere to go but to her own family. This is the point to nail another of those extraordinary legends which cling to the affair – namely the story that Sophie now fled into a nunnery (from which, in the more highly-coloured versions, the Archduke himself freed her). The story is repeated again and again, even in the most recent works about the period,[6] but according to her descendants (who would have no reason to deny it) it is completely false. The first thing that Sophie *did* do after that distressing scene at Pressburg was to go to Vienna, to stay at the apartment of her aunt Zdenka, who was also a lady-in-waiting, in the household of the widowed Crown Princess Stephanie. This aunt did herself eventually go into a nunnery and the confusion may have arisen thus. In any case, Sophie's own movements from midsummer of 1899 until the resolution of the crisis are, in the main, known. From Vienna she went to Kosterlitz in Bohemia to one of her Kinsky uncles; from there to Dresden to stay with a younger sister, Marie, who was married to Karl Adam von Wuthenau; and from there she moved to

Grosspriesen, near Teplitz, to stay with another uncle, Count
Carl Nostitz, where she left her things until her future was
decided. The pattern from then on was to travel between the
country estates of her large family, which included five married
sisters and brothers, and their various neighbours.

As can be seen, there was no lack of choice. Among the
relatives or in-laws with whom she spent the next desperate
months of waiting were, apart from those already named, Count
and Countess Franz and Sophie Kinsky and Count and
Countess Leopold and Cara Nostitz (both in Bohemia); Count
and Countess Jaroslav and Marie Thun in Moravia; Count and
Countess Edwin and Willy Henckel in Silesia and Prince and
Princess Alois and 'Osy' Lowenstein in Salzburg.[7] This broad
geographical choice of castles made it possible for the Archduke,
on his travels, to meet with her discreetly from time to time to
discuss the way out of their plight. Where meetings were
impossible, contact was maintained by coded telegrams, picture
postcards with secret signs, and long letters, often delivered in
person by the good Janaczek.

It was of course the Archduke who stood at the centre of this
blazing circle of intrigue. The main battle was fought out far
away from the public gaze under the chandeliers at court, and
here Franz Ferdinand found himself heavily outnumbered. His
bitterest opponent was Archduchess Isabella (who promptly
brought the matter to the Emperor's attention) and her wide
circle of family and friends. She probably did not need to do
much intensive lobbying, for the majority, especially among the
highest aristocracy, who stood closest to the royal family, had the
same instinctive reaction as Isabella herself, though for purely
objective reasons. A romance between the Heir-Apparent and a
lady-in-waiting would be bad enough if it were purely a passing
affair, but positively devastating to the whole hierarchical order
of which they were all a part if it were taken seriously. In the eyes
of the *Erste Gesellschaft*, or top rung of society, the marriage just
wouldn't do.

The Archduke's other active opponents at court all based
themselves, out of different motives, on this same philosophy.

Foremost was, of course, the Court Chamberlain, Prince Montenuovo, whose whole desiccated being was devoted to the preservation of the existing hierarchy. Franz Ferdinand would have expected nothing else from his old enemy. What surprised and saddened him was that both his brothers immediately joined the ranks against Sophie, and never budged.

In 'Handsome Otto's' case, the motive can hardly have been personal ambition, for this would have been far better served by actually promoting an unsuitable match for the heir. Perhaps he was compensating for the unbridled profligacy of his private life by upholding all the more fiercely the public sanctity of the dynasty. After all, he had been talked into his disastrous marriage with the plain Saxon princess in order to make a sacrifice for that dynasty. Why should 'Franzi' be allowed to do as he pleased?

The virtuous indignation of the younger brother, Ferdinand Karl, was particularly ironic in view of his own fate. For this weak and dreamy boy was soon to fall in love with Fraulein Csuber, the daughter of a mere university professor, whom he then married without the Emperor's consent. As a result he was stripped of all rank, titles, decorations and privileges, cast out of the Habsburg family and condemned to a wretched life in exile as plain Herr Burg, a life which ended with his early death in 1919.

But that all lay in an unforeseen future. At the turn of the century, the fact that both brothers had joined the archducal and princely ranks against the Heir-Apparent made the fight look almost hopeless. Two women who always had the Emperor's ear were also implacably against Sophie. One was Katharina Schratt, the Viennese comedy actress with whom, for decades, the Emperor had conducted a companionable romance which was as correct as it was deeply-felt (they used regularly to breakfast together, though without, so far as one can judge or imagine, ever having spent the previous night together). The other lady Franz Ferdinand had particularly to fear was Franz Joseph's beloved grand-daughter, the Archduchess Elisabeth, only child of the late Crown Prince Rudolph. She opposed Franz

Ferdinand in everything, presumably because he had taken her own father's place on the steps of the throne.

Paradoxically, her mother, the widowed Crown Princess Stephanie, was just as resolutely on the Archduke's side. Apart from the affection they had always had for each other, there was now a special reason for this support. Stephanie was struggling to get an 'unsuitable' match of her own approved; she was determined to marry a Hungarian noble, Count Lonyáy, with whom she had fallen in love. So, throughout the months ahead, she was fighting the Heir-Apparent's battle in reverse.* For this reason, however, she did not now count for very much at court. A much more powerful voice pleading for Franz Ferdinand was that of the Archduchess Maria Theresa, his angelic stepmother, who, as always, stood by him. But that was about all the support he could hope for in the innermost court circle. It did not seem very weighty in the coming struggle for the Emperor's mind.

Franz Joseph's own reaction to 'the Chotek affair' had been predictable. He was aghast at this heavy new blow threatening the empire and the dynasty of which he was the head. His own son had ended his life in circumstances that were criminal as well as humiliating, and though the shadow of Mayerling was now ten years old, the Emperor was never to overcome either the shock or the shame of it. Since then other blots, great and small, had fallen on the escutcheon. The lifestyle of 'Handsome Otto', Franz Ferdinand's own brother, was a permanent reproach to the family honour. Even the women of the imperial house were not, it seemed, to be relied on. Had the Emperor but known it, the wife of Crown Prince Frederick Augustus of Saxony, the Habsburg-born Archduchess Louise of Tuscana, had already fallen in love with a Monsieur Giron, the Belgian tutor of her four children, with whom in 1902 she duly eloped – leaving him in turn for Enrico Toselli, the Italian pianist and composer. Her doubly cuckolded and deserted Saxon prince took it all with admirable phlegm ('I only hope she can decide between the two' was his reported reaction); but the scandal was to shake European society like an earthquake.

* Stephanie won her battle before Franz Ferdinand and remarried on 9 March 1900.

But no matter what embarrassments to the dynasty came before or after it, the affair of Franz Ferdinand and his Countess was uniquely grave, for the Archduke now in love with the wrong woman was Heir-Apparent to the throne. The Emperor's horror deepened when, at the first confrontation with his nephew, he found Franz Ferdinand determined not to choose between bride and throne, but to have them both. A sustained campaign was launched from all sides to break his will.

One of the first to be mobilized personally by the Emperor for the task was Gottfried Marschall, the jovial priest who had once been Franz Ferdinand's religious instructor and who had recently become a bishop. The prelate seems to have laboured at his thankless task for weeks, approaching it from every possible angle.[8] He appealed directly to his former pupil to do his duty as the heir to an apostolic throne; he mobilized the Archduke's sisters to bring their influence to bear on their wayward brother; finally, he tackled Sophie herself during that first stay of hers in Vienna, imploring her to save the dynasty and renounce not only her loved one but the world itself by retreating into a nunnery. (As we have seen, that proposal, despite reports to the contrary, was not followed.) But the sisters remained hesitant; the Archduke remained obdurate; and all that the wretched prelate planted in Sophie's mind was a bitter animosity that was to do him no good at all in his later career.

How many sessions the sovereign himself had with his nephew we do not know, for hardly any documentary evidence has survived. However, one telegram does exist which almost certainly has a bearing on the subject. It was despatched by the Emperor from his Vienna winter palace, the Hofburg, on 5 October 1899, and addressed to Franz Ferdinand at his shooting lodge in Lower Austria. (This was the stag-rutting season, the high point of the hunter's year, and nothing would keep the Archduke from that.) The text, without introduction or a single word of greeting, reads simply, 'Please come here in the next few days and inform me and Otto of your arrival.'[9] A gruff summons like that can have had only one significance during that particular autumn.

The new year, and the new century, dawned with the deadlock still unbroken. But as it now looked as though nothing would stop the Archduke marrying the woman he loved, only two questions remained to be answered. First, would the Emperor agree to a morganatic marriage which would preserve the right of succession for his nephew? Second, if he did agree, how would the position of Franz Ferdinand's wife, and any children she bore him, be regulated for the period before and after he came to the throne?

As all the politicians, constitutional lawyers, archdukes, and amateur court pundits alike in Vienna wrestled with little else but this intricate problem for the next six months, its historical background is worth a brief look. The concept of a morganatic union (*Matrimonium ad Morganiticam, Matrimonium ad Legem Salicam*) went back at least to the Roman Empire and meant originally a marriage between a free and an unfree person. Over the centuries it was extended to cover any marriage between a couple of unequal standing.

The house of Habsburg was itself no stranger to the practice. As far back as 1557, Ferdinand, Count of Tyrol had formed such a union with Phillipine Welser, the daughter of a patrician from Augsburg, and all manner of complications had resulted. There had been two cases in the nineteenth century which had just closed. By far the most famous was the marriage, on 2 September 1823, of Archduke Johann, who lost his heart to Anna Plochl, the comely daughter of a mere postmaster. It was also to prove the most radiant of such unions. The couple settled in Brandhof, a small estate tucked into the waist of a lovely green mountain in Styria (Anna was initially given the title of 'Baroness Brandhof'), and there they lived out an idyllic life that has echoes in legend and song to this day. To this day too, Brandhof itself flourishes, and also the family of the Counts of Meran, descendants of the marriage. A less well known but equally romantic case cropped up forty years later when Archduke Heinrich married the singer Leopoldine Hofman. Franz Joseph, by then of course well-established on the throne himself, repeated his predecessor's formula by bestowing on

Leopoldine the title of Baroness Waldeck. In each case, those legal arrangements which had developed throughout the German-speaking lands (where such unions were known as 'marriages of the left hand') came smoothly into operation. The wife took the ring of her husband, but not his name, rank or privileges. Her children were to be called after her and their rights were subject to restriction éven in matters of property inheritance.

But both these cases were purely family affairs. They posed no political or dynastic problems because the archdukes concerned were far removed from the succession. (Archduke Johann, for example, was the seventh son of the Emperor Leopold II.) With Franz Ferdinand the crown was faced, for the first time, with an Heir-Apparent resolved to marry a woman who could never become an archduchess, let alone an empress.* It was, above all, a constitutional maze that love had drawn Franz Ferdinand into, and to find a way out of it he turned, early in the new year, to his one-time tutor in law, Max von Beck. This highly capable devil's advocate† concentrated not so much on the court – where as a mere *Freiherr*, ennobled only two years previously, he had little influence – but on the political leaders of the day, and above all on the Austrian and Hungarian Prime Ministers, Ernest von Koerber and Kálmán von Szell. If they were prepared to advise the Emperor that a morganatic marriage along suitable lines would not undermine the Monarchy, then the Archduke's cause would be mightily helped.

The agreement of the Hungarian leader was crucial. There was nothing in the laws of the ancient Magyar kingdom, which was so restlessly incorporated in the empire, to forbid morganatic unions. In theory, therefore, Sophie could be acknowledged one day as Queen of Hungary without being accepted as Empress of Austria-Hungary. Worse still, the Hungarians were threatening to use the debate to further their long-term aim of

---

* Other European royal dynasties had to deal with the problem from the throne: Tsar Alexander II of Russia, for example, concluded a morganatic marriage with Countess Dolgorucki, and King Victor Emmanuel of Italy married Countess Mirafiore.

† He was to serve as Austrian Prime Minister from 1906 to 1908.

loosening their own dynastic ties with the imperial crown; and this conjured up the spectre of some Habsburg archduke from one of the cadet branches of the family sitting, as a quasi-independent sovereign, on the Hungarian throne. It was an appalling cat's cradle of dynastic politics tugging against human passion. In one of the few letters on the crisis to have survived, Archduke Rainer (who had succeeded the now defunct Field-Marshal Albrecht as custodian of the Habsburg conscience) is seen laying out the dilemma before Franz Ferdinand in a desperate appeal to his nephew to think again about the fateful union:

> As far as your own affair is concerned, I can only repeat what I said to you a few days ago. If it is at all possible for His Majesty to agree to give his consent, he simply cannot take a decision before the constitutional questions are cleared up, and in both halves of the Monarchy. Your case, because of your position, is quite different from that of any previous archduke. They stepped into the background after concluding morganatic marriages. But you, the first in line, are not prepared to renounce your right to succeed ... H.M., *and especially you*, carry this responsibility for the entire empire ...
>
> Try and preoccupy yourself with serious activity and reflect carefully on the consequences of the step you propose to take, because I do not believe that you will find lasting happiness in this union. To see a wife you love disadvantaged will cause you pain, and should things turn out not as expected and you do not find the domestic happiness you hoped for, everything will be even more difficult to bear. Every man has to face up to painful moments, some more difficult than others. Recalling one's duty helps to overcome these, and the higher one stands the less one can allow oneself to be deflected from fulfilling that duty. For this reason it is not possible for me to support your wishes ...

And the stern voice of duty went on to make it quite plain that, whatever happened in the future, he would *always* speak up against the marriage whenever his opinion was sought.[10]

All this time, what was helping Franz Ferdinand survive the ordeal was not so much recalling his duty to the dynasty as recalling his love for Sophie. As described above, throughout these months they continued to keep in touch, either by secret meetings or by exchanging messages. Whenever these messages could not be delivered by hand, little post offices in the countryside suddenly came to play a big role in their lives. One charming example is provided by the memoirs of a certain Bruno Richter, which the Archduke's family have preserved. Richter had been since 1896 imperial postmaster at Grosspriesen, the little spa where Sophie's uncle, Count Carl Chotek, had his estate and where she spent several of these anxious weeks of 1900.

He writes how, one day in the town, he met Countess Sophie, who was normally nearly always absent in the service of the Archduchess Isabella. She told him that she was now going to stay for a while in Grosspriesen, to which he politely replied that he was very pleased to hear it. He continues:

> Soon afterwards, I was very puzzled when a lengthy telegram arrived from Vienna addressed to Countess Sophie, written in a fashion that gave one a lot to think about. The signature was 'Hohenberg'. When, over the next few days, several more telegrams of the same sort arrived, she asked me, 'Please be so good and bring any more letters or telegrams that arrive for me up to the castle in the evening.' I gladly agreed. Whenever I rang, it was always Countess Sophie herself who appeared and took over the post. It often happened that when I got back from the castle I found an urgent service message announcing another telegram for the Countess, so I had to make the journey all over again.
>
> One day, the Director of the Post rang up himself. 'Postmaster,' he said, 'I must inform you that the letters and telegrams which have been arriving over the past few days for Countess Sophie Chotek come from a member of the imperial house. Take the greatest care to observe any special instructions and refuse to give any information to newspaper reporters . . .' When I met the Countess that same afternoon, I told her about the call. She got very alarmed but I calmed her by saying that we had spoken on an official line and no-one would hear about it.[11]

Without knowing it, the good postmaster of Grosspriesen was

providing a rare, if not unique, first-hand glimpse behind the heavy curtains which screened the romance.

In May of 1900, while the messages were raining down on Grosspriesen, the battle was reaching its climax. On 19 May, Franz Ferdinand suddenly received good news from Beck. The political leaders of Austria and Hungary, the jurist wrote, had now reached complete agreement, though, to avoid complications, they both thought it would be better to hold the wedding when the parliaments of Vienna and Budapest were not in session. The main concession required of the Archduke was 'the usual form of renunciation for his descendants'. The Austrian Prime Minister, Koerber, with whom Beck had just spoken, was to have an audience with the Emperor on the matter the following morning. The best thing Franz Ferdinand could do in the meantime was to take 'decisive action' with his own brothers. But he, Beck, judged the position to be 'hopeful, surprisingly hopeful'.[12]

Beck also enclosed the draft of a final plea which the Archduke was to send to his sovereign, so that full advantage could be taken of this favourable turn of fortune. It was a long and skilfully constructed epistle in which the human appeal of nephew to uncle was blended with the dynastic arguments of an heir-apparent calming his sovereign's fears.

The first approach was sounded in the opening sentences:

> Increasingly weighed down as I am by the agonising situation in which I have for some time found myself, I turn again towards Your Majesty's fatherly heart with the most pressing of pleas to fulfill for me that deepest and dearest of my wishes, on which depends the whole of my future existence, my happiness, my peace, and my contentment ... I can only say again that my desire to marry the Countess does not spring from a passing mood, but flows from the profoundest attachment, tested by many years of suffering ...

The letter goes on to assure the Emperor that, by renouncing 'all family and other rights' for the children of his morganatic marriage, any constitutional objection will be met. He offers his own 'independence of character' as a guarantee that, in future years, nobody would be able to talk him or his wife out of his renunciation pledge and he continues with a passage which was to prove somewhat ironic and over-pitched in view of what was to come in the years immediately ahead:

> There are no difficulties on the ceremonial or representational side, for, as I have already mentioned and permitted myself to promise, the Countess will never show herself either at court or in high social circles and will never make claims of any sort or seek to play any role. I know her character, disposition and her heart too well not to be assured that she will take her place with total lack of pretensions and will live only for our happiness and for our peaceful, contented love ...[13]

The letter concluded with two pieces of gentle moral blackmail. First, the Emperor was asked to acquiesce in order to quieten public opinion, for 'the great majority of the population live in the unshakeable conviction that I am already secretly married to the Countess and have several children by her'. (This was a pardonable exaggeration. Even at this late date, the Archduke's romance was much more talked about in the salons than on the streets.) Second, the Emperor was reminded of the effects a refusal might have on his nephew's health: his nerves, the Archduke pointed out, were already in tatters. The spectre of a second Mayerling – which had already been raised by the Foreign Minister Goluchowski – was a terrible one indeed to invoke with the ageing sovereign.

So, towards the end of May, despite last-minute reservations expressed by the Vatican, the pressures for consent converged powerfully around the Emperor's head: Koerber, his Prime Minister, assuring him that the constitutional problem was manageable, even with the Hungarians; Goluchowski, his Foreign Minister, hinting that a distraught Franz Ferdinand might even blow his brains out and take Countess Sophie with him into the next world; his sister-in-law, the gentle Archduchess Maria Theresa, pleading eloquently for her stepson's happiness; and the Archduke himself, metaphorically down on his knees, for the first and last time in his life. Whether the Emperor gave in with good grace or bad at his final audience with Franz Ferdinand (one semi-fictionalized version has him sternly saying, 'I hope, nephew, that you will never live to regret this')[14], the important thing was that he had consented to a unique departure in the six hundred-year-old history of his dynasty. For the first time the heir to the throne was to marry far beneath him, with all that this entailed for the future of the Monarchy.

Franz Ferdinand's impatience to get everything over was now helped by the fact that his uncle shared his own passion for hunting and for the countryside. As every June came round, the Emperor would leave Vienna for a long sojourn at his lovely villa-cum-shooting lodge at Bad Ischl in the Salzkammergut. He was reluctant to allow even a momentous affair such as this to disturb his schedule and, in the event, he was just able to keep to the long-established routine. But first there had to come Franz Ferdinand's public ceremony of triumph and submission combined.

It was staged in an apartment of the Hofburg which was the core of the dynasty's history, the so-called Secret Council Chamber. This was where, in past centuries, the emperors had met to confer with their chancellors and army commanders and where, in 1848, the newly-crowned Franz Joseph, then a royal stripling only eighteen years old, had read his own speech from the throne. A very different speech in a very different setting had been prepared for the august assembly which gathered there shortly before noon on the morning of Thursday 28 June 1900. Every other adult archduke of all lines of the Habsburg family was there – a total of fifteen, headed by Franz Ferdinand's two brothers, who took their places to the left of the gilded coronation chair, overhung with its heavy purple baldachin. To the right of the chair stood Franz Ferdinand himself, flanked by his two witnesses, Count Albert Nostitz and his future brother-in-law, Count Wolfgang Chotek. In front of them were grouped the government ministers, the senior court officials, the Cardinal-Archbishop Dr Gruscha and his attendants, the privy councillors and provincial governors summoned from all the lands of the empire, the black-frocked notaries and a sprinkling of military figures such as the Adjutant-General and the Captain of the Lifeguards.

The Emperor, resplendent in his Field-Marshal's uniform, stood on a raised platform in front of the throne to make his brief address. In it he called on the assembly to witness this act of grave importance for the dynasty and the empire. The Archduke Franz Ferdinand had 'followed the call of his heart' in desiring to marry Countess Sophie Chotek and he, the Emperor, had given his consent 'out of consideration for his well-loved nephew'. However, as the Countess was of noble but not of equal birth, the marriage could only be morganatic and therefore neither she nor her children could be accorded any of the rights of a marriage between equals.[15] When the Emperor had finished, the Archduke's old adversary, 'that dreadful Polack', the Foreign Minister Count Goluchowski, read out the full text of the declaration of renunciation. Franz Ferdinand then stepped forward. He first took the oath by holding two fingers of his ungloved right hand on a bible held for him by the Cardinal-Archbishop and then seated himself at a small table to sign his declaration and its accompanying deeds in both German and Hungarian versions. Finally, his personal seal was impressed on all the documents by the public notary. The ceremony, which had lasted less than thirty minutes, was over, and they all filed out, the monarch and his archdukes withdrawing to the inner apartments. Many of those present must have silently echoed the words with which Franz Ferdinand had ended his oath, 'So help me God!'

The day after those momentous happenings at the Hofburg, a radiant Countess Sophie, who had been following events from Grosspriesen, met Postmaster Richter again in the streets of the town. 'Well,' she said to her faithful messenger, 'now you know who the sender of all those letters and telegrams is, the heir to the throne. He is coming this Sunday with the express train which is being specially halted here so that he can meet my relatives. If you are interested, go to the station, but don't tell anybody about it.'[16]

The postmaster did indeed turn up (and so, of course, did

civic dignitaries, half the local population and scores of holidaymakers) to watch the Archduke arrive and meet the various members of the Chotek family assembled at the station to welcome him. (Sophie herself had already left for the house of her sister, Baroness Wuthenau, in Dresden, where the formal engagement was to take place.) The passengers of the Vienna–Berlin express waited and watched for half an hour, their curiosity probably greater than their impatience, as Franz Ferdinand warmly thanked his new in-laws, especially Count Carl Chotek and Countess Olga, for their kindness towards his parentless bride-to-be. Then, as the train pulled out, all thoughts turned to the marriage itself, which was to take place in precisely four days time. Among the most excited of the guests was Frau Richter senior. Sophie, on a happy impulse, had invited the postmaster to the wedding, but, like a good civil servant, he had pleaded the call of duty, and had got his mother asked instead. His assumption that the local post office would be in for a very hectic time was borne out. On the wedding day, he counted the arrival of some two thousand telegrams addressed to the bridal couple as well as almost a thousand letters of congratulation.

*　　*　　*

Although it was held only one week after Franz Ferdinand's solemn oath of renunciation, preparations for his wedding had been going on since the end of May, when it was clear that the Emperor would consent to the match. Even the place chosen symbolized that inequality between the partners which had been officially signed and sealed in the Hofburg. It was not the bride's home which was selected, as was normal, nor even a neutral setting, but a castle of the bridegroom's family, Reichstadt in northern Bohemia. This sprawling building, built on a slight rise overlooking the town from the north, numbered nearly two hundred rooms, and the many courtyards and annexes added over the centuries told in stone the story of a rich and varied past. Originally the property of the great Bohemian family of Lobkowitz (who introduced camels into the park – the first to be seen in Europe) it had passed successively through the hands of the last Duke and then the wife of Duke Gaston of Medici. She was followed as owner by three other German dukes, then by King Maximilian of Bavaria, and finally by the Grandduke Ferdinand III of Tuscany before the Habsburgs finally acquired the property in 1824. It had at least one greater claim to fame than those seventeenth-century camels. It was here that Napoleon, by adding all the surrounding estates to the castle, created the so-called 'Duchy of Reichstadt', of which he made his only son the Duke. The creation was as short-lived as it was artificial. At the death of the ill-fated child, who never saw his tiny new kingdom, the duchy and the dukedom faded away with him.

There was a very good reason why Reichstadt was chosen for this happier moment in its history. Its present summer inhabitant was Franz Ferdinand's own stepmother, the widowed Archduchess Maria Theresa, and both bride and groom were well aware how much of their happiness was owed to her. She was there on the castle steps to greet them when they arrived to prepare for the wedding on the afternoon of 30 June – travelling together in the first of a procession of carriages from the station. The other family guests had all arrived by the evening. Even at this late stage, the local newspapers were speculating whether the bridegroom's brothers might turn up (it was already clear that the Emperor himself would not attend). Franz Ferdinand knew better. There would be two other archduchesses present, his own half-sisters, Elisabeth and Maria Annunziata. But all of that phalanx of fifteen uncles, brothers and cousins who had witnessed his oath the week before had now found themselves hindered by other engagements.* He would be the only archduke at his wedding.

This seems to have increased, rather than diminished, the radiance of the wedding day, which could be staged as a purely family affair rather than a state occasion. Despite this there was

---

* One protocol excuse advanced was the death, on 19 June, of a Princess Josephine Hohenzollern. Though not even a member of the reigning dynasty, the Vienna court conveniently went into twelve days mourning.

no stopping the world immediately around them from looking in, as Sophie had fondly hoped with her warning to the postmaster to tell nobody about the 'secret' meeting on the railway platform. Reichstadt, like Grosspriesen, was determined to enjoy its big day to the full. Even on the short drive from the station (where, on orders, there had been no ceremony of welcome) hundreds of citizens of the town, including all its schoolchildren, the girls on the left and the boys on the right, lined the route with flags. Everything in Reichstadt which wore medals and uniform – the volunteer rifle corps, the army veterans union and, of course, the ubiquitous fire brigade – turned up as well. The *'Gott Erhalte'*, the national anthem of the Monarchy based on a melody from one of Haydn's string quartets, was produced by the rifle corps band as the procession neared the castle entrance. Banners in black and yellow, the colours of the house of Habsburg, hung from every window and the sun shone down on it all from a cloudless sky.[17]

The marriage took place the following morning in the castle chapel which the Emperor Ferdinand II had had richly decorated and ornamented during his years of residence. No cardinal, not even a bishop, conducted the ceremony, but the aged Deacon Hikisch of Reichstadt, who had already held his office for half a century. As if to emphasize the homely setting, one of the priests assisting him was the Capuchin monk who served as confessor to Archduchess Maria Theresa. It was a strange wedding cortege which marched slowly in on the stroke of 10.30 a.m. At its head was Franz Ferdinand in full dress general's uniform accompanied by his stepmother and half-sisters (all the Habsburgs together). Next, on the left arm of her guardian, Prince Löwenstein, who was also giving her in marriage, came the bride.

Her wedding dress could have been designed as a silent refutation of those distressing rumours that she had been living in sin for years with her Archduke, bearing him one illegitimate child after another. The thirty-two-year-old woman was attired as the very symbol of maidenly purity. Her gown was of white silk with a train several yards long and a white veil stretching

80

down in front from forehead to toes. Myrtle and orange-blossoms, the symbols of innocence and virginity, were everywhere – wreathed as blooms with the diamond diadem on her head, worked as figures all around the hem of her gown and as blossoms again in the bridal bouquet. It was her hour of triumph as well as her hour of fulfilment, and those lustrous eyes, which, to the admiring congregation, seemed to shine as brightly as the diamonds, showed it. At her other side walked the head of the Chotek family, Count Carl, followed by her other uncles, aunts, sisters and brothers-in-law. After them came the person who would normally have walked with the bridegroom in front, Franz Ferdinand's Household Chamberlain, Count Nostitz, who, in the absence of any archduke, was acting as best man.

That this was no conventional wedding was also echoed in the words that the old Deacon (who had been instructed on no account to refer to the rank of the bride) addressed to the couple after they had exchanged their vows and their rings: 'May these wedding rings also serve for all time as witnesses to your untroubled marital happiness. That is the ardent wish of millions of hearts, and especially of those who now stand near to you ...'

Few wished it more ardently than Franz Ferdinand's stepmother. It was she who had chosen the music which, after prayers, ended the· ceremony; indeed, she had personally conducted rehearsal after rehearsal. It was she, not the best man, who called for three cheers for the bridal couple at the wedding breakfast held in the castle afterwards. Then, at two o'clock, the procession of carriages drove back to the station to begin the journey to their new home. Even the steady rain which had replaced yesterday's sun did nothing to lessen the crowds. Nor did it dampen Sophie's spirits. On the contrary: in her country, rain on your wedding day was supposed to bring luck.

*   *   *

Though the Emperor had not attended the wedding in person, his presence was very much felt – not only in the repeated rendering of the national anthem or even in the diadem which had been his own gift to the bride. More precious than the diamonds was a telegram which Goluchowski had sent to Reichstadt in his master's name on the morning of the ceremony. This raised Countess Sophie 'to the hereditary princely rank with the name of Hohenberg and the title of "Princely Grace"'. The announcement was none the less gratifying for being expected. Hohenberg was one of the oldest names associated with the dynasty. It stemmed from their medieval possessions around Rottenburg in southern Germany, which had been purchased from the local counts in 1486; and though the lands of Hohenberg had belonged since 1805 to the kingdom of Württemberg, Franz Ferdinand himself had often used the title as his incognito for travelling abroad. Sophie had thus been brought as close to the Habsburgs as was possible for anyone who was forever to be denied admission to the family itself. This was to create problems enough in the years ahead, both personal and political. But what, in the meantime, was the immediate reaction of the empire to the Reichstadt wedding?

In the capital, the Viennese, and especially the ladies of society, were their usual rather catty selves. Poor Sophie's case was not helped by the fact that many of the pictures distributed of her dated from a few years back and showed her in dresses which had become distinctly unfashionable by the summer of 1900. But elsewhere, and particularly in the provinces, this middle-aged romance seemed to have touched people's hearts. Franz Ferdinand himself, hitherto a remote and shadowy figure, stepped for a moment right into the limelight, hailed on all sides as though he were some Habsburgian Siegfried, who had fought his way past fire and dragons to possess his Bohemian Brunnhilde. More than once, the press of the eleven-nation Monarchy drew political parallels from this fairy tale come true. Thus one Czech paper wrote, 'He who fights for his love, he who refuses to yield up that which he holds dear despite all the opposition, in such a man one can safely place one's trust, for he will defend everything which he prizes with the same energy ... we can rest assured that he will also win the love of his people and hold it in the same determined way ...'[18]

And from Agram, the capital of Croatia, came this comment, after fulsome praise of the 'chivalrous prince': 'Why shouldn't we rejoice that a noble lady who herself springs from a Bohemian family, will now be the lifelong companion of our future ruler?' The South Slavs, the writer complained, had all too few friends near the throne and Bohemian blood was, after all, Slav blood.[19]

But the most complex and significant of all the reactions came from Budapest, the twin-capital of the empire. There was, on the one hand, the same personal praise for the Archduke's courageous fight. As one Budapest paper wrote:

Archduke Franz Ferdinand has not only secured his own life-happiness; through his marriage he has also risen up in the eyes of the people of this Monarchy ... He has acted like a man, and a nobleman. He has acted straightforwardly, bravely and resolutely, which is what the Hungarian likes to see in somebody who will be called on one day to be his king.

Nonetheless, the Hungarians felt frustrated that, through a Habsburg family decision which found no counterpart in their own ancient Magyar laws (or, for that matter, no sanction within any constitution of the empire), Hungary would be deprived of a queen even when Franz Ferdinand's day as king had dawned. The nationalists tried to exploit this resentment for all it was worth, claiming that the Archduke's oath of renunciation could not be legally registered in Hungary and that his wife, as legal consort, was, for them, their future queen.

In the event, when the bill relating to the wedding was presented to the Hungarian Parliament in October of that year, it was accepted over opposition protests without undue fuss. But the fact that those awkward Hungarians were the only ones to object, even to his marriage, was not lost on Franz Ferdinand, who had already developed a phobia against everything Magyar.

As for the future of his newly-wed bride, one of her own Bohemian papers had summed up her prospects poetically and prophetically in these words: 'Countess Sophie Chotek will never wear a crown upon her head, yet nonetheless she will feel its thorns.'[20]

CHAPTER SIX

————— ⊗ —————

The Squire of Konopischt

THE THORNS seemed as remote as the crown in that summer of 1900. From Reichstadt, the bridal couple, cheered at every station, went by train to begin their honeymoon at home. For them, the setting was very apt. First, because this was a honeymoon that was to last all their lives – Franz Ferdinand's morganatic union was to prove by far the happiest, as well as the most controversial, of the Habsburg marriages of the day – and second, because the newly-weds seemed to slip straight from the altar into domesticity. A letter which the Archduke wrote to his beloved stepmother from Konopischt a week after the wedding already breathes an air of benign security alongside the triumph and the gratitude:

> We are both unspeakably happy and this happiness we owe above all to you. Where would we be today if you had not taken our part in such noble and moving fashion! We can offer nothing in return but the assurance that you have done a truly good work and have made your two children happy for the rest of their days.
>
> ... Soph [sic] is *not* reading this as she is busy just now sorting out begging letters. That means that I can tell you, just between our two selves, dearest Mamma, that Soph is a *treasure* and that I cannot describe my happiness. She looks after me so well, I'm doing famously, much less nervous and feeling so healthy. It is as though I have been born anew. She is always singing your praises and talks only of your goodness and your love ...

May the good Lord, to whom I pray with Soph twice a day
in the chapel, reward you for all you have done for us . . .[1]

That is probably the most radiant letter ever written by Franz
Ferdinand to have survived. Yet it is also tranquil: they might
have been man and wife for ten years instead of for ten days.

The letter also hints at that special quality in Sophie which
had always drawn him towards her. It was not just the physical
attraction of this woman, nor the admiration for a character that
had matured even beyond her thirty-two years. He was also
convinced, quite simply, that she would be good for him – good
for his health, and above all, good for his nerves. The
Archduke's niece by marriage, who saw a lot of the couple
together, put it in these words:

> Apart from her striking looks and very feminine charm, it was
> her air of quiet calm which he found so irresistible. She was
> the ideal partner for such a highly-strung man and she knew
> so well how to handle him. She could nearly always make him
> relax, and whenever he had one of his angry outbursts, she
> would quieten him by simply pressing his arm and saying,
> 'Franzi, Franzi'.[2]

And one of the Archduke's grandchildren capped this description by pointing out that Sophie was often able to calm her
husband down without even uttering a word. Franz Ferdinand
had given her a jewelled brooch in the shape of a lamb, to
symbolize her tranquil nature. When he lost his temper (though
never, apparently, with her) she would just look at him and
gently stroke the brooch until the storm subsided.[3]

It may well have been appropriate for this couple, destined,
among many other things, for fourteen years of almost bourgeois
domesticity, to spend their first bridal nights at home. But
Konopischt was hardly a tender, romantic place to look at. Set
on the so-called Tabor plateau some thirty-four miles outside
Prague, the great rectangular castle, with its four corner turrets
and overpowering central tower, looks more like a fortress than a
home. Indeed, its greatest claim to fame before now had been as
the citadel of the great Wallenstein, Duke of Friedland, Prince of

Sagan, and generalissimo of the Catholic forces in the Thirty Years War, who had been dismissed by the Emperor and finally murdered in 1634 on suspicion of treacherous negotiations with the Swedish Protestant foe. Despite all the changes made since the 1630s, something of that original sombreness hangs over the place today; certainly, it is the very opposite of those smiling yellow-washed eighteenth-century Baroque castles, their balustraded stone stairways tumbling invitingly down to the surrounding gardens, which were dotted all over the empire for Franz Ferdinand to choose from.

Perhaps it was a fortress he had always wanted, and not just a retreat to protect a morganatic bride, for the choice of Konopischt was made before he ever set eyes on Sophie. He bought it in 1887, adding it to his other Bohemian property, Chlumetz near Wittingau, from the great princely family of Lobkowitz, which had also once owned Reichstadt. The money for these two large estates (Konopischt had 12,000 *Joch** of land and Chlumetz 16,000) had come from selling up part of his Modena legacy, an operation attended by much legal argument.

The will of the last Duke of Modena, which had made the twelve-year-old Franz Ferdinand his beneficiary, was a copious and complicated document more than five hundred pages long. One of its many provisions laid down that the entire Italian inheritance, including the small palace in Vienna, could only pass in direct line from father to son and that, moreover, every inheritor had to be a member of the House of Austria. What prompted the old Duke (himself a member of the non-ruling branch of that house) to make this provision was the hope that, one day, a Habsburg might return to rule in Modena. That looked unlikely enough at his death in 1873. Now, in 1900, something much more unforeseen had occurred. The owner of the Este estates and the bearer of the Este name had not only become heir to the Austrian throne but had just concluded a morganatic marriage which excluded his children forever from

---

* The standard measure of land in the Habsburg empire, originally based on the area which a pair of oxen could plough in a day. One *Joch* = approximately 1.4 acres.

bearing his title, a specific requirement of the Modena inheritance.

The lawyers found a solution which was as simple as it was ingenious. Franz Ferdinand proposed to his young nephew Charles (the same unfortunate Archduke who was destined to sit on the throne in his uncle's 'place and rule for just under two years as the last of the Habsburg emperors) that he should eventually inherit these Modena properties, provided he renounced in advance the estates of Konopischt and Chlumetz in favour of his uncle's morganatic children. Even this arrangement was not quite flawless, for it envisaged one transfer from uncle to nephew instead of the unbroken chain of father to son laid down by the last Duke of Modena. But the solution was near enough watertight, and with it Franz Ferdinand thought he had safely secured at least his Bohemian properties for his children.[4] Not surprisingly, he was reckoning without the First World War; the dissolution of the Habsburg empire during the final weeks of that conflict; and the highly questionable action of the post-war Czechoslovak republic in confiscating those Bohemian estates despite the fact that they were private property and not state possessions of the former imperial house.

These nightmares were all unimaginable in 1900 when, with his Sophie at his side, Franz Ferdinand redoubled his efforts to turn Wallenstein's fortress into a homely paradise. As regards the interior, his answer, apart from installing much-needed bathrooms, was to fill the eighty-two rooms from wall to wall with treasures transported from his Italian estates (especially from the famous Villa d'Este near Rome and the country property at Cattaio near Battaglia). To these he added the extraordinary assortment of antiques which he had started to collect all over Europe in a somewhat undisciplined frenzy, and the hundreds of exotic bazaar and hunting souvenirs he had brought back from his world travels. Finally, over the years, came the many hundreds of conventional trophies of stag, chamois and roebuck (his thousandth head of which was mounted in silver) – all shot in his native mountains and forests. The resulting impression was vividly described by a government official from Prague who visited Konopischt at the time:

> The antlers of a Scandinavian elk, the skins of the black and
> brown bear, of the African and Asiatic lion, of the leopard and
> the panther, and the heads of the wild cat and wild boar all
> present themselves for admiration in the corridors. The foot
> of a giant elephant, shot by the Archduke in Kalawana in
> 1893, serves as an ashtray; the foot of another such colossus
> from Ceylon as a wastepaper basket. In one room, on whose
> walls hangs a portrait of the Emperor Franz Joseph in
> hunter's clothes, are assembled special mementos of memor-
> able shooting days – a white partridge, a white crow and heads
> of deer and chamois with a single horn for antlers.
>
> Alongside the treasures of the house of Este, whose
> precious pieces Franz Ferdinand won possession of only after
> legal proceedings with the King of Italy, one sees other special
> items of all descriptions and all origins. Thus the splendid
> chandelier which hangs in the hall of knights once cast its light
> on a Galician synagogue ... the imposing, artistically de-
> corated chests ... were taken from the so-called 'best rooms'
> of Upper Austrian peasant houses ... The Tyrolean room is
> as authentic as the Moorish room with its richly patterned
> carpets and cushions. The tent room is also genuine ... and
> the fabrics spread out were woven by the busy fingers of
> Algerian Jewesses. There they were intended for robes; here
> one admires them as hangings ...
>
> A rich variety of amazing objects, which scarcely another
> collector anywhere can claim to have assembled under his
> roof, awaits us in the third floor of the castle – a historical
> display of arms composed of the rarest and costliest specimens
> all down the centuries. There is a room full of powder horns,
> another of spears, pikes and lances ... and finally the Hall of
> Armour itself, with its array of breastplates and helmets of the
> knights of old and their steeds, decorated in gold and silver
> and collected from the castles and palaces of Este ...[5]

What this open-mouthed visitor did not mention – doubtless because it was not completed at the time – was the St George's
Hall, filled with 3750 representations of that Roman legionary
turned martyr who, by some mysterious process, had become
the patron saint of England. The Archduke's display surpassed,
at least in quantity, even the collection at Windsor Castle itself.

St George and his expiring dragon appeared at Konopischt in every form: woven in silken flags and pennants; set in stones or ivory inlay; painted in oils or watercolours; portrayed in prints or etchings, medals and coins; carved out of wood; modelled in silver; cast out of bronze; or just factory-produced in cheap pottery images. Not even his surviving daughter can explain the reason for this passion. Presumably Franz Ferdinand saw himself in the role of the saintly knight. But what was the dragon he was always ruthlessly spearing? Was it Austrian inefficiency, Italian irredentism, or Hungarian chauvinism – his three political bugbears? Or was that fiery serpent the Court Chamberlain in Vienna, Prince Montenuovo, who was able to make the Archduke's life doubly uncomfortable after his marriage? Nobody, it seems, ever asked about the riddle, and nobody was told.

Franz Ferdinand had worked to far better effect outside the castle walls. By buying up and then demolishing the handful of buildings which had constituted the tiny hamlet of Konopischt (a sugar factory simply ceased to exist but a brewery, whose light and well-flavoured beer was popular throughout the district, was prudently re-erected in Beneschau) he gradually extended the dimensions of the surrounding park to nearly five hundred *Joch* – the size of a modest estate in itself. This vast area he then carpeted between the trees with shrubberies and flower beds. Eventually, they stretched almost as far as the eye could see, even if that eye was placed where the owner himself had his apartment, high up on the third floor of the castle. (The best view of all was from the lavatory on that floor, where visitors were often taken to admire it.)

The Archduke's determination to see nothing but the cultivated beauty of nature when he looked out of his windows reached even beyond the boundaries of this vast park, where the farmland of the estate began. He gave orders that ploughing must everywhere be halted one metre from the field's edge and that, all along these unploughed strips, wild flowers and hedge roses should be planted, in order to carry the garden panorama into the far distance. To make sure the cattle would not nibble everything away, hundreds of large basket-shaped muzzles were ordered for the herd. The peasants were appeased, though still dumbfounded, once they heard that they would not have to bear the expense. But the farm manager never got over the loss of his soil.[6]

'The Archduke always had this passion for flowers,' his daughter recalls. 'He was always pressing them in his books and always reading about them to add to his knowledge. Though an amateur, he could eventually talk on equal terms with the experts, and knew all the Latin names, even for the varieties.'[7] But roses were his special love, and over the years literally thousands of cultivated rose beds of all varieties were spread out in a great floral mosaic to match those miles of hedge roses which began where the park ended. Despite the poor quality of the Tabor plateau earth (cracked open by a few days of sun and ankle-deep in mud after a short spell of rain) this great carpet of roses, unique in the empire, was somehow stitched together and kept intact by a small army of gardeners. Guests often lost themselves in the floral maze. Even the Archduke, who seemed to know every blossom, sometimes used a small pony trap to make his long-range inspections. This maze was also his moat. The flowers of Konopischt, like its turrets, were there to keep everyone and everything that was unwelcome or unlovely at a distance from Franz Ferdinand and his bride. To remind them of what they had both gone through to reach their haven, the first gravel walk at the top of the gardens was named 'Oberer Kreuzweg'. This was the street in Dresden where Sophie's married sister, Countess Wuthenau, had the apartment which Sophie had lived in through much of the marriage crisis, and where the Archduke had often come on secret visits.

They had many other places to live. Apart from the Belvedere Palace in Vienna (now allotted to him as Heir-Apparent), there were the various shooting lodges he had used as a bachelor to which, as a married man, he added the castle of Blühnbach in the Salzburg province, with its surrounding mantle of mountain forests which had been famous for their stag and chamois even in medieval times. But Konopischt was always home, the more so as two of their children were born there. The first, Sophie, came in July 1901, a year after the wedding. It was a forceps birth after nearly seventeen hours of labour for the thirty-three-year-old mother. 'I was half dead with fright,' the Archduke wrote soon afterwards to Baron Beck. The daughter was followed by two sons, Max in September 1902 and Ernst in May 1904. (A fourth baby was stillborn in 1908.) Habsburgs they were not, but with two healthy Prince Hohenbergs in the nursery, the ancient title of the dynasty which the Archduke had chosen for his bride seemed secure for the future. This one hope, at least, history was not to dash.*

Four months after the birth of his second son, Franz Ferdinand wrote another letter to the Archduchess Maria Theresa. It is a further epistle of joy in which the gratitude of the stepson, the pride of the father and the fulfilled contentment of the husband all vie with each other for pride of place:

> ... By far the cleverest thing I ever did in my life was to marry my Sophie. She is everything for me: my wife, my doctor, my adviser – in a word my whole happiness. Today, four years later, we love each other as on the first day of our marriage and our bliss has not been clouded for a single second. And then our children! They are my whole pride and joy. I sit with them all day long in amazement that I can love them so much. And then the evenings at home when I smoke my cigar and read my papers. Sophie knits and the children tumble about, knocking everything off the tables. It's all so cosy and precious ...[8]

Though he now had this firm and happy base to his existence at Konopischt, the Archduke was often away from it. His absences were dictated partly by the desire to keep an eye on, and enjoy, his other properties; partly by the need, which grew over the years, to put in a minimum of time at Vienna or, on military and representational duties, elsewhere; and partly by the old itch to travel which still nagged at him as a staid married man. His daughter has described a typical year for the family:

* There are close on a dozen male Hohenbergs surviving today and the current head of the house is an ambassador of the Austrian Republic.

Christmas was nearly always spent at Konopischt. Only once did we go to Chlumetz instead and once, in 1912, we had to spend it at the Belvedere in Vienna because the Emperor was quite ill at the time. I remember that even then we had two enormous Christmas trees sent from the forests of Konopischt. Then, in January and February, we were all mainly in Vienna, but with trips back to Konopischt. After that, in March and April, we would usually go south. We either went to Miramar Castle near Trieste, which was then a Habsburg property, used by several members of the royal family, or to the Adriatic island of Brioni, where we lived in a hotel. Sometimes we would go to the Alps instead – to St Moritz, for example, where we also put up in a hotel.

May and June were normally spent in Konopischt again, though always with a trip to Vienna in June for the big horse-race meeting in the Prater, and the carnival of flowers. In June also we often went to Donau-Eschingen to shoot roebuck with the Fürstenbergs. In July, we would sometimes go to a Belgian seaside resort for a few weeks. August was spent either at Lölling in Carinthia or at Blühnbach, where we would often remain for the stag shooting until October, though from there my father would pay periodic visits to Bad Ischl, where the Emperor always went for the summer. Occasionally, towards the end of September, we would go for the stag to Eckhartsau, another Habsburg family property.* Then, to round off the year, November and December would be spent mainly in Konopischt again. Konopischt was always home to us children. It was, quite simply, the place where we left our things.[9]

As Franz Ferdinand was heir to the Austrian throne, this highly agreeable annual routine of his entered the calculations of the diplomats, and especially those of Heinrich von Tschirschky, the German Ambassador in Vienna, who courted him on all possible occasions. As the envoy once reported, in rather a resigned tone, to his Foreign Office in Berlin, 'So far as Archduke Franz Ferdinand's travel plans are concerned, he is

---

* And one of baleful significance to the dynasty. It was to this little castle, on the boundaries of Austria, Hungary and Slovakia, that Franz Ferdinand's nephew Charles fled from Vienna in November 1918 after he had renounced power as the last of the Habsburg emperors. It was to be his last domicile on Austrian soil.

now spending a couple of months at Miramare. He probably won't be in Vienna for any length of time after that as the roebuck season starts then and anyway he is rarely ever in Vienna during the springtime.'[10]

Since roebuck and stag figure so prominently in the travel accounts of both the daughter and the diplomat, this might be a good moment to examine that other great passion of Franz Ferdinand's private life, second only to Sophie and before his beloved roses – namely shooting. The Archduke certainly regarded St Hubert even more highly than St George in the calendar of saints, but it was a veneration that was to do his reputation little good. As we have seen, he had already met with enough criticism early on in life for devoting too much of his time and energy to the pursuit of game; after his death, this criticism was magnified into the ugly image of a ruthless slaughterer of animals, who shot out of sheer blood-lust and not from any love of the sport.

The man who probably did most to popularize the legend was Bruno Brehm, a German writer whose works sold in the hundred thousands in the 1920s and 1930s. Three of them formed a trilogy on the last years of the Habsburg Monarchy. In the first, *Apis und Este*, the reader is at one point taken up to the mountains near Blühnbach where the Archduke is depicted conducting a single-handed massacre of a herd of chamois being driven towards him – bucks, does and kids are falling indiscriminately to his rifle while his wife purrs contentedly at his side. The story also has a local forester's daughter fleeing hysterically from the scene and uttering treasonable screams in dialect as she goes because this unsporting slaughter is too much even for her well-conditioned nerves to bear.[11] Similar tales were spread of the Archduke at work with all feathered and lowland game.

Only one or two people can be found alive today who actually saw Franz Ferdinand shoot. To their descriptions, however, can be added various second-hand accounts given by the children of his contemporaries, some of whom recorded these impressions themselves in diaries or memoirs. There can be no doubt that he loved shooting, and loved shooting big bags, which meant a great deal of killing. There is also little doubt that, on any given day at any given target, he enjoyed shooting more game than anyone else. This was not merely due to his native pride, which rose to the point of haughtiness outside his own family. It was perhaps even more due to an inner desire, as the odd man out in the imperial family, constantly to prove himself. The frustrations of a long wait for the throne may also have played a psychological role. Here again, an interesting comparison can be drawn with that other European Heir-Apparent who shared some of the same years of waiting with him – Edward, Prince of Wales.

Edward felt no need to prove himself to society, not even as Prince, let alone as King. He knew that he would lead society unchallenged until his dying day. So, despite the fact that he was a rather indifferent shot, he happily surrounded himself with the finest marksmen of his kingdom, who invariably performed better than he did. So long as everyone enjoyed themselves, this did not bother him a scrap. Indeed, he would be furious if any of his guests made tactful attempts to make the gap look less obvious.[12]

With Franz Ferdinand, things were very different. His niece by marriage, the then Archduchess Zita, recalls being at pheasant shoots where both Franz Ferdinand and her own husband, Charles, were among the guns. Though not as deadly and not as dedicated as the Heir-Apparent, the young Archduke was an excellent shot himself, so that if he was having a particularly good day and standing next to his uncle the onlookers would not notice that much difference between the two as marksmen. Whenever he sensed there was a danger of that happening, Charles would deliberately aim wide at a few birds so that his uncle could remain '*Schützenkönig*' or 'king-gun' (the practice, largely confined to continental shoots, of totting up everybody's individual bag to establish who has shot the most). We may be sure that if the Heir-Apparent's own nephew, himself next in line to the throne after the renunciation oath of 1900, went out of his way to flatter his uncle as a sportsman, then the lesser mortals of the aristocracy would not have lagged behind.[13]

None of this, however, detracts from Franz Ferdinand's own skills. As a performer with the shotgun against driven pheasant and partridge ('*Flugwild*', as he would have called it), he was certainly in the highest European class, though without being at the very top of it. The trouble with the encomiums published on this subject in the memoirs of members of his suite is that several of the writers never seemed to have fired shotguns themselves and, in all cases, appear to have had no standards of comparison outside the Monarchy to go on. Thus his doctor writes reverently of seeing the Archduke fire more than thirty shots against game birds before missing.[14] Capital marksmanship certainly, but it has to be placed against the skill and astonishing speed of Lord Ripon, who once killed twenty-eight pheasants in sixty seconds at Sandringham and who, on another occasion, was seen to have seven dead birds in the air at once.[15]

Then there is the question of the quality of the birds produced. Anyone who has ever shot over the same terrain enjoyed by the Archduke at the beginning of the century (and it has not changed much in configuration) will know that the typical driven partridge of Austria – if indeed it is driven at all – is the one which rises fairly easily from the maize fields. The typical pheasant is the so-called 'tree-pheasant' or 'park-pheasant', a much simpler target than the very high 'tower-birds' which many English estates were specially fashioned to produce. (As we shall see, even the Archduke was to be in some difficulty when confronted by these for the first time, in the Great Park at Windsor.)

Where Franz Ferdinand was almost in a class by himself was with the rifle. For preference he would, for example, shoot roebucks on the run – clapping his hands to get them moving when he saw them motionless in front of him – and even so he rarely missed the *Blatt*, that vital target area behind the animal's shoulder which, if struck, means a clean and instant kill. More remarkable still, he was often observed to take aim with his Mannlicher rifle when a stray pheasant or partridge sped past during a roebuck hunt, and bring the bird down stone dead with his bullet.[16] Very few European sportsmen would have attempted the feat, let alone brought it off time after time.

There remains the charge of 'mass slaughter'. That he killed, in his lifetime, vast numbers of game birds and beasts is a matter of record: a thousand stag had fallen to his rifle before the turn of the century, for example, and, by the time of his death, the total had topped the three thousand mark. The tally of pheasant, partridge and ground game shot during his life cannot be estimated with such accuracy, but the highest estimate puts it at something well over a quarter of a million.* An enormous tally, to be sure, yet the point to note is that, unless he had been a very mediocre shot, it could hardly have been otherwise with his favourite sport.

He was the heir to the throne; he was asked to all the best shoots (and owned one or two of them himself); and he was undoubtedly an exceptionally fine marksman. Moreover, the sheer profusion of game in the Europe of his day led, as a matter of course, to bags which would appear incredible to the present-day generation of sportsmen. For a party of six guns to shoot less than a thousand birds on a main day at any first-class estate would have been considered disappointing sport. Today, many smaller estates would be happy to get that number over an entire season. But it took daily bags well over the thousand mark to raise the eyebrows of Edwardian-age marksmen in enthusiasm or envy: the all-time record of 6125 pheasant shot at Tótmegyer in Hungary on 10 December 1909, for example; the bag of close on 3000 grouse (a far more difficult target) returned at Broomhead in Yorkshire on 27 August 1913; or the 7000 rabbits killed at Blenheim Palace in Oxfordshire on 7 October 1898. Though not in that league, Konopischt itself was nothing to be ashamed of. Two days shooting there, on 24 and 25 October 1913, yielded 6300 pheasants.

The matter can be summed up thus: almost any contemporary European sportsman of great skill, wealth and leisure could have matched Franz Ferdinand's tally had he pursued his

---

* Vladimir Aichelburg, in his brief but authoritative handbook, *Franz Ferdinand und Artstetten* (Vienna, 1983) has calculated from surviving records that the grand total of all game of all types shot by the Archduke during his life was 272,511.

passion with the same lifelong dedication. Some passed that tally. There hangs at Newby Hall in Yorkshire today, for example, the gun with which Lord Ripon, perhaps the finest of all the fine shots in the England of his day, accounted for most of the 556,000 head of birds and ground game which he killed between 1867 and 1923. Nor is there any evidence to suggest that the Archduke was any less of a fair sportsman than His Lordship; indeed, as we have seen during his tour of India, Franz Ferdinand is occasionally found complaining about the unsporting methods of his English hosts. If the Archduke was a monster simply because he shot so much, then so was King George V of England, King Alfonso XIII of Spain (comparable royal exponents of the shotgun) and practically every sporting grandée on the European continent of the time. Today, it is the tycoons who have taken up the tradition as best they can.

What was Franz Ferdinand like as a private person when he did not have a gun in his hand? What were the other tastes and characteristics of this middle-aged married man, now with several more inches around his waist than he had when a young lieutenant, but still with that same piercing, enigmatic gaze which seemed to come from two sets of eyes?

He was, first of all (as that letter of 1904 to his stepmother suggests) an excellent family man. His daughter, who can certainly be regarded as an authority on this subject, recalls:

> He was marvellous as a father to us children. We were always taken with him on every possible occasion, whether travelling, or, when we were old enough, out shooting at home. We had private tutors to educate us but he took an enormous interest in our lessons and we used to rehearse little poems and speeches to deliver to him in all languages – even Hungarian!
>
> He was firm with us, but never harsh or unjust. As for those famous tempers that came and went like midsummer storms, we certainly saw him sometimes bang on the table and raise his voice. But it was always with adults, never with us.[17]

The warmth and geniality which the Archduke always radiated at home seemed to many observers to freeze once he stepped into the outside world, as though his blood had turned to ice once he crossed the threshold. Certainly, to the people at large, he remained until his life's end a remote, cold and somewhat frightening figure. This was partly due to circumstances: the long spells of foreign travel, of illness and convalescence also spent largely abroad had kept him out of the public eye, and even his first years as a healthy, married man were spent largely in seclusion. His natural temperament also played a role. He had absolutely no talent for what the twentieth century was later to describe as public relations. Indeed, he would have spurned the concept had it been developed in his own day. The peoples he hoped to rule over he regarded as sacred charges, placed in his hands by a God working mysteriously through his dynasty. But he never made the slightest attempt, as heir to the throne, to court their affection and had he ascended that throne he would have ruled in the same lofty style – paternal to the point of authoritarianism. He was, as the author Karl Krauss wrote with delightful understatement, 'not a hand-shaker'. Franz Ferdinand said as much himself. He once told his nephew Charles, when the young Archduke and his wife were spending a relaxed day with him in Upper Austria, 'Make no mistake, you won't have an easy time with me as Emperor.'[18] The young couple were already under no illusions on that score.

But the factor which compounded both the remoteness and the severity was his mistrust of humanity – possibly instinctive in him as a young man but certainly ingrained for ever after the humiliating intrigues which had surrounded his illness. Again, he admitted it himself, this time in a well-known remark he made to the Austrian Chief-of-Staff, Conrad von Hötzendorf (a man we shall hear more of later), when the General was discussing personnel questions with him in Vienna. 'We start from different standpoints,' the Archduke declared. 'You regard everybody as being an angel by nature, and that will lead you into a lot of trouble. I regard everyone I meet as being a scoundrel at first sight, and then let him gradually change my mind if he can.'[19]

Healthy scepticism has always been regarded as a political virtue in rulers, yet Franz Ferdinand, if he really meant those words, was carrying things a bit too far. In any case, Imperial Vienna in decline contained more fools than scoundrels.

Franz Ferdinand certainly emerges, even in his own words, as a somewhat forbidding figure to all but his family. There were two things, however, which smoothed the jagged edges. The first was that, like so many seemingly austere beings, he was capable of both great charm and deep emotion when the mood seized him. There were also sudden outbursts of gaiety – unpredictable, like his bouts of temper – as though a genial spirit, imprisoned within that stern frame, had managed to make its brief escape before being recaptured. The Archduke had another attractive quality not uncommon among characters of his stamp: a loathing of flattery, combined with a respect for anyone, high or low, who was prepared to speak his mind and damn the consequences.

Baron Morsey described how, after he was persuaded to overcome his misgivings and join the Archduke's personal staff, he was greeted with these uncompromising words by his master: 'However uncomfortable it may be for you, always tell me the truth to my face – even if you are afraid you may be thrown out for it!'

Standing up to the Archduke was something that nobody ever was thrown out for. Morsey goes on to describe the case of a certain Lieutenant Schwarz, a man of humble origins who occupied a lowly post running the garden administration, and who always did speak his mind – quite unperturbed by any archducal displeasure or explosions. As a result, he was held in the highest regard. 'Watch your step if Schwarz is in a bad mood,' the Archduke once warned Morsey, adding, 'Even I have to look out for myself then.'[20]

As for the Archduke's mental qualities, he was by far the most intelligent and perceptive Habsburg of his generation, once, that is, Crown Prince Rudolf had blown out those brains which he certainly also once possessed. He could cut to the bone of the most complicated problem in a few words – even if those words were all too often laced with sarcasm. Yet though he had a sharp intellect, he was no intellectual, preferring always the practical to the philosophical. Moreover, he was not a deeply cultured man, for even that vast pile of antiques and curiosities which he crammed into Konopischt owed its existence as much to a frenzy for collecting as to a love of beauty for its own sake. Though he grew up in a momentous musical age (with the great new symphonies and concertos of Johannes Brahms joining the established classics of Beethoven, Mozart, Schumann and Schubert in the repertoire of the Vienna Philharmonic), there is no evidence he ever heard them, let alone enjoyed them. Music for him, as for the Emperor, was something you could whistle, and preferably songs from popular operettas or old folk tunes. The hurdy-gurdy seems to have been his favourite instrument.

It was a similar tale with literature. He had great respect, but little time, for Goethe, Schiller and the other giants of German letters. But he devoured newspapers and, later, the heaps of official documents which came his way. His reading, like his mind, was directed towards the practical: books on flowers, gardens, weapons, furniture and, above all, the design of old houses and castles. He was in fact a great conservationist as well as a great conservative, and here his deep love for his own fatherland played a big role. Though he pulled down much at Konopischt, what he rebuilt on the estate was all in the traditional peasant style. He cast the same keenly nostalgic eye over Artstetten, the property his father had left him. Its pointed turrets irritated him as being quite out of style for a castle in the Danubian valley. At considerable expense, he demolished them in 1912 and had the original onion-shaped towers put back. One of his last great labours, left unfinished at his death (and promptly cancelled because of the enormous cost) was the restoration of the ancient castle of Ambras in the Tyrol. There was doubtless a special reason for his attachment to it. This was once the fortress where those forerunners of Habsburg morganatic marriages, Ferdinand of Tyrol and Phillipine Welser, had lived.

Finally, before we leave his private character for his political personality, we must look at a trio of miscellaneous charges levelled against him: that he disliked children, apart from his own; that he had no time for dogs, except as necessary adjuncts to his shooting; and that he was very mean with money. Though the accusations, even if proven, would hardly amount to criminal offences, each of them is mildly damaging. Each is, in fact, also inexact, at least when stated in such bald terms. The intense warmth with which family relationships were cultivated within the seclusion of Konopischt always meant that anything outside this emotional hothouse stayed in the cold. But what probably turned the Archduke's indifference to other children into a kind of resentment was the tragedy of Sophie's fourth baby, which was stillborn in 1908. After that, his hopes of founding a large family (and three offspring was a fairly modest total by the copious standards of the time) were dashed, as the doctors strongly cautioned against another pregnancy. There was nothing that his formidable willpower could do about it. In these circumstances, the sight of a farmyard with anything up to a dozen peasant children running around among the chickens may well have made him grumpy, for he was not a man who took any defeat easily, even if it were at the hands of the Almighty.

The story that the Archduke disliked dogs because he never allowed one in the house was put about by the head of his Military Chancery between 1911 and 1914, Colonel Karl von Bardolff. Though told in good faith, it rests on ignorance of the facts. Dogs were always kept as domestic pets in Konopischt until an incident which happened when the children were still quite small. Max, the elder of the two brothers, had dressed himself up in costume and ran into the room to greet his parents. A collie (never the safest of animals) leapt forward to attack this unrecognized intruder and would have bitten the child had the Archduke not wrenched his son back in time. From that day on, no dogs were allowed within the castle walls – but the ban was ordered out of concern for the children, not out of dislike for the animals. All this happened before Bardolff entered the Archduke's service.[21]

Franz Ferdinand's attitude to money did him far more harm, for the Austrians and, even more, the Hungarians (specialists in the art of living graciously above their income) expected to find generosity to the point of extravagance in the heir to the throne. There is no denying that in his case the extravagance seemed more in evidence than the generosity. Like so many of his pleasure-loving subjects, he usually spent more than he had on the acquisition and running of his various estates, to say nothing of the ceaseless quest for antiques. Even the Este inheritance (or, rather, that portion of it which he was able to turn into cash) was not enough to meet his needs, and at one point he had to borrow the considerable sum of ten million gold schillings from the Sieghart bank, as well as relying on the imperial treasury for what would nowadays be termed 'bridging loans'.[22]

But what made him very flinty-eyed as regards the running of his own estates (and it was there that many of the stories of meanness originated) was the discovery he made very early on that he was being let down by idle officials as well as being deliberately fleeced by corrupt ones. Moreover, when he turned for outside help and advice to administrators called from the Habsburg family trust, he found to his horror that they were no better. This prompted a long, heartfelt letter to the Emperor in which he set out to expose the dishonesty and inefficiency which was costing them all so dear. Concrete examples were given: a sugar factory where the sales figures for beet were regularly distorted until Franz Ferdinand had acted to put things right; farm rents which appeared on the books at suspiciously low figures; prices for felled timber pitched far below the real market levels until the official responsible was sent packing into premature retirement. By now, the Archduke had so got the bit between his teeth as to propose that he himself should conduct a complete overhaul of estate administration within the imperial family. There was a long silence before the Emperor replied that, on the whole, it would be better to leave things as they were rather than run the risk of 'a well-proven system which has worked for so many years to the benefit of our interests being disturbed by experiments'.[23] It was a classic example of the total immobility in which the old monarch's thinking had become encrusted, an immobility which was to cause his heir so much anguish on the political arena.

Before leaving Konopischt for Vienna, however, it is worth taking another look at the remarkable peasant who ran not only the Archduke's Bohemian estates but almost everything else outside his family and political life – Franz Janaczek. We have seen how indispensable he became to Franz Ferdinand before his marriage. The extraordinary thing was that even after Sophie moved into Konopischt as the chatelaine, Janaczek's native tact was such that he continued to expand his dominion without ever giving offence to the new mistress of the house. He became, quite simply, a member of the family as well as a servant of the family, so much so that when the first-born baby girl was carried out of the bedroom by a joyous Archduke, she was put straight away into Janaczek's arms for inspection before anyone else was given a look.

Equally remarkable was the way in which this uneducated country lad (he had started off as a keeper on the Eckartsau estate in Lower Austria) eventually became one of the Archduke's principal advisers on the purchase of antiques and the furnishing of apartments in both Vienna and the countryside, without, of course, ever neglecting the shooting. A telegram he sent from the capital to the Archduke in Bohemia sums it up: 'I report with humble duty that the Chancery offices are drawing up a register of the stag, chamois and deer trophies ... Härdtle is coming to the Belvedere tomorrow to look at the material and the frames. Jaray will make the furniture for Blühnbach and will be submitting drawings of various old styles.'[24]

Here, at least, was one member of the household who earned his keep, as well as his master's respect and gratitude, until the Archduke's dying day. He also kept faith with his master's confidence, repeatedly refusing right down to his own death on 8 December 1955, at the age of ninety, lucrative publishing offers for his memoirs. He was in the family's service to the end.

CHAPTER SEVEN

―――――✂―――――

Belvedere: Pomp without Power

THERE MAY WELL HAVE BEEN no other suitable building in Vienna
for an Heir-Apparent to live in; nonetheless, to allot the
Belvedere as an official residence to a man of Franz Ferdinand's
stamp was asking for trouble. That same Archduke who was so
impatient to see what he would look like as ruler as to have his
portrait secretly painted in full imperial costume found himself
living in a palace which vied both in size and splendour with the
Hofburg and Schönbrunn, the winter and summer residences of
the dynasty which would only be his as Emperor. In the cold
magnificence of the Belvedere he could almost feel the sceptre in
his hands already. The itch to grasp it properly became at times
unbearable.

Prince Eugene of Savoy, servant of the Habsburg emperors
and comrade of Marlborough, had built the Belvedere, and his
elaborate coat-of-arms, chiselled in stone, still crowns the
entrance. It was the Prince's relief army which, in 1683, had
driven the Turkish janissaries from the gates of Vienna and
subsequently put them to flight for good. All Christian Europe
breathed again, and the joy of the Habsburg Monarchy flowed
out in sculpture and gold leaf. The disciplined extravaganza of
baroque was born from that victory, and Prince Eugene's
creation became one of its masterpieces. For his site, he had
bought up an area of pasture lands which sloped up quite steeply
from the Rennweg, just outside the confines of the old city. The
slope dictated the layout: a lower palace close to the road, the
larger upper palace straddling the crest above, from where the

retired warlord could look across to those wooded Vienna hills
down which he had led his columns to break the long Turkish
siege. The architect was a former officer of engineers in that
army, Johann Lukas von Hildebrandt. He was a German who
had worked in Italy, and the twin construction of the Belvedere,
which he created for his master between 1714 and 1722, married
Teuton solidity to Latin caprice. The lower building is basically
single-storeyed, with large oblong windows, red–brown tiles and
five separate roofs which bind the wings compactly to the main
body. From the outside, at least, it comes as close as baroque can
ever get to being modest and homely. A place to be lived in; and
it was indeed used for most of the time as the residence.

The upper palace, joined to the lower building by a stiff maze
of gravel paths and fountains, strewn with statues which seem to
bolt the gardens to the ground, is a very different proposition.
This is above all a place for ceremony, and Hildebrandt designed
everything to impress as well as enchant. The first thing the
visitor sees, for example, is the central double staircase in
marble, with a balustrade topped by simpering white cherubs
holding up black wrought-iron lanterns nearly twice their size.
And when the first floor is reached, a series of seven inter-
connecting salons stretch out on either side – those to the left of
the staircase having been hung originally with paintings of the
Flemish school (including one large hall covered with nothing
but Rubens canvasses) and those to the right with works of
Italian masters. At the centre, facing the staircase and looking
out over the formal gardens, is Hildebrandt's decorative
masterpiece, a large oval chamber whose Corinthian wall
columns, fireplaces and flooring are all in rich red marble. One
cannot imagine just taking tea there.

The Belvedere was to have an unhappy history as a palace of
doom. When Prince Eugene died in 1736 there was no male heir,
and everything passed into the hands of his niece, Princess
Viktoria von Sachsen-Hilburghausen. They proved disastrously
extravagant hands. Within a few years, the great man's fortune
had been squandered, and in 1752, only thirty years after its
completion, the Belvedere passed into the possession of the

ruling dynasty. It was not to fare any better under the Habsburgs. It was in the red marble chamber of the Upper Palace that the Archduchess Maria Antonia said farewell to Vienna at a court gala staged in April of 1770 before leaving for Paris – and ultimately for the guillotine – as the bride of Louis XVI. The parallel with Franz Ferdinand's destiny scarcely needs drawing.[1]

What counted in his lifetime, however, were the Belvedere's happier associations. It had been built by an immortal warrior who had rescued the Austro-Hungarian empire by feats of arms, just as the new tenant was resolved to go down in history as the man who would save it from collapse by feats of rejuvenation and diplomacy. To this end, every fresco and every statue seemed to be urging him forward.

The sumptuous setting of the couple's Vienna residence also needs to be borne in mind to appreciate to the full the pain inflicted by the famous protocol pin-pricks the couple had to suffer whenever they visited the capital. These visits increased in frequency after the first year or two of their marriage, which were devoted to founding a family in the domestic paradise of Konopischt. As the visits lengthened so, too, did their determination grow to win a fuller recognition of Sophie's place in society, determination which encountered implacable opposition at court. There is no doubt that the Emperor's spokesman in these matters, Prince Montenuovo, neglected no opportunity to wield the rules of protocol for all they were worth against the Archduke as a morganatically married prince, just as he had used them to the same effect against Franz Ferdinand the sick and prickly bachelor. But here again, some revision is needed of the popular picture which portrays Franz Joseph's Chamberlain as a Satan in knee-breeches, gratuitously inflicting humiliation after humiliation on a defenceless couple.

Spanish court etiquette was a ponderous legacy which the Habsburgs had inherited from their period of joint rule in Madrid and Vienna. This over-extension of the dynasty's powers had been ended by that extraordinary Emperor Charles V who, two years before his death in 1558, had divided the empire for all time into its separate Austrian and Spanish halves. But the suffocating ceremonial of the Escorial lived on at the Hofburg even after this political divorce. Just how suffocating it could be in the Escorial can be judged by the fact that on one occasion, when an emperor had suddenly been taken ill in Madrid, he was almost left to die while court officials argued furiously among themselves as to who had the right to render or summon aid.

Yet such tales from Madrid in the fifteenth century need to have set beside them the story of another sick emperor in Vienna in the early twentieth. Franz Joseph had suffered for many years from bronchial asthma, and the illness got steadily more serious as time went by. One night, when the monarch was already in his eighties, he was stricken in the early hours by a terrible choking fit. He rang for help and, within minutes, his personal physician, who lived in the palace, hurried to his sovereign's bedroom. Though there were no ceremonial problems in Vienna about summoning aid, etiquette reared its head high the moment the doctor entered the room. Realizing it was an emergency, he had simply put on a dressing gown, seized his bag of medicines, and run. But the sight of that dressing gown was too much for the Emperor, even *in extremis*. With what might well have been his last breath, Franz Joseph rose up from his pillows and angrily croaked out the one word, '*Frack!*' ('Tail coat!') – thus indicating that, whenever summoned to the presence, and in whatever circumstances, the doctor was expected to don the formal garb prescribed for all civilian audiences.

The point of this anecdote is to show that protocol was not something which Prince Montenuovo had invented; nor was it something which he alone esteemed. In one form or another, it has been a prop of all forms of government in all ages. Franz Joseph himself, as that sick-bed incident illustrates, was the greatest stickler in his empire for protocol, for the simple reason that he was its greatest beneficiary.

The rules of etiquette were the iron bands which held the rotting Habsburg tree upright. After fifty, then sixty years on the throne, Franz Joseph could no more survive without them than he could have dispensed with those gigantic daily intakes of official papers which he absorbed from dawn to dusk. To him, and most of those who surrounded him, a dynasty without protocol was a dynasty without meaning – and also without internal defences. And as the old Emperor, in the closing stages of that almost unbelievable sixty-eight-year reign of his, became a semi-divine figure to his courtiers, the rules of etiquette became almost interchangeable with forms of prayer. As an Apostolic Majesty, everything he did, and everything he received was, after all, by divine sanction.

It is against this background that one has to judge the so-called insults which Prince Montenuovo inflicted on Sophie whenever she came with her husband to the Belvedere. On her wedding day, she had been given the title of Princess (not a royal title in the Habsburg Monarchy); eventually, in 1909, the Emperor raised her in rank again, to become the Duchess of Hohenberg. Even then, however, she could not be entitled to any of the formal privileges of an archduchess, for the simple reason that she was not, and could never become, a fully-fledged member of the royal family.

It can of course be argued that, had he been well-disposed to either Sophie or her husband (and had he not been such an autocratic and pedantic character by nature), Montenuovo might have used his influence to help them out of some of their pettier embarrassments. It was, for example, an appalling humiliation for the Archduke, whenever he attended a performance even at a private theatre, to be obliged to sit in a separate box from his wife. Sophie's own nervousness at these moments waxed almost to the point of suppressed hysteria, as this anecdote recounted by the then Archduchess Zita shows:

> I remember an occasion when my husband Charles and I attended the same public performance of a play as the Archduke Franz Ferdinand and his wife. She was by now Duchess of Hohenberg, and when I greeted her I wanted to show her the usual courtesies to a lady of rank, the wife of our 'Uncle Franzi', who happened also to be much older than I. At the time, I was barely into my twenties, she well into her

forties. So I took her hand and kissed it. She gave a terrified look around her, and recoiled as though she had been stung. 'Please,' she implored, 'never do that again in public. It's just what people who want to make difficulties are looking out for. I've even had threatening letters through the post after things like that!'[2]

It is not certain whether, even if Prince Montenuovo had approached the Emperor to try and put a stop to extreme situations like that, he would have found a ready ear. During this final period (the Archduchess Zita's experience of life at court in pre-war Vienna only started fully with her own marriage in 1911) Franz Joseph was like some stone Methuselah, sanctified but also petrified by the years. What does seem certain, on the other hand, is that he needed absolutely no persuading to deny those formal rights which were simply not Sophie's on any reading of the book of rules. Only archdukes and archduchesses, for example, had the picturesque privilege (imported, needless to say, from Madrid) of driving about the capital in carriages which had thin golden threads decorating the spokes of the wheels. Sophie was confined to plain wheels for the equally plain fact that she did not qualify in rank for the special embellishment. There were similar obstacles – insuperable, according to the protocol codes of the day – about her ceremonial appearances at court. These concerned above all the 'Hofball' in carnival time, where the Emperor (whether he actually turned up or not) played host to the members of his family and those deemed fit to be invited with them. There had been one painful occasion in 1909 when, by design or accident, Sophie had been left stranded without any partner, and had been obliged to walk in on her own.

Whether her husband's explosion at this affront was particularly violent or whether someone else persuaded the Emperor that such public humiliation was really going too far we do not know. But, thanks to a fading card preserved by one of the grand-daughters of Prince Montenuovo[3] we do know that, at the next carnival season Sophie (by now raised to the rank of Duchess) enjoyed her hard-earned triumph. The card shows the seating plan for the ladies' tea-tables at the Hofball of 1910. Across the bottom, Prince Montenuovo's wife has recorded in her own handwriting, '*Erstes officielles Erscheinen der Herzogin von Hohenberg*' ('First official appearance of the Duchess of Hohenberg').

The 'placement' was not without its ironies. Of the four tables, Number One (presided over by Archduchess Maria Annunziata, half-sister to Franz Ferdinand) and Number Two (headed by the Emperor's daughter, Archduchess Maria Valerie) are conventional enough – a blend of Czech, Austrian and German princesses with a sprinkling of foreign ambassadors' wives. Sophie is seated at Table Four, headed by the Grand Duchess Alice from the Tuscan branch of the great Habsburg family tree. But seated next to her are two of the daughters of her one-time employer, the Archduchess Isabella, and at the top of Table Three (spaced well away from Table Four by the diamond-shaped arrangement) is the chatelaine of Pressburg herself – still, ten years after the tennis-court scandal, Sophie's archenemy. One wonders who had worked out the seating arrangements.

Poor Sophie's placing at table, or rather her non-placing whenever her husband had to dine at court, had always followed a similar relentless pattern. As she could not be asked to anything as ceremonial as a meal for a visiting sovereign, Prince Montenuovo resorted to the inexplicable device of laying one plate too many, usually at the corner of the table, which remained unoccupied. The empty glasses and the gleaming unused silver must have ruined Franz Ferdinand's digestion. To begin with, at any rate, the mockery even applied to similar functions at the Belvedere where she was herself the hostess. She was conspicuously absent from her own table, for example, when, in 1901, her husband gave a gala dinner for the German Crown Prince, who was visiting Vienna.

None of this affected the Emperor's personal courtesy towards the controversial couple, however difficult he had always found his nephew. Franz Ferdinand's daughter relates that in September of 1900, when the newly-weds showed themselves for the first time in the capital, the Emperor received them 'in the kindest possible way'. Moreover, at the end of that month, he returned the visit by calling on them at the Belvedere, where he spent an hour inspecting all the changes they had made.[4] But these were private gestures. Publicly, it was always protocol which reigned.

Another very important factor has to be recalled in this context – the passionate letter which Franz Ferdinand had himself penned to the Emperor in May of 1900, when he was pleading for his own happiness. In it, after all, he had promised his uncle that if the marriage were allowed, 'the Countess will never show herself either at court or in high social circles and will never make claims of any sort or seek to play any role'.[5] Now it may well have been expecting too much of human flesh and blood (and especially of hot blood such as Franz Ferdinand's) to suppose that such a promise of lifelong self-banishment undertaken on his wife's behalf could have been adhered to in practice as the years of married life rolled by. Nonetheless, the pledge had been given, and the Emperor would have been entitled to remind his nephew of it as the arguments over Sophie's status at court grew fiercer.

Finally, there is one significant aspect of the affair which only fully emerged years later. Franz Ferdinand himself applied to his wife's family those very same rules of etiquette which he fought against so bitterly whenever they were directed against her. In German, as in French, there are two forms of address, the formal *Sie* and the intimate *Du*, reserved in society for those equal in birth, background or standing.* Among the plethora of titled brothers-in-law and uncles which Franz Ferdinand acquired by his marriage there were only two whom he ever addressed in the intimate style. Both qualified first because they were foreign (which always made things easier) and second because they ranked as so-called *Standesherren*, that is nobles of

---

* A poignant extension of the background qualifications came into existence during the years of Nazi oppression, when every inmate of a concentration camp was, forever afterwards, *Du* to his fellow-sufferers. The inmates included both of Franz Ferdinand's sons.

the German empire whose families once had certain territorial rights – Count Schönburg-Glauchau and Baron (later Count) Wuthenau-Hohenturn. All Sophie's other male relatives, being Austrian, were expected to treat her husband as an archduke who was also their future sovereign. This meant that, in addition to the formal *Sie* being always used, even in private conversations at home, the even more formal *Kaiserliche Hoheit* or Imperial Highness would occasionally be thrown in as well from their side. As for the ladies, almost all the Archduke's sisters-in-law and aunts by marriage remained *per Sie* with him for life. There was only one exception – Henriette, the youngest of the Chotek girls. She, for some reason, captured his affection and was often taken with him on family holidays to the mountains or the coast. It must have been a considerable relief to Sophie to feel that at least one of her own flesh and blood was treated by her husband as though she were a normal member of the family.[6] But the point to note is that this awkward and complicated arrangement might well have been ordained by Prince Montenuovo rather than by Franz Ferdinand himself, though the Court Chamberlain would doubtless have raised his eyebrows at the breach of etiquette as regards the favoured Countess Henriette. Montenuovo was merely a tyrant in the execution of a tyrannical social system. Neither the Emperor nor the Archduke could have broken free from that system even if they had tried.

What were the feelings of Franz Ferdinand's own children in all this? His daughter recalls:

> We never asked our parents about the problems they were facing, and I can never remember them sitting down and explaining any of the difficulties to us. The situation was just left unmentioned as though it didn't exist. But of course we knew it did. We were always nervous at being taken along to court because we sensed that we were somehow in a special category. Even at children's parties, we were sometimes 'placed' very oddly.
>
> There was never any tension at home about it, however, though we noticed certain things even if we didn't talk about them. In Vienna, for example, we would see our father being driven away in one of the so-called 'golden' carriages, and

then our mother leaving separately in the ordinary carriage used by ladies-in-waiting at court. The thing I remember most vividly was the business with the sentries at the Belvedere. The moment father left the palace, even when our mother was still there, the sentries were withdrawn and they did not return until he did. I remember this so well because we sometimes used to play soldiers in the empty boxes.[7]

To the children themselves – Sophie, Max and Ernst – their strange position may have meant little more than being 'oddly placed' at Vienna tea parties or being presented with suddenly unoccupied sentry-boxes to play in at their father's palace. But, unknown to them at the time, clouds of rumour and intrigue were always forming over their little heads. As they grew out of infancy – all strong, healthy and intelligent – and as the Emperor himself inched reluctantly towards dotage or death, one great question arose. Would Franz Ferdinand, on inheriting the throne, break that oath of June 1900 so that his own sons might eventually be enabled to succeed him? Those who, then and later, argued No, pointed above all to the solemn and sacred nature of that oath and to the Archduke's sense of duty, not just to the dynasty but, as a devout Catholic, to the God before whom he had made his pledge. Certainly, the two boys were never made to feel that they were being prepared surreptitiously for higher things. Quite the contrary. Without exception, Franz Ferdinand's secretaries and personal aides – members of the household who would have been in constant contact with the whole family – have testified that he wanted for his sons nothing more ambitious than to be brought up as landed noblemen. Thus his secretary, Nikitsch-Boulles:

Franz Ferdinand seemed even to envy his children their tranquil future. In the entire education that he prepared for them, there was nothing which might be construed as a preparation for any eventual succession to the throne. He wanted his boys to enjoy the untrammelled existence of country squires and not the artificial life imposed by court . . . He had similar intentions for his daughter. He believed that she would be a thousand times happier at the side of a socially suitable partner whom she loved than was ever possible with those marriages of convenience – which so often went wrong – entered into by princesses of the royal house.[8]

(In this last respect, as in others, the Archduke's only daughter was fully to live up to his expectations. Six years after his death, when aged nineteen, she married Count Friedrich Nostitz-Rieneck, with whom she was to enjoy more than fifty years of happy married life.)

Baron Alfred Morsey, one of the last recruits to Franz Ferdinand's household, is even more emphatic about the Archduke's intentions. In his unpublished memoirs, the Baron describes how his employer greeted him with these words: 'Please bring it home to my children that to rule and wear a crown is a heavy burden imposed from heaven and that one should never yearn for such things. My children are destined one of these days after my death to become simply large Bohemian landlords.'[9]

Though the young Baron (who had been recruited from the staff of the imperial state archives in Vienna for service with the Archduke) little knew it at the time, much tragic irony lay buried in that last sentence. 'One of these days' was to come for Franz Ferdinand with terrible swiftness. Moreover, the ultimate aftermath of the catastrophe was such that in 1919 the republican successors to the Monarchy were to deprive his sons of the last acre of their Bohemian estates.

But nothing that Franz Ferdinand could say or do about the succession could disperse the suspicions about his real motives which swirled around at court. The well-founded belief that the Hungarians, as part of their relentless campaign to win more and more independence from Vienna, would accept the Duchess of Hohenberg as Queen of Hungary, and might one day, after Franz Ferdinand's death, select an archduke of their own to be their king, gave the threat constitutional substance. Not surprisingly, perhaps, the young Archduke Charles and his wife – who fully expected before Sarajevo to continue into the 1930s as next in line to the throne, with their uncle reigning as Emperor – were the most affected by doubts. The Empress Zita relates:

Sometimes it was only a chance remark which, rightly or wrongly, made one wonder. For example, I remember Uncle Franzi once saying to me, when we were talking about a very industrious land agent, 'That man works so hard. I just can't understand anyone doing that unless it is for his own children!'

Obviously, one could interpret a remark like that to mean that he was thinking of his own case and his own children. My husband quite certainly had this dread. He felt that after succeeding to the throne, his uncle might somehow manage it so that his sons could inherit and then an impossible situation would arise. Archduke Charles would continue to be the Heir-Presumptive,* but due to the Hungarian factor, the Monarchy could become divided into two camps about its future sovereign.[10]

We shall never know the answer to the riddle because Franz Ferdinand was never called upon to face it. In the absence of any evidence of intended double-dealing on his part, it is only fair to presume him innocent. But it is also fair to add that even if, as Emperor, he had not actually succumbed to temptation over the succession, he would certainly have felt its pangs.

Meanwhile, the resident-in-waiting at the Belvedere had to fight down a very present temptation, namely, the itch to win more and more influence over the Monarchy's affairs at the expense of the ageing sovereign. The relationship between Franz Joseph and Franz Ferdinand was a complex one. The great personal bond between them was their love, as good Austrians, of the hunt. True, the Emperor's approach to shooting was very different from that of his nephew. For Franz Joseph, it was something to be pursued serenely (as with everything he did) and made to fit into the normal pattern of life. The imperial villa at Bad Ischl, set in the middle of the fashionable Salzkammergut, became a busy country court during the roebuck season, and was the genial symbol of pleasure combined with duty. As we have seen, there was nothing so

* Only 'presumptive' because, in the event of the Duchess of Hohenberg dying and Franz Ferdinand concluding another marriage, this time dynastically acceptable, the male children of that union would come first in the succession line. (See Appendix II, p. 288.)

relaxed in the Archduke's attitude. Moreover, he preferred seclusion in which to enjoy his sport. The remote and rugged beauty of his Blühnbach estate, which was virtually sealed off from the public, typified this.

Nonetheless, the common love was there, and without it, it is hard to see how any real human contact could have been kept up between the two men. From the earliest days, the ruler's letters to his nephew are strewn with references to their mutual passion. Thus, only a few weeks before the scandal over Sophie broke, the Emperor wrote to Franz Ferdinand reminding him that the funeral and requiem mass for his 'Uncle Ernst' would be held that coming weekend in Vienna, and that the Archduke's presence at the ceremonies seemed 'unavoidable'. But when the Emperor added, 'I am sorry that your shooting will be disturbed,'[11] he was not being sarcastic. April was the time to stalk that very elusive quarry, the capercailzie, and the writer knew full well what it meant to forego that excitement.

Uncle and nephew shared other tastes and prejudices. Each had distinctly middlebrow ideas about music and literature, for example. Each preferred the practical to the intellectual approach. Each was a dedicated military man. Each was an autocrat. And both the ruler and the prince who hoped to succeed him were obsessed with the need to hold dynasty and empire together (though their thoughts as to how best the sacred aim might be achieved were poles apart). Yet, despite all this, neither their minds nor their hearts ever came really close, except in very brief moments of common stress or mourning. Nor can too much be read into the courteous style of the Emperor's letters to his 'dear nephew'. The old gentleman would have been equally courteous (though not, of course, as familiar) had he been writing to the widow of a level-crossing keeper complaining about her inadequate pension. What matters is not what went down on paper but what happened in the flesh, and in this respect the then Archduchess Zita, who saw it all happening around her, is an invaluable witness:

> When they came together in the family circle everything was always perfectly harmonious. But we all knew that it was a

very different matter when they were alone. The Emperor, who was old and tired during those last years, hated above all any scenes. His nephew nearly always made scenes, and sometimes frightful ones, at their private audiences. That was the main reason why he often got what he wanted. But it was also the reason why the Emperor sent for him as little as possible. Apart from political differences – and, of course, the constant problems arising out of the marriage – they were just too different in temperament. So there was always electricity in the air when they were together.[12]

The truth of the matter is that every time the Emperor saw his nephew before him he saw a dual phantom, and a dual reproach. The first came out of the past, the shadow of his own son Rudolf, who ought, by rights, to have been standing there in Franz Ferdinand's place. The second shadow was cast forward across the future. Like the venerable head of an old-established family firm threatened with shutdown, the Emperor wanted to surmount the crisis, as he had surmounted so many others since the middle of the nineteenth century, by clinging to the old methods and playing doggedly for time. This meant that the pattern of life, as well as the established pattern of rule, was never varied by one millimetre unless the heavens fell in. That annual holiday in Bad Ischl, for example, would begin on 15 June, as it had done for well over sixty years. And the first Sunday morning after arriving at Ischl, the Emperor would set out by train for Gmunden to visit the German royal families of Hanover and Württemberg, both of whom had properties there. It was always the same carriage which waited for him outside Gmunden station, and though the old monarch must have outlived more than one coachman in his time, he always gave the same tip. (Inflation, in those literally golden days, played little havoc with the money.)

The Archduke's pattern of life, as we have seen, could not have been in greater contrast: always on the move, sometimes spending 200 out of the 365 days in a year in a train, and often setting off on a sheer impulse. This was the same restless energy, the same drive for new horizons and new experiences, which he wanted to bring to the throne. Time, he was convinced, could no longer be relied on to save the empire. On the contrary, to survive, the empire had to catch up with the clock of history.

While he was still waiting for his own hour to come, all Franz Ferdinand could do was press the Emperor and his ministers for modernization and reform. The most effective helper he ever found to exert such pressure lived and worked with him in the Lower Belvedere for nearly six years: Major (later Colonel) Alexander Brosch von Aarenau, the handsome officer shown riding to his death in that painting in Vienna's War Museum. Their instrument was Franz Ferdinand's so-called 'Military Chancery'. In the first years of its existence this had been little more than a post office, passing on, for the Archduke's perusal, only such documents as the Emperor's Adjutant-General, Baron Arthur Bolfras, thought fit to send over. Its first two heads had been amiable nonentities who found even this limited work too much for them.

But when, on 16 January 1901, Brosch, then a relatively young staff officer, was put in charge, the chancery was transformed from a post office into a power house. The staff was rapidly increased from two officers to fourteen (almost the same size as the Emperor's own Military Chancery), and its responsibilities were expanded accordingly. Within little more than three months, Franz Ferdinand was receiving, on the Emperor's orders, every document of significance from the War Ministry. Briefings from other ministries followed and, increasingly, the ministers themselves as well as the ambassadors accredited to the Emperor's court came for audiences at the Belvedere also. Increasingly, too, the traffic in ideas became a two-way flow, often leading to collisions. Those ministers whom the Archduke liked or found opposed to his ideas he and Brosch intrigued to install or get rid of – succeeding, for example, in appointing Baron Schonaich to the War Ministry in 1906 and then, when he proved a disappointment, in getting him shifted in 1911. Nor did the Military Chancery confine itself to official matters. It became more and more involved in day-to-day politics and polemics and to this end built up its own little press corps to get its opinions over to the general public. These 'Belvedere organs' included the fortnightly *Österreichische Rundschau*, the weekly *Armeezeitung* and the *Reichspost*, the Vienna Catholic daily edited by the eminent Friedrich Funder. None of these journals could reach the broad masses. But they saw to it that the Archduke's reformist ideas reached that patriotic élite on which he was counting for so much.

To find the political spokesmen and sponsors for that élite – men who put loyalty to the dynasty and a dedication to the unity of the empire above everything – Franz Ferdinand had cast his net wide. His Austrian favourites included the banker Alexander von Spitzmüller, the leader of the Hungarian-German Peoples Party Baron von Eichoff, the jurist Heinrich Lammasch, and his own nominee for the post of Chief of Staff, Conrad von Hötzendorf. From the national groups he drew supporters such as Baron Rauch for the Croats, Vaida-Voivod and Maniu for the Rumanians, Count Ottokar Czernin for the Czechs (or rather, for the Bohemian nobility), the young Milan Hodza for the Slovaks and Bishop Lányi and Josef Kristóffy – who were among the few prominent Hungarians he liked and trusted – for the Magyars. The Archduke's selection showed an eye for talent, though of very different varieties. During the war which followed Franz Ferdinand's death, Spitzmüller became a very capable Trade Minister; Czernin a brilliant but very erratic Foreign Minister; while Professor Lammasch ended up as the very last Chancellor to serve under the Monarchy. Vaida-Voivod eventually became Prime Minister of Rumania and, later still, Hodza ended his fanatical career as head of a puppet state under Hitler. At the beginning of the century, however, one and all of this mixed company saw the Archduke as the guarantor of their people's salvation – and, of course, of their own bright future.

Inevitably, a tension and a rivalry sprang up between the Belvedere and Schönbrunn. Ministers, generals, civil servants and courtiers alike tried, unless they were irrevocably committed, to look two ways at once – towards the setting sun of Franz Joseph and towards the rising sun of Franz Ferdinand. There was much blurred vision as a result. Yet though Brosch himself once ironically called the Belvedere 'His Majesty's most loyal Opposition', it was not, and never could be, a rival government. So long as the old Emperor drew breath, power, which in his case stretched to latent despotism, remained in his hands and the hands of those he appointed. What the Belvedere had was influence, which is the next best thing.

Though Brosch found a very capable successor for himself – Colonel Karl Bardolff – when he finally persuaded a reluctant Archduke to release him for field service in the autumn of 1911, the Military Chancery remained his creation and he left it at its zenith. He was one of the most remarkable young Austrians of his generation, endowed with brains as well as bravery and – an even more remarkable blend – combining tact with panache. No-one outside the family circle came closer to Franz Ferdinand and no-one outside that circle was more devoted to him. It is well worth while, therefore, taking another look at the Archduke's character, as seen by this most loyal and perceptive of his servants.

Two years after leaving the Belvedere (and less than a year before his own death in battle), Brosch put down at great length on paper his thoughts on Franz Ferdinand 'as a human being and as a soldier'. When he had finished, he thought of burning the document, which was, in parts, extremely frank. Fortunately, he put it aside instead, and it was found among his private papers.

> ... The Archduke is open to suggestions, and, in fact, it is easy to convince him of a good thing provided he does not mistrust the speaker in the first place; but one must know the right way to go about it, for the Archduke will on no account tolerate direct contradiction. What he will accept, on the other hand, more than most people, is the unvarnished truth; indeed, he demands it. So if one knows how to be frank with him in an acceptable manner which avoids contradiction, one can achieve almost anything. Of course, that means using a lot of finesse and tact and choosing the right moment; in other words, it's a wearisome business.
>
> The Archduke is sharp and often harsh in his judgements and somewhat hasty as well, so that it often happens that he is

unjust to people. But once he realizes this, he doesn't hesitate
to put things right ...

Towards those who work with him, the Archduke
displays a magical amiability: during the whole six years, I
never saw an unfriendly gesture or heard a gruff word. Once
one has won his confidence – which naturally takes quite some
time – then his trust in you endures and knows no limitations
... The head of his Military Chancery is the best-placed in
this respect because he is called on to report more than anyone
else. His influence is therefore, without doubt, the greatest,
and the only danger is that, instead of acting as intermediary,
he might become ambitious and try to steer things himself ...

People are right in supposing that the Archduke is a man
of great energy; unfortunately, it operates explosively. The
Archduke always works in bursts. Steady calm is something
he simply doesn't know, and thus he gives the impression of
an unconsidered impulsiveness which could be dangerous ...

He has the characteristic habit of all Habsburgs of
avoiding immediate action over anything unpleasant or
momentous, preferring to wait in case some miracle will show
him the solution ...[13]

Though there were some passages in that very private report
which, had they come to Franz Ferdinand's eyes or ears, might
well have brought about one of his famous explosions, the
Colonel's underlying verdict is one of deep and affectionate
respect. That these feelings were fully reciprocated is shown by
the letters which the Archduke continued to send to his former
right-hand man after Brosch had rejoined his regiment (and
found time, at last, to marry). Thus, for the new year of 1912 –
the first in six that they had not worked together – Brosch, in
offering the usual good wishes, had described how he saw his
mission as a serving officer. Franz Ferdinand replied:

What you wrote to me in your letter, and above all your ideal
concept of a good soldier, moved me enormously. I can only
say: true Brosch, that's how the traditional Austrian soldier,
loyal to the dynasty and with his heart in the right place, must
think! Whatever happens, may you preserve those ideals, and
your youthful energy and capacity for work.[14]

Such was the remarkable team which tried, from a suite of offices in the Lower Belvedere, to shake the Emperor out of his lethargy and shore up a crumbling empire. It is time to look at what, precisely, they sought to achieve.

CHAPTER EIGHT

────── ⊗ ──────

The Monarchy:
A Blurred Vision

THE SPLENDID BOSNIAN SOLDIERS of the palace guard; the peasants in their white hand-woven robes which seemed to draw into the capital a breath of wide eastern spaces, of the Carpathians and steppes; the flower-sellers, bearing a whole garden of blossoms in front of them; the wet-nurses from Iglau, cooks from Prague, nannies from Pressburg; the short-skirted housemaids from Slovakia; the Jews from Galicia in their long kaftans; the recruits and officers with the colours of all the famous regiments of the army stitched on their collars; the wood-carvers of Tyrol, the porters, basket-weavers and gypsies; Ruthenians and Triestinos; the fair-headed sons of the mountains and the dark-skinned people from the Adriatic coast . . . like a magnet, Vienna drew them all towards her, and Vienna herself was in every province and land.[1]

That word picture of the street throng in Franz Joseph's capital was written long after he and his empire had vanished. But it can still serve to bring to life the tangle of peoples and principalities which, over the course of more than six centuries, the Habsburgs had gathered around their crown. And this was the cat's cradle of a legacy which the prince who succeeded Franz Joseph would have to unravel before he could weave a new political pattern strong enough to endure in the twentieth century. One presumes that Franz Ferdinand, who confidently expected to be that prince, sometimes studied a detailed map of the distribution of races within his empire when pondering over the problems of reform. If so, one may safely presume also that he would have sighed despondently when removing his spectacles.

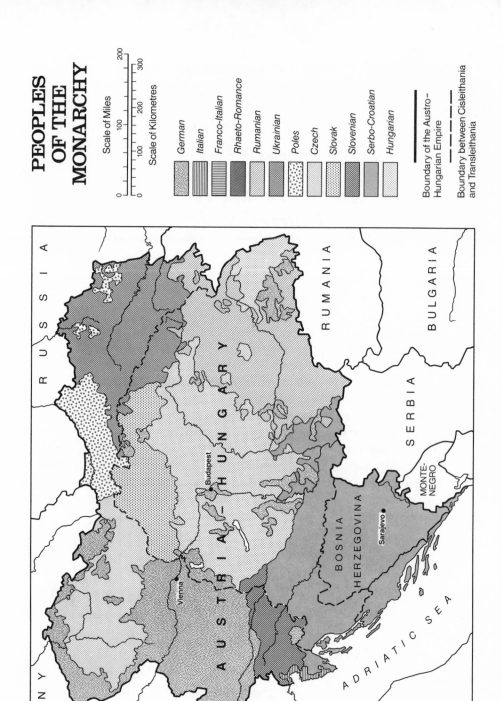

PEOPLES OF THE MONARCHY

Scale of Miles
Scale of Kilometres

German
Italian
Franco-Italian
Rhaeto-Romance
Rumanian
Ukrainian
Poles
Czech
Slovak
Slovenian
Serbo-Croatian
Hungarian

Boundary of the Austro-Hungarian Empire

Boundary between Cisleithania and Transleithania

RUSSIA

GERMANY

AUSTRIA–HUNGARY

Vienna

Budapest

BOSNIA HERZEGOVINA

Sarajevo

ITALY

ADRIATIC SEA

RUMANIA

SERBIA

BULGARIA

MONTE-NEGRO

One such map is reproduced opposite. It shows no fewer than eighteen different racial groups within and around the borders of the Monarchy; and what is even more muddling than the variety of races on the map is their intermingling. Only the Austro-German bloc in the east presents a solid ethnic heart-land, which is just nibbled at, in the extreme south, by a Slovene preserve (still there today, and still a periodic headache). Elsewhere, everything is a jumble: wedges of German-speakers among the Serbs, Magyars, Rumanians and Poles; Poles among the Ukrainians; Hungarians among the Rumanians; Italians among the Slovenes; Slovenes among the Serbs. As to numbers, when the eleven major nationalities were counted in the last imperial census of 1910, the Austro-Germans were shown to be still the largest group at just over twelve million, followed by the Hungarians with ten million, the Poles with nearly five million, the Ruthenians with nearly four million, and the Rumanians, with three and a quarter million, heading the list of smaller minorities.*

This unholy confusion of tongues and peoples had never been created as a state. Like Topsy, it had just grown. It was the product of racial migrations going back to the Dark Ages; of the ebb and flow of great invasions, like that of the Turks; of victory and defeat in many a lesser battle; of marriage pacts and dynastic legacies; of geo-politics and the course of rivers and mountain ranges; and, sometimes, simply of economic pressures or commercial enterprise. It was natural that the house of Habsburg, which presided over this medley of races (and also provided, through the crown, the one single link they had with each other), should have bestowed upon itself a sense of

---

* The exact breakdown:

Germans	12,011,081	Rumanians	3,224,728
Magyars	10,067,917	Croats	2,888,171
Czechs	6,643,059	Serbs	2,041,899
Slovaks	1,967,520	Slovenes	1,371,256
Poles	4,977,643	Italians	771,054
Ruthenians	3,999,100	Others	979,990

'mission' as the divinely-sanctioned preserver of unity and order among them.*

Other empires of the day made similar moral claims – the British, for example, sincerely believing that they were 'civilizing the natives' while at the same time obliging them to work for the greater power and wealth of the mother country. But whereas the kings and queens of England, surrounded by their saltwater moat, were perched off the north-west corner of Europe, almost ludicrously far removed from their imperial possessions, the Habsburgs lived slap in the middle of their lands, so that any tumult, even on the fringes, pressed immediately upon the centre. Moreover, though the Austro-Hungarian Monarchy certainly had its first and second-class citizens in practice, they were all white, all European, all proud of some glory in their past, and all theoretically equal before the law of the day.

Finally, and most important, all were stirring, with varying degrees of agitation, under something which had not yet touched the natives of Britain's empire – the call of nationalism. There had been the great explosion of 1848, Europe's year of revolution, when the dynasty had been driven by the Vienna mob into temporary exile in the provinces. Franz Joseph had himself come to the throne in the wake of that revolution, succeeding his discredited uncle Ferdinand as a sop to the 'new age' which the crown was nonetheless determined to keep at bay.

A second great impetus to nationalist movements everywhere had been sparked off eleven years later when Garibaldi set about transforming the hotchpotch of Italian states into one nation – a transformation which, incidentally, was to cost the Habsburgs many of their own Italian provinces. Though there had been no domestic upheaval of 1848 proportions as a result of those losses, the earth had continued to tremble, and the tremblings grew steadily louder. How was a dynasty which stood

---

* The claim becomes alive if the list of royal and feudal titles – nearly fifty in number – contained in the Archduke's own draft Accession Manifesto is studied. (See Appendix II, p. 290.)

Artist's impression of the historic scene in the Hofburg on 28 June 1900 when the Archduke, in return for being allowed his morganatic marriage, renounced all royal rights for his wife and children.

His reward: the wedding in Reichstadt, boycotted by the Emperor and all the Archdukes. The couple's 'guardian angel', the bridegroom's stepmother, Archduchess Maria Theresa, stands at Sophie's right.

Married bliss. The happy couple caught in picture postcard pose on a stroll at home.

The 'official' picture of the newly-married pair. 'Soph', he wrote, 'is a treasure!'

Franz Ferdinand with his eldest child and only daughter, Sophie. 'He was marvellous as a father to us children . . .'

Part of the famous rose gardens at Konopischt, which took him more than twenty years to perfect.

The former gamekeeper who rose to be the head of the Archduke's household, a post for which this special uniform was designed.

or fell by being supra-national to survive sitting on the top of this nationalist volcano?

For the first decade after the revolution, the young ruler, guided initially by his 'iron chancellor', Prince Felix Schwarzenberg, tried to stultify nationalist stirrings by a mixture of force and bureaucracy. These were the years of absolutism combined with centralism, when the army saw to it that all power rested with the crown and the civil servants saw to it that all administration centred on Vienna. Given both the spirit of the age and the complexity of the empire itself, it was an unreal experiment which could last only as long as the Emperor and his ministers could preserve their hallowed image. The Monarchy's humiliating defeats in the Italian wars of reunification had put paid to that, and the search for new devices to maintain stability began. In 1860, for example, a somewhat bogus essay in federalism was proclaimed by the so-called 'October Diploma'. Under this, the Emperor relinquished some of his centralized powers, but only to autocratic Diets of selected nations. This farce of trying to make the guardians of the old order function as representatives of the new was overtaken, a year later, by the much bolder innovation of setting up new-fangled parliamentary institutions by imperial decree. Having realized that neither the army nor the nobility could be relied on to save it from nationalism, the dynasty thus turned to its own version of democracy to do the trick.

Under this 'February Patent' of 1861, a two-chambered Parliament was set up in Vienna, elected on a complex curial system which greatly favoured the Austro-Germans. The mere fact of its establishment in the capital certainly represented a swing back to centralism; but this was accompanied by only a very small and controlled swing away from absolutism. The empire's first parliament was the creation of the crown, not of the people, and the crown took care to keep all vital matters of state in its own hands. Indeed, it went so far as to appoint the president and vice president of both chambers. As a result, even the elected house of representatives became more of a platform for airing racial squabbles than a forum for solving them. Some national groups stayed away altogether; others turned up only to walk out; those of the 343 who came and remained spent much of their time banging desk-lids and hurling ink-pots.

Thus, by the mid-sixties, Franz Joseph had spent nearly twenty years cutting and shuffling the constitutional pack, all the time taking good care that none of the court cards fell out. He had still failed to find any dependable instrument to share with him (and under him) the task of keeping his empire stable and unified. There seemed nothing else to try. Then, a totally different experiment was virtually forced upon him. Stability in the nationalist age was sought, not by unifying the Monarchy, but by splitting it in two, and dividing both land and power with the Hungarians.

The empire's ten million Hungarians were the inevitable partners for the Austrians in any such venture, not merely because they were by far the largest of the other racial groups but also because they were the most compact, the most talented, the most virile and the most confident. It is worth taking a closer look at them, in view of Franz Ferdinand's lifelong obsession both with the Hungarian nation as such and with the compact which his uncle was now about to strike with them.

Hungary came into existence in the closing years of the ninth century when the Magyars, who were a Finno-Ugric people from the Upper Volga area, struck south and occupied the central Danube plain. They had crossed the Carpathians as a federation of seven 'hordes' under their first leader, Arpád, and the process of transforming that uneasy tribal alliance into a stable kingdom proved a long and bloody one. A hundred years after Arpád's appearance on the scene, his great-great-grandson, Stephen, was still struggling in the battle for supremacy. But as his own father, Géza, had already been received in the Christian church and had taken a Bavarian princess for his wife, Stephen had the happy thought of turning to Pope Sylvester II for blessing and support. The Vatican responded, and this massive infusion of moral backing from Rome settled the issue in Stephen's favour. On Christmas Day of the year 1000 he was crowned King, with an apostolic crown and cross sent, according to legend, by the Holy Father himself.

Both the time and the manner of Hungary's emergence into statehood made themselves felt down the centuries. The Magyars became the historic people *par excellence* of the Danube basin. They could claim to have been a kingdom, for example, nearly two hundred and seventy years before the Habsburg dynasty was even founded. And the fact that their nationhood had been sanctioned at its birth, making their realm a spiritual fiefdom of the Papacy, gave to 'the lands of St Stephen' an aura of holy magic unparalleled among the kingdoms of Europe before or since. This survived all the tribulations which followed – occupation by foreign rulers from Anjou, Luxembourg and Poland; invasion by the Turks; and finally, through marriage-pacts and battle, absorption into the Habsburg Monarchy, which established direct rule over the whole of the country in 1699, after the Turks had been put to flight for good. Throughout, the Hungarians preserved not only their unique language (in itself a protection against assimilation) but also their unique sense of God-given destiny. It mattered little that the aroma of incense grew stale over the centuries or that the ancient Papal blessing was used to sanctify not just the crown, but also feudal privilege and greed. For peasant or prince, the lands of St Stephen remained something mystical, precious, eternal.

Even this elemental force operating in the century of nationalism had, however, to await its moment in history to break through. Discussions on a radically new relationship between Budapest and Vienna had begun in 1865, when it was clear that the Emperor's other constitutional experiments had failed; but, once again, it was the dynasty's defeat on the battlefield which sent it scurrying for cover at home. In July 1866, after a disastrous war of only seven weeks against Prussia, the Austrian armies were routed at Königgraetz in Bohemia; the empire was then expelled from the German Confederation and lost its remaining Italian province of Venetia into the bargain. After this, the Hungarians barely needed to press against the negotiating door in Vienna for it to swing open. Franz Deak, the moderate statesman who was the architect of their campaign,

made success certain by prudently refraining from increasing his
earlier demands.

The result was the historic *Ausgleich* or Compromise of
1867. Henceforth, though all the peoples of the Habsburg
Monarchy remained under Franz Joseph's sceptre, the orb of
his empire was split into two. The Western Austrian 'half' was
shaped like a great crescent which curved down from Galicia,
through Bohemia and the Austrian heartland itself down to
Bosnia. The eastern Hungarian 'half' was based on the old 'lands
of St Stephen' of the central Danube basin, but now greatly
enlarged with dominion over non-Magyar races living in the
empire's so-called 'military frontiers' which bordered on
Turkey.

The two halves were separated for all purposes of domestic
rule, each with its own prime minister, government, domestic
taxes and law. They were still linked by the crown, however,
even if the Hungarians regarded it as primarily their national
crown, and also by three joint ministries for foreign policy,
defence and their relevant financing. Just to make things more
complicated, the heads of these ministries were made responsible to two bodies, each of sixty members, chosen from the two
national Parliaments and known as 'delegations'. To make
things more troublesome as well in the future, it was agreed that,
every ten years, there had to be fresh discussions between the
joint ministers and the delegations on such key financial
questions as to how the Monarchy's debts should be paid off and
how its customs revenues should be divided up. This was to
prove a sure recipe for decennial mayhem.

This strange combination of divorce and remarriage had
some ludicrous side-effects. To begin with, a physical boundary
of some sort had to be found, and the Leitha, an obscure little
river which trickles down the flat expanses of the Burgenland
east of Vienna, was selected as the marker. Henceforth,
everything on the Austrian side was known for short as
Cisleithania and everything on the Hungarian side as Transleithania. That at least sounded like a fair balance. But the formal
titles of the two halves were horribly lopsided. They had no

doubts in Budapest as to how their new state should be designated; they called it, of course, 'the lands of the sacred Hungarian crown of St Stephen'. Yet how, in legal documents, should Cisleithania be described – this random grouping which included Upper and Lower Austria, Salzburg, Tyrol, Styria, Gorizia, Istria, Dalmatia, Bohemia, Moravia, Silesia, Galizia and Bukowina? It was not until 1915 that anyone thought of calling it simply Austria. For nearly fifty years before that it was burdened with the cumbrous title of 'the lands and kingdoms represented in the Imperial Council'. Compared with its Hungarian equivalent, that was not much of a name to shout in battle or on the hustings.

But the really damaging imbalance created by the pact of 1867 was that between political and social advance in the two halves of the Monarchy. Over the next half century, the Hungarians carried out a relentless programme of Magyarization among their Serbs, Croats, Slovaks, Rumanians and Ruthenians despite all the liberal promises made in the so-called Nationalities Law of 1868. Within fifteen years of that law being passed, Magyar was made compulsory in all non-Magyar schools, and eventually teachers were even made liable to dismissal if they had not carried out their linguistic duties efficiently. Parallel drives were launched to swamp and smother non-Magyar books and newspapers.*

The deprivation of civic rights was even harsher than this cultural blitz. No fewer than 407 of the 413 seats in the Budapest Parliament were held by Magyars, despite the fact that they were actually in a minority in the new state as a whole. Government posts as well as parliamentary seats were also a virtual monopoly of the Magyars. On the other side of Leitha, however, non-Austrians crowded the ranks of the civil service while the highest offices of state could be filled by men of Polish or Bohemian descent – even if they were usually noblemen.

---

* Ironically, a similar campaign in reverse is being applied today by Rumania against the Hungarian population which came under its rule in Transylvania after the Second World War.

But the greatest contrast came when, in January 1907, the Emperor gave his consent to a bill which accorded the vote to every male of Cisleithania, irrespective of his race or creed, who had reached the age of twenty-four. With this step, one half of the Dual Monarchy had dragged itself into the twentieth century, whereas the other remained stuck in the age of feudalism.*

By choosing to run their enlarged multinational state along lines that were both archaic and chauvinistic, the Hungarians drove the two segments of the empire steadily apart while at the same time discrediting its reputation abroad. In this way, the settlement of 1867, which, for the Magyars, brought the triumph of national over imperial loyalty, spelt doom for the imperial concept itself. Franz Joseph's historic plunge was a reform which shut out all further reform. He soon sensed this himself and, after 1867, went into a state of deep political hibernation which lasted to his death fifty years later.

What could the nephew do about it all, while waiting – as it turned out in vain – for that death? To begin with, he tried everything in his power to rouse the Emperor from his Hungarian coma. Among the Archduke's surviving political papers there is, for example, the draft of a letter of June 1907 in which he complains bitterly about the fuss being made over the fortieth anniversary celebrations of the Dual Monarchy's creation – celebrations which, as heir to the throne, he was obliged to attend. We do not know whether this letter was ever despatched as drafted, but the fact that it is written in the Archduke's hand in pencil, with frequent underlinings added in red, makes it, more than any formal document, a truly vibrant echo of what Franz Ferdinand really felt.

> Your Majesty has ordered me to go to Pest. Order will be obeyed. Please don't misunderstand me but I hold it my duty to tell Your Majesty the truth. I regard these celebrations as a distorted concept. The anniversary jubilee is being held at a

---

* And not just politically. It was calculated that at the turn of the century, the 324 largest private estates of Hungary accounted for nearly 20% of the country's total agricultural land.

time when the rulers there (people who I can only describe as traitors) are constantly agitating against everything – dynasty, empire, army. They have broken every promise they have made, universal suffrage, army levies, etc ... I don't know if Your Majesty realizes what attacks are made on you in officially subsidized newspapers ... I can only say it's an outrage, a scandal.

The letter ends with a plea from the Archduke that he should be spared the pain of going to Budapest in person for the festivities. 'That would be for me a journey to Canossa and I beg that I be spared such an embarrassment.'[2] (He was not spared, but managed to offend everyone in Budapest by leaving almost as soon as he arrived.)

Even for a man of Franz Ferdinand's temperament, the style of that letter, considering that it was intended for the Emperor himself, was pretty fierce. But the Archduke was often much fiercer when corresponding with his own advisers on this sore subject. Thus the following outburst comes in one of his letters to the faithful Baron Max Beck: 'The so-called "decent Hungarian" simply doesn't exist, and every Hungarian, whether he's a minister, a prince, a cardinal, a townsman or a peasant, a peddler or a servant, is a revolutionary coming from the dregs. (Dregs can't apply to the cardinal I suppose, but he's certainly a republican.)'[3] And the following passage occurs in a draft of a letter to the German Emperor William, penned in the summer of 1909: 'The so-called noble and knightly Magyar is in fact the most monstrous, despicable, deceitful and unreliable of fellows and all the problems we have in the Monarchy arise only because of them.'[4]

What comes out in explosions like these (and many such examples could be quoted) is the Archduke's smouldering dislike of the Hungarians, as well as his fury at the political challenge they presented. He may well have tried to persuade himself that, as befitted the future father of this quarrelsome Habsburg family of nations, he could learn to love them all equally once they, for their part, had learnt to be equally obedient. But the truth is that he was temperamentally incapable even of liking the Hungarians as people, let alone of loving them. Everything about them (beginning with that bizarre language) irritated and frustrated him; even the customs which the rest of the world found so charming. As a young officer, for example, he frequently attended Hungarian regimental dinners where the hussars performed their traditional *csardas*. On one such occasion, he turned to his companion and snorted, 'Just look at that animal dance! That's one of the first things I shall do away with!'[5] The remark caused much consternation, as well it might, less for the threat being taken too seriously than for the mere fact that it had been uttered.

Throughout his years as the second man in the empire, the Archduke tried to wriggle out of taking any Hungarians with him on his official travels, although they represented half of the Dual Monarchy. His antagonism was just as evident at the pettiest personal level. The then Archduchess Zita, his niece by marriage, recalled a significant episode:

> Once, my husband Charles agreed to be the godfather of a groom on his estate. The groom happened to have a Hungarian name, and when our uncle Franz heard about it he wrote a letter demanding an explanation. To him, this little gesture appeared as a gratuitous way of favouring Hungary! My husband promptly replied that it was all quite harmless. Though the man may have had a Hungarian name, he was a native of Lower Austria and no more Magyar than anyone else on the estate. After that, there was silence.[6]

It was a sobering thought for all concerned that the prince with such violent prejudices was no ordinary archduke but the heir to the throne itself. What on earth would he get up to with the Hungarians once the crown was his? Before examining the Archduke's own ideas for that event (which were a great deal more nebulous than is often supposed) it is worth looking at how he was preparing himself for the battle, when forced to work in the Emperor's shadow.

To operate at all, the Archduke knew that he needed a power base. He had laid the first plank of this on 8 April 1901 when – out of the blue as far as his uncle was concerned – he announced that he had agreed to become patron of the League of Catholic Schools. In the Austria of the day this was tantamount to a declaration of war on anyone who sought to weaken the dynasty by weakening those special links which the Habsburg rulers, as 'apostolic majesties', possessed with Rome. Though Europe was not about to fight the Thirty Years War all over again, the tug-of-war was intensifying in the Dual Monarchy between the devout Catholics who held true to the imperial concept and those who, for various reasons and in varying degrees, wanted to move closer to Protestant Germany. The Archduke made the point quite bluntly in his speech of acceptance. Praising the 'religious and patriotic work' of the League, he stressed its particular importance 'in this time of the "away-from-Rome" movement, which is also an "away-from-Austria" movement'. This trend, he said, could not be fought energetically enough, and accordingly he pledged himself to help in word and deed.[7]

The speech raised the hackles not merely of the liberal pan-Germans in Austria. The outcry in Hungary – which, unlike the Austrian lands, had a very substantial Protestant population – was even louder. The heir to the throne, cried the Budapest papers, should not allow himself to be drawn onto ground which was so sensitive and dangerous for the Monarchy. The monarch himself had misgivings. Writing from a visit to Hungary a fortnight after the Archduke had dropped his political bomb-shell, the Emperor, while accepting that his nephew had acted with the best motives in patronizing such an admirable organization, nonetheless warned against such 'demonstrative behaviour which, in view of your exceptionally high position and with regard to your own future ... was precipitate to a high degree'.[8] And, almost by the same post, came a more formal reprimand in the shape of a decree forbidding any member of the imperial house to accept the patronage of 'any type of league, corporation, congress or assembly' without the previous consent of the sovereign.[9] As far as the Archduke was concerned, however, the glove had already been thrown down.

The second and broader plank of Franz Ferdinand's power base was the armed forces of the empire, on whose loyalty and unity the dynasty itself stood or fell. Two years after leaving the Belvedere, Brosch wrote of his former master that even if the Archduke had achieved nothing else in his life hitherto and were to achieve nothing more in the future, his work in the military sphere alone would guarantee him a proud place in the empire's history.[10] Whether the devoted courtier spoke louder in that verdict than the professional soldier we shall never know. What is certain is that in this field, as in all others where the heir to the throne tried to leave his mark, he had to scratch out a laborious path ahead.

When, on finally recovering his health in 1898, Franz Ferdinand was placed, on a very broad and vague assignment, 'at the disposition of the Supreme army command', he had hoped that the appointment would make him, in effect, the General-Inspector of the empire's armed forces in peacetime as well as their designated Commander-in-Chief in war. In fact, he had to wait fifteen more years before, on 17 August 1913, the formal title was bestowed upon him. To begin with he had no official power and very little unofficial influence. He was only allowed a field command at military manoeuvres on three occasions between 1898 and 1903; at all other times he was simply a frustrated observer. And though he was always pressing for better coordination between cavalry, infantry and artillery, the old establishment, personified by the Chief-of-Staff Count Friederich Beck,* usually managed to turn a deaf ear to innovation – helped, of course, by the old Emperor, who was a past master at the art.

Then, in the autumn of 1906, came the Archduke's great chance. The old establishment had made a complete and utter hash of joint sea and army manoeuvres in the Adriatic, which Franz Ferdinand, representing the Emperor, had attended. He was able, without exaggeration, to submit a blistering report, suggesting that it was high time that Count Beck, and, for that matter, the War Minister, Baron Pitreich, were replaced. What followed was an impressive tribute to the growing prestige of the

---

* Not to be confused with Baron Max Beck, the Archduke's former tutor and confidant who had played such a key role in the marriage crisis.

Archduke and his fast-expanding Military Chancery. A harassed sovereign was obliged not merely to agree to the dismissals, but was also persuaded to accept his nephew's nominees for both posts – General Conrad von Hötzendorf as the new Chief-of-Staff and Baron Schönaich as the new War Minister.

The appointment of Conrad, who was to go down in history as the supreme 'hawk' of the Habsburg Monarchy and the tireless advocate of a 'preventive war' against the Slav and Italian enemies which supposedly threatened the dying empire in the south, was especially remarkable. Conrad, who had caught the Archduke's eye at manoeuvres in the South Tyrol the year before, had had no experience of staff work of any sort during the previous fifteen years and was most reluctant to exchange a field command for the hothouse of Viennese intrigue. Indeed, he turned down the idea when the Archduke first summoned him to the Belvedere to sound him out. Nor was Franz Joseph himself any more enthusiastic to have this outspoken officer, who clearly disliked the Monarchy's passive diplomacy as well as the way it was running its army, made his Chief-of-Staff. But on 18 November 1906 Franz Ferdinand finally got his way with both of them and Conrad's appointment was officially announced.

It proved to be an uneasy relationship all round, with Conrad often threatening to resign (and once carrying his threat out and having to be coerced into returning). The Emperor, despite the fact that he had urged Conrad always to tell him the unvarnished truth, found this commodity – so rare in the self-mirroring world of the Hofburg – extremely unpleasant whenever it was dished up. 'I get annoyed whenever I read one of your memoranda,' he once exploded to the General, banging his fist on the table as he did so in a rare loss of imperial composure.[11]

As for the Archduke, he had found a strange and stormy companion in his odyssey to rescue the dynasty. Both shared the same quick temper, the same passionate devotion to the Monarchy and its armed services, and the same furious impatience with the muddle and lethargy which were crippling both. There were also great gulfs between them. Whereas, for example, Franz Ferdinand was a devout Catholic of the old school, Conrad, very much under the influence of Darwinism, was more of an agnostic. But true believer or not, the two men shared the same supreme agony in their private lives. The General, like the Archduke, had fallen head over heels in love with a lady he was not supposed to marry; and, like the Archduke, he braved all opposition and all scandal to win his prize.

Conrad's fate was a young dark-haired beauty called Gina von Reininghaus, wife of the ennobled Styrian brewer of that name, who had married her when she was only sixteen and had already had three children by her when, at the age of twenty, she first met the General at a dinner party. At that time, 1900, Conrad was also married; but, seven years later, meeting her again after the death of his own wife, he decided on the spot that he could not live without her. He was now, thanks to Franz Ferdinand, the famous Chief-of-Staff; she was now, thanks to her ardent husband, the mother of six children, and that, as she told the infatuated General, made a total of seven reasons why she could never belong to him. Conrad nonetheless laid siege to her as though he were storming a fortress. He appeared so often at the Reininghaus residences in Vienna and Graz that the beer baron himself became resigned to one day losing his wife to this resplendent soldier. And from 1907 onwards, whenever away on manoeuvres or foreign travels, Conrad would write a passionate letter to Frau von Reininghaus every single day. It was not until 1915, however, that she could steel herself to do the socially unthinkable and get a divorce in order to marry Conrad, hoping that any clamour might be drowned by the noise of war.[12] This proved a false hope. For weeks on end, the scandal vied with the battlefields for the attention of the Viennese.

It is ironic that during all the years when Franz Ferdinand and Conrad worked together, travelled together and conducted manoeuvres together, the heir to the throne never seems to have realized the private torment, mirroring that which he had once felt, which his Chief-of-Staff was going through. Nor does Conrad ever seem to have disclosed his secret: after audiences with the Archduke he would withdraw to his tent or his sleeping-car, night after night, to write his love letters to a respectable married woman back in Vienna or Graz.

Indeed, among all the 1800-odd pages of Conrad's memoirs, only one occasion is recorded when the question of marriage cropped up between the two men, and the Archduke referred to his own historic struggle. On a car journey through the South Tyrol in August 1910 – made to inspect Austrian defence fortifications in the mountains – the Archduke raised the question of one of the Monarchy's most capable Corps Commanders who had blotted his copybook by turning Protestant in order to marry a divorced Catholic. The Archduke criticized the officer; Conrad just as stoutly defended him. It was surely the supreme right of any man, he argued, to choose the woman of his choice and, having made that choice, it was only manly to fight for it. At that, Franz Ferdinand smiled and said, 'Yes, actually that's what I did myself.' Now, if ever, was the moment for the General to mention, however obliquely, his own torment. But after a short silence they started talking again about gun positions.[13]

Though the two men never got close on any deep personal level, it was a very different story on the professional level. Here, despite periodic clashes, they managed between them to pull the antiquated Austrian army into the twentieth century, against all the entrenched opposition, within the short space of less than eight years. Though the ideas mostly came from Conrad, it was only thanks to the Archduke's support from the Belvedere that they could be realized.

As a result, by 1914, the army had been properly introduced to both the telephone and the automobile (though, characteristically, Franz Ferdinand was not so enthusiastic about motorization for Hungarian units); a miniature air-force had been created; the artillery, which was to prove one of Austria's most powerful fighting arms in the Armageddon ahead, had been reorganized from top to bottom; machine-guns had been introduced; up-to-date fighting manuals had been prepared and issued; the technical services had been overhauled, and Conrad's so-called 'open system' of military deployment, revolutionary for its time, had been successfully tested in manoeuvres.

Another sadly neglected sphere to which the Archduke devoted special attention was the need for closer cooperation between land and sea forces. This leads us on to what was by far the most important single contribution Franz Ferdinand made to the armed services of the Monarchy, the creation of a modern navy. Though it had been a Habsburg, Archduke John of Austria, who had led the Christian armada which smashed the Turkish fleet in the great battle of Lepanto three centuries before Franz Ferdinand's time, the dynasty had taken precious little personal interest in the sea ever since. Almost the only exception had been Archduke Maximilian who, before embarking on his ill-fated venture as Emperor of Mexico, had served from 1854 to 1862 as naval Commander-in-Chief of his fatherland, and had worked wonders to bring the Austrian navy from the age of sail to the age of steel. The victory which that navy scored against the Italians at Lissa in 1866 – a victory doubly treasured by the Austrians as some compensation for their humiliating series of defeats on land – owed as much to the doomed Maximilian as to the capable Austrian admiral of the day, Wilhelm von Tegetthof.

But with Franz Ferdinand there arrived on the scene the most influential as well as the most determined of Habsburg naval patrons. Moreover, he flourished at a time when fleets had become the symbols of national virility, when the sons of drapers as well as the sons of princes were decked out in sailor suits in every capital of Europe. This was a powerful factor in Franz Ferdinand's thinking, as the young Archduchess Zita, who often heard him holding forth on the subject, recalls:

> Certainly, that world cruise of 1892–3 had left a deep impression on the Archduke. Having seen British warships everywhere, controlling not only the oceans but many of the lands behind these oceans, he realized once and for all what sea power could achieve. More immediately, of course, he wanted to build up the navy to defend the Adriatic coastline of the Monarchy and to fight, if need be, beyond that in the

Mediterranean. But he thought of it not just in terms of Italy, whom he saw as the Monarchy's greatest enemy, but also of Germany, who became the Monarchy's closest military ally after their fratricidal war. The Emperor William was building his enormously powerful navy – and creating serious tension with England in the process – and the Archduke always felt that unless we too had a respectable fleet, we would look insignificant in the alliance with Berlin.[14]

Whatever the motives, it was thanks largely to Franz Ferdinand's enthusiasm (he was made an admiral in 1902 despite the fact that he had never even served aboard a warship, let alone commanded one) that Austria-Hungary entered the World War with a navy which was at least respectable (though scarcely overpowering) by the demanding standards of the time. The grand plan was to build 16 new battleships, 4 large and 8 small new cruisers, 24 additional destroyers, 72 torpedo-boats and 12 submarines.[15] Though the war interrupted that programme, by 1914, the Austrian flag flew over a fairly balanced fleet of more than a quarter of a million tons whose pride was the four 20,000-ton dreadnoughts of the *Viribus Unitis* class. The Archduke and Sophie, who loved these naval occasions, attended most of the major launchings themselves. However, when it came to the ceremony for the last of the quartet, Franz Ferdinand sent a representative instead. The name of this ship happened to be *Szent Istvan*, and it was being built in Fiume by the Hungarian 'Danubius' shipyard. Even the bracing sea air, it seemed, could not dispel the Archduke's distaste for everything Magyar.

Where the real military clash with Hungary came was, of course, over the control of the imperial army itself. To put it simply, Franz Ferdinand regarded the army as the Praetorian guard of the crown. It should know no politics and no rifts of race or creed but always be true to the motto '*Inseparabiliter ac Indivisibiliter*', 'Inseparable and Indivisible'. For the Hungarians, however, the army was the battle symbol of St Stephen's crown which had to be prised loose from the grip of Austria at every opportunity. Unfortunately for Vienna such a golden opportunity cropped up every ten years, when, as laid down in the pact of 1867, the terms of the Austro-Hungarian Compromise came up for renewal.* The last such battle in the Archduke's lifetime came round in 1907, and he was forced to watch it from the sidelines. (Indeed, the Emperor gave instructions that details of the negotiations were to be kept secret from his nephew, knowing that there was only trouble to be expected from that quarter.[16]) Nonetheless, Franz Ferdinand brought to bear all the influence he could to ensure that military concessions to Hungary were kept out of the talks. So indeed they were, and the main advances which Magyar nationalism scored when the pact was finally renewed on 8 October 1907 were in the economic field – the right, for example, to have their own Hungarian signatory authorizing all future trade pacts which the Monarchy concluded with foreign states.

Yet the Hungarians pressed tirelessly forwards on other fronts to achieve their dream of establishing a truly national Hungarian army, with its own chain of command and its own language of command, as the pillar of an independent Magyar state. Thus, as the price for furnishing more recruits for the joint armed forces of the Monarchy, they floated the idea of transferring more executive power from the crown to county and municipal authorities in Hungary and extending the rights of Hungarian constitutional courts. One effect of this – and doubtless also one of its aims – would have been to complicate any political reforms Franz Ferdinand might have launched as Emperor. Another would have been to block, through resistance by the civil power, any emergency attempts he might have made to mobilize army units to enforce his will. Hungarian fears in this respect were not groundless. As early as 1903, the Austrian general staff had drawn up secret plans – rather indiscreetly labelled 'War Contingency U' (for '*Ungarn*' or 'Hungary') – for a concerted march on Budapest by troops drawn from Vienna,

---

* In Franz Ferdinand's view, the renewal period ought to have been extended to an interval of at least twenty-five years, to spare the Dual Monarchy the repeated strain of these negotiations.

Bohemia, Poland and even the native Hungarian province of Croatia.[17]

At the end of this drawn-out haggle, which went on, in one form or another, well into 1908, the Hungarians, having agreed to raise their recruit contingent by two per cent, demanded, as a counter-concession, that no more money should be spent on increasing officers' pay. As this had been a cherished personal aim of the Archduke's the frustration which had been welling up inside him for more than twelve months over the negotiations with Budapest now boiled over in anger. To Conrad he wrote from Switzerland:

> You can well imagine, my dear Conrad, the fury and desperation I have been going through lately over the situation at home and especially over the behaviour of the two war ministers. On the one hand we shout for all the world to hear that we have a surplus of two hundred million crowns, and hand out twenty million to the civil servants and another twenty million to the railways – and then cannot raise a miserable nine million for the poor officers. And all because of the screams of some Hungarian traitors. In fact this is just their pretext. The underlying reason is that the Monarchy is now utterly in the hands of Jews, Freemasons, and Socialists ... and that all these elements seek to bring about disaffection and decay in the army – and especially among the officers corps – so that one day, when I really need the army, I can no longer rely upon it.[18]

The Hungarian nationalists would have been very interested in the concluding passage of that outburst. Indeed, in their eyes, it would have justified all they were so desperately seeking to achieve before Franz Ferdinand did succeed to the throne.

* * *

How could the Archduke, as Emperor, have set about his sworn task of cutting the Hungarians down to size and, in the process, placing the eleven-nation Monarchy on a more stable basis? As he never lived to make the attempt, the question is speculative, even unhistorical. Nonetheless, it is worth stressing that, well before his death, he was cooling off towards the reform always associated with his name. This was the so-called 'Trialist Solution', the creation of a third Habsburg kingdom of South Slavs, to be built around a Great Croatian state with Bosnia-Herzegovina, Dalmatia and the Adriatic port of Trieste tacked on.* But quite apart from the problem of forcing the Hungarians (they could scarcely have been persuaded) to relinquish the 2.8 million Croats allotted to them in 1867, other huge snags emerged the more the Archduke pondered the plan with various advisers. To begin with, if the South Slavs were given their separate kingdom, would the North Slavs keep quiet? At the heart of the North Slav problem was Bohemia, the homeland of his own wife; and though there is no evidence whatever that his marriage ever influenced his racial politics, that state of affairs could hardly have continued in the face of an all-out agitation for nationhood by her fellow-Czechs.

Nor were the Croats themselves always behaving as dependably (that is, loyal to the Monarchy as a whole) as was expected of them. Many of their leaders had chauvinistic ideas of their own; indeed, in October 1903, believing that it was Budapest rather than Vienna which would one day help them to annexe Dalmatia, they issued the so-called 'Fiume Resolution', which committed them to fight 'shoulder to shoulder with the Hungarian nation in the struggle for constitutional rights'. The resolution, signed by almost every Croatian party, shook the Archduke to the core. Trialism, he realized, would not provide him with a loyal and docile kingdom along the southern marches of the empire but might easily produce another Magyar monster in miniature. The thought of incessant fights over parliamentary franchise, taxes, army recruitment, military manuals and the like being waged from Vienna against two adversaries instead of one was too much to contemplate. Though the 'South Slav Solution' continued to be floated from the Belvedere, if only to frighten the Magyars, both heads of the Military Chancery,

* Though not classed among the so-called 'historic nations' of the Monarchy, the Croats had in fact been an independent multinational kingdom before even the Austrians themselves. As far back as 924 the Croatian King Tomoslav had ruled over part of the Dalmatian coast, only to have it taken from him eventually by Venice. In 1097, the Croatian kingdom was swallowed up whole by the Magyars.

Brosch and Bardolff, pronounced themselves against it. As for the Archduke, his own growing disenchantment with the idea came out at the end of a draft letter he composed in the summer of 1909 to the German Emperor. While stressing the need to break the arrogant chauvinism of the Magyars, he bluntly dismissed the concept of Trialism as a 'disaster'.[19]

Three years after the Croats, with their Fiume Resolution, had triggered off the Archduke's disillusionment with a South Slav kingdom, a totally new reform plan caught his imagination. This was the scheme put forward by the Rumanian professor Aurel Popovici to divide the Dual Monarchy up all over again and construct sixteen new units based as closely as possible on race. Popovici's book, *Die Vereinigten Staaten von Gross-Österreich*, was widely hailed when it appeared as the magical *vade mecum* for all the empire's political ills. What appealed to the Archduke most of all was the stress it laid on a strong, if need be a dictatorial, central power, based in Vienna, to counterbalance the national assemblies and judicial freedoms accorded to the member-states. But though he retained some aspects of Popovici's ideas in his own thinking, one hard look at those seventeen new units* ought to have convinced any realist of the absurdity of the blueprint. The existing boundaries of demarcation between the various crown lands of the empire were not mere dotted lines which could be swept up and redrawn at will. They were paths worn deep by the custom and pride of centuries. Popovici might reshuffle his races as much as he pleased on paper, and the result may well have made as much ethnic sense as was possible out of such a tangle of peoples. But his racial reforms rode across history – whether Austrian, Magyar or Slav.

There are few regions on earth where traditions are so alive, so irreconcilable and, above all, so concentrated as in the Danube Basin. The Monarchy had too much history crammed into too

---

* German-Austria; German-Bohemia; German-Moravia and German-Silesia; Czech-Bohemia; Czech-Moravia; Magyar-Hungary; Transylvania; Croatia-Slavonia; Polish West Galicia; Ruthenian East Galicia; Slovakia; Krain; the Voivodina; Trente; the Szeklerland; Trieste; and Dalmatia with Bosnia-Herzogovina.

little space to accommodate Popovici's dream. And those who criticize the Habsburgs for making no progress with the problem would do well to remember the far greater mess made by the Western democracies, in the name of progress, when the defeated empire was dismembered. Those rearrangements ordained by the Versailles Peace Conference between 1919 and 1921 actually left more former citizens of the Monarchy living on the wrong side of their natural ethnic borders than in Franz Joseph's day. Neither Hitler nor Stalin was to do much better later on in the century, despite their massive exercise of tyranny. Emperors and dictators alike were dealing with roots too strong to be crushed and too deep to be pulled apart by force. The Archduke came at the end to realize this himself. His last known thoughts on the subject were addressed to his diplomat friend Baron Johann Eichoff in the spring of 1914. The Baron, who was full of ideas about constitutional reform, was asked to devise a plan 'in which the boundaries of the old crown lands would remain untouched'.[20]

*   *   *

In the first days of July 1914, the twenty-seven-year-old Archduke Charles, who had just succeeded his murdered uncle to the Habsburg throne, carried out the dead man's instructions and unlocked a desk in the private study at the Belvedere, not knowing in the least what he would find there. What he picked up was a bulky document, over ten thousand words long, entitled 'Accession Programme',* and it is the nearest thing we have to the course Franz Ferdinand had plotted for himself as sovereign. It is important to stress that it was, for the most part, only the outline of a policy, and a pragmatic unofficial outline at that. Nor is the authorship or the date certain, though it is likely that the principal draftsman was Colonel Brosch, working with a number of legal experts (above all Professor Lammasch, who

---

* It was first published in the Vienna *Reichspost* of 28 March 1926 and is commonly referred to as Franz Ferdinand's 'Programme for Government'. The original document, which differs only in small detail from the published version, is deposited in the 'Nachlass Franz Ferdinand'.

was destined to be the empire's very last Prime Minister) and that the document was produced between 1908 and 1911. Franz Ferdinand would obviously have been consulted over almost every line, and, though he is nowhere mentioned, his own explosive style is sometimes reflected in the text.

The programme can be said to pick up all the different fragments of the domestic kaleidoscope which have been looked at briefly above and bring them together in one pattern: the position of Sophie as the new ruler's wife; the position of Archduke Charles as the new Heir-Presumptive; the need to preserve the unity of the army; the need to preserve German as the official imperial language; the need to ensure protection for all nationalities of the empire; and the strong question marks over Trialism. The Hungarian menace to the Monarchy runs through the text* like a crimson thread. Of the thirteen major problems listed as first priorities for the new sovereign to tackle, no fewer than seven bear directly upon it: parliamentary franchise in Hungary; equal rights for all nations in Hungary; preservation of the empire's unity and of unity of the army; maintenance of the basic Compromise of 1867 (meaning that, until its terms could be revised, this should not get any worse for Vienna); the revision of some of the 1867 agreements; and the promise of a coronation in Hungary only after the necessary constitutional reforms had been carried out.

When this and other problems are elaborated upon, the need to bridle Magyar chauvinism is spelt out in detail. This affected, for example, the question of Sophie's new status. According to the programme, she would remain a Duchess even after her husband became Emperor, thus keeping faith with the letter of the 1900 pledge. But she would also have bestowed upon her, by her husband's decree, 'the title and dignity of consort of the Emperor and King, with all the privileges arising from this position as first lady at the court of the All-Highest'. This change was to be implemented on the very first day of the new reign. Such speed, the programme explained, was necessary not merely

* A summary appears in translation as Appendix II, p. 286.

to pre-empt discussion and avoid embarrassments with foreign rulers attending the funeral of the departed sovereign but also 'to frustrate any Hungarian attempts to make political capital out of the issue by unilaterally declaring the Duchess to be their own Queen'.

As for the coronation of the new Emperor as King of Hungary (which, according to a Hungarian law of 1791, had to take place within six months of the accession), this could only follow and never precede the reforms needed. Moreover, the crown must resign itself to the fact that at least some of these reforms would never be accepted voluntarily by Budapest and would therefore have to be imposed on the Hungarians by imperial decree – thus involving the threat of force or even its actual use.

Much thought is given to the creation of new official colours and crests for the Monarchy to avoid the confusion whereby three different flags were hoisted in Vienna on state occasions – plain black and yellow, or black and yellow with the imperial eagle for the dynasty, and the red-white-green for Hungary. A common flag was needed and so was a common German language, and this would mean rescinding all the concessions made to Budapest over the use of Hungarian as a parallel language for many civil and military purposes.*

The concessions demanded of the Magyars are clearly stated. What is not clear is how even the firm hand of Franz Ferdinand would have imposed them on Budapest. Count Ottokar Czernin, that unstable political dilettante (and fellow Bohemian magnate of the Archduke's) who was always pouring constitutional advice into Franz Ferdinand's ear, came out with his preferred solution loud and clear in various lengthy memoranda. Hungary, he said, had to be 'degraded to the status of an Austrian province'. The best way to ensure this in practice would be to appoint 'a black-yellow (i.e. Monarchist) general as

* It was, above all, the unity of the imperial army he was concerned with over the language issue. As he wrote to a friend and supporter, the Austrian diplomat Baron Biegeleben, on 6 January 1909: 'If the army is torn apart we cease to be a great power.'

the first Hungarian prime minister' of the new reign.[21] But Czernin also put his finger on the difficulty when he wondered out loud where the Archduke would find the necessary men of iron to subdue Hungary. Where indeed, for the Austrians could not hold a candle to the Hungarians when it came to toughness and fanaticism and Hungary was, after all, the second pillar of the empire. To rebuild that empire from the bottom up might, even in peacetime, have brought the entire edifice down. In wartime, as Franz Ferdinand's nephew found when the crown was placed on his head in 1916, even the attempt was unthinkable.

Franz Ferdinand himself had probably ended up by coming to these sober conclusions and his vituperation against the Hungarians is partly to be explained by the realization of his own limitations in the struggle against them. At all events, the Draft Manifesto of 'Franz II' with which the accession programme concludes goes no further than to promise his best endeavours to guarantee 'each racial element of the Monarchy its own national development, so long as this is sought within the framework of the empire'. The formula could mean anything or nothing according to how it was applied.

The supreme irony of Franz Ferdinand's Magyar phobia was that he shared so many of their personal qualities – a fiery sense of mission, an explosive temperament, a deep feeling for history, the conviction of his own beliefs, and an impatience for anything which contradicted or frustrated those beliefs. Had he been born a Hungarian nobleman instead of a Habsburg archduke, he would have been the greatest Magyar chauvinist of them all.

CHAPTER NINE

The World Outside

IT WAS A PARADOX that so much blame for the war which followed the Archduke's death was to be heaped on Vienna. More than any other city of Europe, this capital of a supra-national empire had seemed best equipped to fend off that Armageddon of nationalism.

The previous chapter opened with a street scene depicting the racial panorama of the Monarchy's peoples. At the top of the social scale, on the parquet floors rather than the pavements, the Vienna mixture was even richer. Quite apart from the variegated nobility thrown up by the Dual Monarchy, the Habsburgs had accepted in their midst over the centuries, and bestowed Austrian titles upon, families gathered from every corner of the continent. To take the counts alone, the selection at the outbreak of war included the Almeidas from Portugal; the Ansembourgs and Baillet de Latours from the Netherlands; the Buquoys from Spain; the Demblins from Lorraine; the Bombelles from France; the Degenfelds from Swabia; the Eltzs from the Mosel; the Dauns from the Rhineland; and even from distant Ireland, the Taaffes, who in the last quarter of the nineteenth century had provided Franz Joseph with one of the most enduring of his prime ministers.

Yet this appearance of a city open to all the talents of the old Europe (or, at least, open to all its Catholic parts) was deceptive. The diplomatic picture contradicted the social one, for, as the new century dawned, Austria-Hungary found herself increasingly pinned down and isolated. The crux of the problem was the empire's estrangement from Russia, her great neighbour in the north-east, and her great rival in the south-east, where, throughout the Balkans, St Petersburg played patron to the Slav peoples.

The rift had opened up nearly fifty years before. During the Crimea War of 1853–6, Franz Joseph had remained studiously, and foolishly, neutral when Tsar Alexander, fighting the combined armies of England, France and Turkey, had needed him most. For a while, the so-called 'Three Emperors' League' of 1872 between the sovereigns of Russia, Austria-Hungary and Germany had papered over the crack, as Bismarck, its dominant political personality, had intended. The League was converted into a secret alliance in 1881 and renewed three years later, but then collapsed under precisely the sort of strain Bismarck sought to avoid – a collision in 1886 between St Petersburg and Vienna as to who was to sit on the throne of Bulgaria. Russia and Austria, never to be allies again, lapsed from there on into a jealous competition for the spoils of the crumbling Ottoman Empire. On the broader plane, Europe quickened its slide into that fixed pattern of rival alliances which was eventually to ensure that a conflict between any two of the major European nations would engulf the entire continent in war.

The process was gradual but remorseless, like the formation of a two-sided glacier. It had begun with the signing, on 7 October 1879, of a treaty between Austria and Germany. Bitter memories in Vienna of Bismarck's triumph over the Habsburg Monarchy in the struggle for supremacy between them then lay more than a decade back. Austria, shaken by the spectacle of a victorious Russian onslaught against Turkey the year before, needed a strong protecting arm which only Berlin could provide. As for Bismarck, the political master of Europe was well aware that, in the long run, the two German-speaking empires, linked by so many ties of history and culture, were destined to be partners rather than enemies in any continental power game. He needed security himself against the increasing hostility of Russia, and this pact with Austria seemed doubly reassuring since, after 1866, Germany was bound to be the senior partner.

The outcome was the so-called Dual Alliance, whose principal clauses pledged each party to help the other with all forces at its disposal in the event of an attack led by, or joined in by, Russia. Three years later, the axis was extended southwards when, on 20 May 1882, the accession of Italy turned it into a Triple Alliance. The maxim that 'two's company and three's a crowd' certainly applied in this diplomatic context. The new pact mixed pledges of military help with promises of benevolent neutrality according to who was attacked by whom and by how many. But just as the 1879 agreement had Russia in its sights, here the prime objective was to curb France.

It was not inevitable that these two target countries should themselves join hands (for Bismarck's aims were genuinely defensive). But it was at least natural that, faced with this powerful-looking military bloc running down the heart of Europe all the way from the Baltic to Sicily, the two nations exposed and vulnerable on its flanks – France and Russia – should grope towards each other for mutual protection. Despite the ideological differences between the two capitals, Paris had always remained the spiritual home of Russian society and French its 'civilized' tongue. More to the point, the French banks, by a series of enormous loans and credits which began in December 1888, had paved the path towards an alliance with gold, or rather with four per cent paper bonds.

In 1891, an 'understanding' was reached between the two governments. A year later, this blossomed into a military convention which, in turn, provided the basis for the formal alliance between the two countries, signed on 4 January 1894. Though this latest of secret European pacts was also defensive in origin (the prime aim being to protect both parties against German aggression), it gradually acquired more offensive undertones as the French and Russian general staffs elaborated their plans for war.

Thus the pattern of confrontation was set between the central powers and the wing powers of the continent, and it was soon the turn of the former to feel apprehension at being closed in – a fear that, in Germany's case, was to grow into the grand obsession with 'encirclement'. So, when the twentieth century opened, only one great European power – the greatest of them all in wealth, temporal possessions, prestige and naval and commercial strength – remained uncommitted to either side: England, as Britain was then called on the continent.

Unlike Austria-Hungary, who lived at the very crossroads of the continent, England had always revelled in her isolation, seemingly impregnable behind her sea-green moat. But the new order of things springing up across the Channel forced her to think again. She was, above all, concerned with the growing challenge from Wilhelmian Germany which, after Bismarck's fall in March 1890, had started building warships of such power and in such numbers as to dispute England's traditional supremacy. The British Government was prepared to accept that Germany should have the most powerful army of Europe. But, once that army could swim, it became a different matter.

In the dying years of the old century, when the English and the French had stood at the point of war over colonial disputes, it had seemed that England might break out of her isolation by actually pairing up with her naval challenger. Throughout the first year of the new century, discussions had continued between London and Berlin – sometimes between the two sovereigns, Edward VII and his new nephew William II, and sometimes between their ministers and officials; sometimes businesslike and sometimes desultory – to try and produce the framework for an Anglo-German alliance or understanding. (Bismarck himself had made three attempts to achieve this, in 1879, 1887 and 1889, so the idea was not novel.) But then, on 19 December 1901, England formally pulled out of the talks. Lord Salisbury's government, mulling over the disadvantages of permanently alienating France and Russia, her most important rivals everywhere overseas, by joining forces with the Central Powers, had decided that the German game was not worth the colonial candle.

The real reason for the disengagement probably went deeper and was not confided to any Cabinet minute. Psychologically, England was very close to a change in her insular politics, as shown by the overtures which Mr Joseph Chamberlain, the Colonial Secretary, was allowed to make to Berlin in 1898. But she was still not quite ready to commit herself. While hard-bitten bachelors often suddenly decide on marriage, with nations, the great leap takes longer.

It did not, however, take much longer, thanks largely to the shock of diplomatic isolation England experienced during the Boer War. Her monarch played an influential role in the final decision. Edward VII, though he had not one drop of French blood in his veins (and scarcely a drop of English), adored France and everything that went with it – especially its food, wine, wit and lovely women. On the other hand, that cosy collection of kingdoms, dukedoms and principalities which had been the Germany of his ancestors was becoming increasingly foreign and increasingly frightening – a unified empire headed by a bombastic young ruler whose military and economic challenge grew with every year that passed.

The King did not create single-handed the historic 'Entente Cordiale' between England and France, which started life merely as a convention signed on 8 April 1904 between the two countries to regulate all their colonial rivalries. Yet the royal hand had a powerful part in the building of it, notably through the enormously successful visit he had paid to Paris – now known to have been planned by him without even consulting his ministers – eleven months previously.[1]

A formal alliance was never signed between the two Western democracies. In typically pragmatic style, the English moved, over the next decade, from colonial conventions to military discussions and from military discussions to military under-standings. In honour, as well as in self-defence, they could not have stood aside when, in 1914, the German army struck at France through the Low Countries. An Anglo-Russian *rap-prochement* only made the commitment geographically wider. Three or four years before the Archduke's murder set that German army marching, the dies for a quarrel were thus cast in Europe, with the Triple Alliance of the Central Powers now facing the Triple Entente.

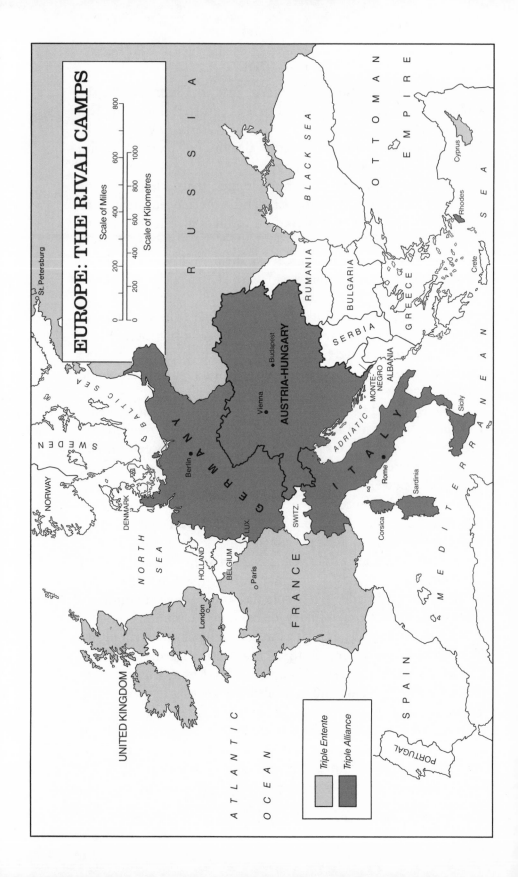

EUROPE: THE RIVAL CAMPS

Scale of Miles

0   200   400   600   800

Scale of Kilometres

0   200   400   600   800   1000

Triple Entente

Triple Alliance

ATLANTIC OCEAN

UNITED KINGDOM

London

NORTH SEA

NORWAY

SWEDEN

DENMARK

BALTIC SEA

St. Petersburg

R U S S I A

HOLLAND

BELGIUM

LUX.

G E R M A N Y

Berlin

AUSTRIA-HUNGARY

Vienna

Budapest

RUMANIA

BLACK SEA

SWITZ.

FRANCE

Paris

I T A L Y

Rome

SERBIA

MONTE-
NEGRO

ALBANIA

BULGARIA

ADRIATIC

GREECE

O T T O M A N   E M P I R E

Corsica

Sardinia

Sicily

M E D I T E R R A N E A N   S E A

Crete

Rhodes

Cyprus

SPAIN

PORTUGAL

It is worth looking back for a moment to see where Franz Ferdinand stood when the decisive steps in this progression were taken. He was a boy of fifteen, and an infantry lieutenant only in name, when the Austro-German pact was signed in 1879. When the fateful breach in the Three Emperors' League occurred in 1886 he was in the midst of his carefree five-year spell as a captain of cavalry at Enns, very intent on enjoying life and largely oblivious to politics. In 1891, when France first joined hands with Russia, he was absorbed with politics of quite a different sort – fuming under Magyar chauvinism in the Monarchy as colonel of a Hungarian Hussar regiment at Sopron. At the turn of the century, when England was struggling towards a union of some sort with Europe, Franz Ferdinand was absorbed with the problems of his own personal union to a Bohemian countess. It was only the last move in the European power game, the gradual linking of England and France, that he witnessed as an established political figure, the heir-in-waiting to an empire at the Belvedere, and with a chancery of his own. By then, the pattern was already set.

But what did he think of the five powers who, together with Austria-Hungary, made up that pattern? To begin with those outside the Monarchy's camp, he seems to have a coolness bordering on hostility towards France, despite the fact that her language was the only foreign tongue he felt at home with. France was not merely the incarnation of republicanism, she was also the centre of Freemasonry, anathema to a Catholic dynasty. Above all, she had been the sponsor of the Italian *Risorgimento* which had robbed the Monarchy of its fairest southern provinces. 'The cannon of Solferino,' he once remarked, 'were the first chimes of our Monarchy's death-knell, and it was France who gave us this splendid concert.'[2] Yet he did not waste much of his characteristic sarcasm on France. Indeed, in his letters and memoranda there is hardly another reference to the country. Paris was, in fact, a blank gap on his political horizon and his treatment of the French embassy in Vienna could be casual to the point of wounding. All the envoys of the major powers expected an audience with the Heir-Apparent reasonably soon after presenting their credentials to the Emperor. One French ambassador, according to his English colleague, was, however, kept waiting for no less than eighteen months before being received at the Belvedere.[3] All in all, Franz Ferdinand seems to have given France up as a bad job.

The Archduke's feelings towards England, though also pronounced, were much more mixed. As we have seen from the journals of his travels, he felt anger – spiced, no doubt, with a certain envy – at the arrogant assurance with which Britannia ruled over her quarter of the globe. It was not merely that the English believed themselves to be the most superior beings on earth. What infuriated Franz Ferdinand (and many another distinguished foreigner) was that this self-appointed station was taken so casually for granted. Such sublime assurance could be even more irritating than the strident cockiness of the Magyars, for it was so much more difficult to dent.

Yet, on the other hand, the Archduke had already learned, as a young prince touring the Indies and Australasia, to admire the solidly comfortable dignified lifestyle which the English had exported to all corners of the earth, and, even more, to respect that formidable sea-power which kept it all in place. And the more deeply Franz Ferdinand immersed himself in the modernization and expansion of his own small navy, the more he looked with something akin to awe at this greatest of all fleets.

London was not merely the maritime capital of the world. It was also, especially during the nine years (1901–10) of King Edward VII's reign, its social capital, and this too played a steadily growing part in the Archduke's calculations. One of Franz Ferdinand's first appearances as Austrian Heir-Apparent on the European stage had been his attendance in his Emperor's name at Queen Victoria's funeral. He joined the splendid gathering of the old order in London again two years later, for the postponed coronation of her son. Yet to begin with he joined it without Sophie.

It was on Russia, the third power of the Triple Entente, that Franz Ferdinand set his fondest hopes. His dream, consistently pursued from first to last (and just as consistently dashed) was to revive the Three Emperors' League between Russia, Austria and Germany, which had lapsed while he was still a young subaltern. He wanted it brought back into being primarily to give his own Monarchy added security, but also to restore stability to an increasingly turbulent continent. Most of the princes and statesmen of that continent had presided over the construction of its lethal alliance system without seeing the abyss to which Europe was being led. The Archduke was a notable exception. For him, to rebuild the bridge between Vienna and St Petersburg was to strengthen the prospects of peace in general as well as to promote the cause of conservative monarchies in particular.

It was ironic that his own visit to St Petersburg in 1891 (his first independent diplomatic mission in the Emperor's name) should have taken place when Russia was already setting out on the road towards her alliance with France. Alexander III bestowed on Franz Joseph's nephew the Order of Saint Andreas; made him Colonel of a Russian regiment of dragoons; and enabled him to shoot a few bears. But these were routine civilities between imperial host and royal guest. The personal goodwill generated had little or no political impact, as the Archduke himself was forced to acknowledge four years later, after Nicholas II, feeble young successor to the murdered Alexander, had sealed the pact with Paris. One of Franz Ferdinand's aides (admittedly not the most trustworthy when it comes to precise quotes) records the following archducal explosion against the new Tsar in 1895:

> Does he have such a thick bandage over his eyes that he can perceive nothing of his own interests? He is playing a pretty game which will cost him dearly; so dear that one fine day he will pay for it with his own skin! The power of the Romanovs rests on feet of clay and in fraternizing with the French Freemasons Nicholas is smashing up his own statue![4]

Though, soon after this, events in the Balkans – the perpetual sparring ground between Austria and Russia and destined to become their battleground – made a *rapprochement* between the two empires even more remote, the Archduke struggled on. He lobbied successive Austrian foreign ministers on the subject; lectured every influential diplomat he could find; got articles published in his own press organs; and urged his sovereign at every opportunity to play the St Petersburg card. On one or two occasions it was tentatively played, but only as a court card.

Franz Ferdinand battled on to the very end. In the last year of his life, he restated his fears and convictions to another of his aides:

> If we all go on arming like this, all of us in Europe will be ruined even before war breaks out. Europe must get a different constellation of alliances if it is to escape all the dangers of war. The only salvation for us is the Three Emperors' League, which I will continue to work for with all my strength. We also need the League for domestic reasons, in the cause of the conservative concept. What would be the point of fighting Russia? Not even Napoleon could succeed. And even if we beat Russia – which to my mind is totally out of the question – a victory like that would still be the greatest tragedy for the Austrian Monarchy.[5]

It was a poignant prophecy.

So much for the Archduke's attitude towards the Monarchy's rivals. What did he think of its principal allies?

Of the partnership with Italy, as already indicated, he thought nothing at all. Indeed, the complicated Austro–German pact with Rome, which Bismarck had hesitantly engineered, struck Franz Ferdinand as a grotesquely dangerous farce. He would rather have had his hands around Italy's throat than enfold her in an artificial embrace. He once put it very bluntly indeed to General Conrad: 'Our main rival is Italy, against whom, one day, we shall have to wage war. Venice and Lombardy must be won back again.'

For once, the Archduke was a jump ahead of the Chief-of-Staff with those words, since it was normally Conrad who urged 'preventive wars' against Austria's relatively weak neighbours in the south. To ask whether Franz Ferdinand would ever have carried out his threat had he survived to become Emperor is a fascinating but pointless speculation. What we do know is that throughout his lifetime he did his utmost to weaken and, if possible, snap the link with Rome. The Italians were well aware of the threat he posed to them. As the German ambassador in Rome, Herr von Jagow, once wrote, 'As long as the Emperor Franz Joseph is alive, the Italians feel protected, but they all ask "What will a government of the Emperor Franz Ferdinand bring?"'[6]

Berlin, too, needed little reminding of the problem. The Italians were constantly urging on Germany the need to have the Triple Alliance reaffirmed ahead of the expiry date, in order to get it extended before the Archduke succeeded to the throne. In 1912, when such a renewal was under discussion, the Emperor William went so far as to plead with Franz Joseph not to tell his nephew what was going on, for fear that Franz Ferdinand would try to torpedo the talks.[7] Such was the hostility among the anti-Italian camp, headed by Conrad and the Archduke, that German diplomats in Vienna debated openly among themselves the possibility of war breaking out between their two allies, and even Sophie makes a rare appearance in their calculations. 'The Duchess of Hohenberg,' the German ambassador wrote in 1911 to Berlin, 'anxiously cares for her husband's wellbeing and will certainly do everything to prevent him having to take part [as war-time Commander-in-Chief] in such a campaign.'[8]

It goes without saying that wild horses would not have dragged Franz Ferdinand to Rome on any peacemaking mission. Even his own sovereign realized he was helpless in the matter when, at a Christmas audience in 1913, Conrad raised the question of the Archduke paying a courtesy visit to the court of what was, after all, an allied state.* The General's account of the exchange which followed is enlightening about more than just Franz Ferdinand's Italian phobia:

H.M.   You think such a visit would have any effect?

---

* The previous Italian monarch, King Umberto I, had visited Vienna in October 1881 and Italy naturally expected that, at some stage, Franz Joseph would return the visit. But the Emperor demurred at going to Rome itself, out of deference to the Vatican which, like the Dual Monarchy, had fallen victim of the *Risorgimento*. As the Italian court refused a meeting in another Italian town, the return visit never took place.

Conrad   I think it is necessary.

H.M.   He won't go.

Conrad   But Your Majesty has only to command him!

H.M.   Oh, you know him, how strange and unpredictable he is. Nobody knows that better than you do.

Conrad   Indeed, Your Majesty, I have felt it on my own back.

H.M.   I will try, but I don't believe he will go.[9]

Whether the Emperor tried hard, or even tried at all, is not recorded. What we do know is that the Archduke never went.

Towards Germany, Austria's one-time conqueror and now senior partner, Franz Ferdinand felt only loyalty, admiration and respect. He well knew that the alliance with Berlin was the central pillar on which the external security of the Monarchy rested. As an Austrian, he shared in the common culture of the German-speaking peoples. Moreover, as a Habsburg prince, he was also bound by multiple ties of marriage and kinship to the German kingdoms: his murdered aunt, the Empress Elisabeth, had been a Wittelsbach from Bavaria, for example, and his sister-in-law, Maria Josepha, was yet another princess of Saxony to have married into the Vienna court. This, the old Germany of nation-states, was the only one for which he, like Edward VII, felt affection. There was something about the united imperial Germany, now presided over in such flamboyant style by William II, which disquieted him. The closest he got to defining it was an excess of the Prussian spirit which, he once remarked to an aide, was like the hypertrophy of any one organism in the human body. 'In the same way, the excessive development of any one element in an assembly of states must inevitably lead, sooner or later, to the ruin of the whole.'[10]

Even in private, however, Franz Ferdinand never spelt out the real problem, perhaps because he never brought himself to admit it. It was, of course, nationalism, the essence of that Prussian spirit he disliked and distrusted. The Hohenzollern dynasty had been nourished by it and the German empire had been founded on it. Yet the stuff which served as cement for the Hohenzollerns could only prove to be dynamite for the

Habsburgs. Some of that dynamite was, indeed, already primed and in position at the heart of the multinational state. The most violent threat was the pan-German movement led by radicals like Georg von Schönerer, who wanted to take the Austrians out of the Dual Monarchy altogether and join them with their German-speaking cousins and neighbours in the north. They linked up, and in some cases were synonymous with, those anti-clericals of the 'Away from Rome' movement which the Archduke had denounced in his first political act.

Yet the real danger to the ornate Habsburg mansion was not so much this dynamite as the uncertain timbers against which the charges were placed. Even that mass of Franz Joseph's Austrian subjects who did not subscribe to Schönerer's ideas were still largely uncertain about their own identity. Could there be such a thing under the Habsburg sceptre as an '*homo austriacus*'? Was he merely the unimpassioned administrator of the imperial estates, with loyalty only to the crown, as the dynasty had indeed encouraged and trained him to believe? ('Is he a patriot for me?' an earlier emperor had tersely demanded when one of his subject's patriotism was being praised.) Or could the Austro-Germans have a pride and profile of their own, to match the nationalist strivings of all the other nations of the empire?

The cultural pull of that giant magnet to north, as well as the demands of their own dynasty, made the riddle impossible to solve. Indeed, the dilemma had been unconsciously carved in stone in the Archduke's day. In Vienna's Heldenplatz, at the centre of the great Hofburg Palace complex, stands a great statue erected to the memory of the Habsburg soldier-hero Archduke Charles. On one side is engraved the legend, 'The tireless fighter for Germany's honour', and on the other, 'The heroic leader of Austria's armies'. It was not altogether surprising that, on a March day twenty-four years after Franz Ferdinand's death, that same statue (and indeed the whole of the vast square around it) should have swarmed with Viennese cheering the arrival of their new ruler, Adolf Hitler. The idealists, as opposed to the mere opportunists in their midst, could point to the words under one flank of the prancing horse. It was even less surprising that Austrian nationalism, which stayed at home that day, also grew fresh roots from then on. The Austrians, who never knew their identity in Franz Ferdinand's lifetime, found it at last – through losing it.

All this lay a generation ahead. Under the Monarchy, even such a passionate believer in the Habsburg mission as the Archduke himself could never shake off a certain ambivalence about '*Deutschtum*'. This was inevitable, for though there were Austrians, 'Old Austrians' and 'Greater Austrians' (the Archduke's favourites), there was no Austrian language. 'The German language is the language of the dynasty, of officialdom, of the army, of the educated upper classes and so on and must be used for all official purposes,' Franz Ferdinand wrote to Freiherr von Schiesl, the head of the Emperor's Civil Chancery, in 1908.[11] Moreover, Franz Ferdinand would think of himself, and refer to himself, as 'a German prince' despite the fact that his Monarchy had been expelled from the German Confederation when he was a toddler of three. And – the ultimate irony – he knew that on succeeding to the throne he would be crowned King of Hungary and perhaps also King of Bohemia, but, unless he changed things, he could never be crowned King of Austria. There was no such title, and never had been. For their own German-speaking subjects, the emperors remained simply archdukes of Austria, and archdukes, dukes or counts of its provinces. The link between the dynasty and the people of its heartlands – feudal, personal and the opposite of national – could not be better symbolized.

This ambivalence played its part in Franz Ferdinand's relationship with the German Emperor, which was by far the closest and most important of his personal ties. He started off, when an impressionable young man, as an open-mouthed admirer of this larger- and louder-than-life sovereign. '*Ein Mordskerl*' ('a devil of a fellow') was his first verdict on William II. That verdict never changed, but though a genuine warmth of feeling was added to this early hero-worship, there were also one or two things to be subtracted from it. On the personal plane, there was always the contrast of styles between the two men, which became more marked as they grew older.

Franz Ferdinand, for those reasons of character and domestic constraints we have already examined, always avoided publicity. William II could not exist out of the public eye. As a self-conscious autocrat, he craved popularity; the Archduke, an instinctive autocrat, despised it. Like many another European royal he found the brash speech, theatrical garb and enormous retinues of the German sovereign at times embarrassing. There may have been just a touch of dynastic snobbery mixed with this: William II was, after all, very much the *parvenu* among emperors and also very much man-made, as opposed to an Apostolic Majesty.

But, snobbery aside, the German Emperor's heavy-handed sense of humour could also cause real hurt, as on one occasion before his marriage when the Archduke was paying a visit to Berlin. His host, waiting for him at the station, decided to play a theatrical joke. 'You don't imagine I've come to meet *your* train do you?' he asked the astonished Franz Ferdinand. 'I'm really expecting the Crown Prince of Italy.'[12] Reassurances, accompanied by loud guffaws, doubtless followed. But given the Archduke's well-known feelings about Italy and its royal family, it was a tactless piece of fun.

There were also marked political differences between the two men. To the end, they never saw eye to eye over Italy. The Emperor William tried time and time again to persuade the Archduke that Italy was a valuable, if minor, member of their alliance and that, moreover, she would stay true to that alliance if the time of testing came. Whenever the two men met, especially in the years just before the war (which was to prove Franz Ferdinand's scepticism more than justified), the Emperor hammered away at the Archduke in vain with his theories. One such sustained attempt is reported by the Emperor himself in a memorandum sent to his Chancellor, Bethmann-Hollweg, from Corfu, where the Archduke had been staying as his guest at the Villa Achilleion, formerly the Mediterranean refuge of the Empress Elisabeth.[13]

Then there was Russia, the cherished object of the Archduke's diplomatic dreams. Whereas Franz Ferdinand saw the Tsar as a conservative sovereign who, for all his faults, belonged back in the bosom of his fellow-emperors, William II, though always courting the Russian ruler, regarded him essentially as the great father of Slavdom, and therefore the enemy of all things Germanic. And it was the same consuming hatred of the Slavs which largely accounted for the German Emperor's consistent enthusiasm for the Magyars* – an enthusiasm which, predictably, found no echo with the Archduke. Franz Ferdinand's most ardent desire was one day to dismantle the Dual Monarchy in its 1867 form and promote his South Slav subjects in a new imperial dependency at the expense of the Hungarians. The German Emperor, on the other hand, regarded Dualism as the only stable basis for Habsburg rule and the best guarantee of stability for everyone in the Danube basin. They often debated the point, but it was a polite dialogue of the deaf.

The fact that despite these substantial differences of temperament and outlook the two men became close friends derived, in great measure, from the circumstances of the Archduke's marriage. Without wishing it (and, quite possibly, without fully realizing it), Sophie became a factor in European diplomacy. Prince Bernard von Bülow, German Chancellor from 1900 to 1909, claims the credit for building this particular bridge to Franz Ferdinand's heart. In the autumn of 1903, William II was on his way to Vienna after a spell of military manoeuvres and stag-shooting, and his Chancellor joined the royal train at Wiener Neustadt, which is about an hour's journey from the Austrian capital. When they fell to discussing Princess (as she then was) Hohenberg, the Emperor roundly declared, 'Of course, I shall take no notice of Franz Ferdinand's wife.' When his Chancellor demurred, he only grew more heated. 'If I give way, I'll find my own sons one day marrying maids of honour – or even chambermaids!'

* It is worth noting that the Berlin-Budapest axis survived in various forms down to Hitler's day until it was finally smashed, in favour of the Slavs, by the Red Army.

Bülow knew that his master had just been staying with Archduke Frederick at his Hungarian shooting lodge at Moson-magyaróvár and that the Archduchess Isabella had also been present. Clearly, she had not missed the opportunity to win over an important ally like the German Emperor in her feud with Franz Ferdinand and his morganatic bride. But Bülow continued to press his royal master that, for reasons of state, the heir to the Austrian throne had to be won over by all means possible.

The debate continued between the two men as the train clattered on through Baden and Mödling, with Bülow seemingly getting nowhere. Then, as their train was pulling in to Vienna's Westbahnhof, and the green hat plumes of the Austrian welcome party were already visible, he produced his final appeal. 'Your Majesty now has the choice of making the future Emperor of Austria our friend or our enemy for life!' It was the perfect cue to summon on stage William II, the great dramatic actor, and it worked. Forgotten were all the arguments over pedigree and all the indignant persuasion of Archduchess Isabella. The visitor embraced his host, the Emperor Franz Joseph, on both cheeks and then turned to greet Franz Ferdinand, who was standing next in line on the platform. After they had shaken hands, William II asked, as though it were the most natural question in the world, 'And when may I have the honour of paying my respects to your wife?' The Archduke's face thereupon flushed with joy, and the call was duly made that same afternoon.

Whatever Prince Bülow may have embroidered in his account[14] (and he was a deft embroiderer when it came to stitching his own image for posterity), he could not possibly have exaggerated Franz Ferdinand's reaction. Only two years before, the Archduke's wife had not been allowed to sit at her own table for the dinner offered by her husband for the German Crown Prince. Now that Prince's father, the German Emperor himself, was coming to the same Belvedere Palace at his own request to kiss Sophie's hand. Franz Ferdinand never forgot the gesture, which made the alliance between the two countries an alliance between the two men. A little bit of history had been made that morning on a Vienna railway platform; and, had the Archduke ever become Emperor, the fragment would have amounted to much more.

The first great trial of this strengthened relationship, both on the personal and the political level, came five years later, when Austria formally annexed the two Turkish frontier provinces of Bosnia and Herzegovina which she had occupied and administered for the past thirty years.* This annexation crisis of 1908 was the gravest which the Monarchy passed through in foreign affairs during the Archduke's lifetime, as well as the acid test as to whether he personally belonged among the 'warmongers' of Vienna or not. It is, therefore, worth a close look.[15]

With the preparations for the annexation and the final decision to take the plunge, Franz Ferdinand had little or nothing to do. Successive governments in Vienna had mulled over how and when the provinces might be legally wrested from the Ottoman Empire and absorbed into the Habsburg Monarchy from the day an Austrian military garrison first set foot in them. The regional opposition was weak and could always be brushed aside. The danger lay in the opposition of outside powers, above all Russia, against whose Balkan expansionism Austria had been allotted the occupation in the first place. On the other hand, the temptation to convert that occupation into outright ownership was very persuasive. Bosnia and Herzegovina constituted a major extension of the Monarchy's security belt and possession seemed anyway to be nine-tenths of the law. Other states before and since acted no differently, though with other methods and other justifications, when given the chance to consolidate their vulnerable frontiers. Israel's colonization of the Jordanian West Bank territories seized by her soldiers in the 1967 war is the most striking of recent examples.

But though, for thirty years, all the European powers had gone on the tacit assumption that the two provinces might well fall entirely to Austria one day, they – and especially Russia –

---

* The award had been made through Bismarck, acting as the 'honest broker' at the Congress of Berlin in 1878. His mediation was called upon by both Austria and England, who were concerned at the great extension of Russia's influence in the Balkans following her defeat of Turkey the previous year.

had also gone on the very explicit assumption that no action would be taken without due warning and mutual agreement. Indeed, whenever the cloudy relations between Vienna and St Petersburg brightened for moments under the influence of royal meetings, this assumption was spelt out. Thus, in 1897, when Franz Joseph visited St Petersburg to greet the new Tsar Nicholas II, the two powers agreed among other things to accept the status quo in the Balkans. Subsequently, they went one step further and pledged themselves to an equitable distribution of the spoils whenever the moribund Turkish empire in south-east Europe gave up the ghost altogether. Austria made it quite clear that Bosnia and Herzegovina were to be counted among her share of the spoils, a claim that Russia did not reject though reserving the right to have a closer look at the matter when the time was ripe.

Six years later, the Tsar returned the visit and Franz Joseph took him straight from Vienna to his hunting lodge at Mürzsteg, now, as then, a lovely and secluded spot by a trout stream where two mountain valleys cross on the borders of Styria and Lower Austria. There, for four days between 30 September and 3 October 1903, and in between much stalking of stag, the so-called 'Mürzsteg Programme' was drawn up by their advisers. This reaffirmed the need for preserving stability in the Balkans, adding a new undertaking to cooperate in the international policing of Macedonia, that troublesome southerly province of Turkish Europe where serious unrest had broken out earlier in the year. Franz Ferdinand, who was at Mürzsteg himself, must have imagined for a while that although imperial host and imperial guest now stood in opposing military camps, they might still be able to realize his dream and join hands across the divide. In the long run that could not be, though, as things turned out, it was not the two Emperors who made the near-fatal muddle of 1908, but their ministers.

A decisive change for the worse – quite unnoticed at the time – had come in 1906 when, both in Vienna and St Petersburg, foreign affairs passed from the hands of safe plodders into those of political adventurers. The new Foreign Minister for the Tsar was Alexander Petrovic Isvolsky, a man of modest origins, exceeding ugliness and overwhelming ambition, the third quality doubtless being developed to compensate for the other two. His private ambition was to raise himself in the social register by finding a high-born wife, an aim which, after many rebuffs elsewhere, he finally achieved by marrying the elegant Countess Töll, daughter of the Russian minister to Weimar. His political ambition was far grander and far more difficult to achieve: to win back in Europe the prestige which his country had just lost in the Far East through her disastrous defeat by Japan in the war of 1904–5. That meant primarily one thing – control of the Dardanelles and with it, uninhibited access for Russian warships from the Black Sea to the Mediterranean. England and France, the two powers traditionally opposed to this historic aim, were now, after all, Russia's partners. Surely that left only Austria to be squared, and her priorities were on land, not on sea.

Franz Joseph's new Foreign Minister, Baron von Aehrenthal,* was as different as could be from Isvolsky in appearance. 'Tall, broad-shouldered, a little bowed, very short-sighted with drooping eyelids that gave an air of weariness ... reserved and somewhat lazy ... Aehrenthal stood in utter contrast to the shorter, more restless, more excitable and sometimes pushing Calmuck, Isvolsky,' was how one contemporary of both men described the pair.[16] Nonetheless, there were many parallels between them. Like Isvolsky, Aehrenthal was a career diplomat promoted to the key political post of his empire. Like Isvolsky, he suffered from certain social complexes – caused, it was said, by the fact that his grandfather had been a Jewish grain merchant from Prague, ennobled barely a century before. (The racial origin, the commercial connection, and the relative newness of a mere barony would all have been black marks in the relentlessly caste-ridden society of the day.) Finally, like Isvolsky, Aehrenthal had a consuming political

* Aehrenthal had spent most of his career in St Petersburg where he had ended as Ambassador; Isvolsky had been Russian Minister in Copenhagen, a relatively minor assignment.

ambition: in his case to crush Serbian chauvinism which, he believed, threatened to destroy the Dual Monarchy in the south, and so to plant the black and yellow Habsburg flag safely for years to come in the Balkans. On 15 September 1908 – after exchanging feelers for a whole year – these two political adventurers met in great secrecy at Buchlau Castle* in Moravia to trade their respective dreams.

Aehrenthal's impatience over the annexation question had quickened as 1908 dawned, for this was the sixtieth jubilee year of Franz Joseph's reign and every loyal fibre of the Monarchy, from the fire brigade of the remotest mountain village upwards, was quivering with commemoration fever. What better gift could he and the army generals present to their sovereign than two new provinces for his sceptre? And when, during the same year, the revolution of the Young Turks took place in Constantinople, Aehrenthal and the 'hawks' of Vienna were presented with something which was half-way between a genuine reason and a plausible pretext for swift action.

To the threat of pan-Slav agitation for a 'Greater Serbia' was now added the most unexpected of embarrassments, the pressure of democracy from, of all places, the Turkish capital. The new liberal leaders of Turkey had announced the calling of a Western-style parliament for the whole of the Ottoman Empire, which implied that representatives of Bosnia-Herzegovina, still in law part of that empire, might well be summoned to sit in it. A legal trap in the 1878 settlement, never sprung due to the paralysis of the old Turkey, was now opening up: if war with the Young Turks should break out over the parliamentary issue, for whom should the inhabitants fight, their legal sovereign, the Sultan, or their effective ruler, the Emperor of Austria? Thus, it was not the senility of the Ottoman Empire which had finally spurred Austria into striking so much as its attempted rejuvenation. What made Aehrenthal's task even easier for jubilee-style diplomacy in a jubilee year was that it had been his fellow-

* It belonged to Count Berchtold, who erected a tablet to commemorate the meeting. Ironically, only six years later, as Austrian Foreign Minister himself, he had to face some of its long-term consequences.

schemer in St Petersburg who had set the ball rolling. In a highly secret *aide-mémoire* sent to the Austrian Foreign Minister on 2 July 1908, Isvolsky outlined the bargain: Russia would have Austrian support in settling the Black Sea Straits question and, in return, Austria could expect Russian compliance over the annexation of Bosnia-Herzegovina.

And this was the essence of the pact which was indeed sealed at Buchlau. What was either deliberately fudged by Aehrenthal or clumsily misunderstood by Isvolsky was precisely when and how Austria was to set about grabbing her share of these Turkish spoils. The Russian left the castle believing that Aehrenthal was in no immediate hurry and that, in any case, consultation of some sort would precede final action. Whether he was justified in that assumption we shall never know. There were no witnesses to the Buchlau talks and nothing was put down in writing at the time. But that either trickery or confusion was at work is shown by the contrasting behaviour of the two conspirators after they had parted.

Aehrenthal got down to business almost immediately. On 26 September he let the German Chancellor into the secret, though without giving Prince Bülow any timetable. Three days later, personal letters signed by the Emperor Franz Joseph were despatched to Austrian ambassadors in all the major capitals abroad for presentation, on 5 October, to the heads of state to whom they were accredited. The letters announced, without more ado, that the annexation of Bosnia and Herzegovina would be proclaimed forty-eight hours later, on 7 October. Isvolsky, who had embarked upon a leisurely progression through Germany, Italy and France to canvass support for the Buchlau pact, was thunderstruck to learn, from newspaper headlines just before his train reached Paris, that Austria had already cashed in her share.

He was not alone in his reaction. Without exception, the other political leaders of Europe showed – depending on their individual viewpoint – anger, annoyance or dismay at the news. King Edward VII, that most genial and effective of all the royal diplomatists of the day was, for example, deeply hurt that the

Emperor Franz Joseph, whom he had visited at Bad Ischl less than two months before, had not dropped even a hint about annexation. As for the German Emperor and his Chancellor, they were very much more shocked and offended that their closest ally had only given them the same short notice of this *fait accompli* as everyone else. The strongest reaction of all came not from the despoiled Ottoman Empire itself, but from Serbia, who saw her own dreams for a South Slav kingdom in the Balkans destroyed. The Skupshtina, or Belgrade national assembly, met to vote credits for war; mobilization was set in train; the '*Narodna Odbrana*' or National Defence Society (an organiz-ation destined to play a sinister role in the tragedy awaiting Franz Ferdinand) was created to defy the Austrian move; and Serbian leaders were despatched on rescue missions in all directions, some touring the Western capitals to seek diplomatic backing, others heading north for St Petersburg to ask outright for armed help from the Tsar. Within days, the annexation crisis of 1908 – in so many respects a dress rehearsal for what was to come six years later – had erupted far beyond the frontiers of the two provinces. Indeed, it was to dominate the whole of European politics for the next six months. What do we know of Franz Ferdinand's role in it all?

Though the Archduke, as heir to the throne, could not publicly disavow this handsome jubilee gift to his sovereign, he was apprehensive from the start about the Monarchy embarking on any trial of strength until it had put its own divided house in order (i.e. tamed the Magyars). One of his closest political advisers, Leopold von Chlumecky, describes in his diary how Franz Ferdinand, who was in Bad Ischl with Colonel Brosch at the time, reacted when, in the summer of 1908, he was let into the secret of the forthcoming annexation. 'He opposed the move, and it was only after Brosch had talked him over for ten days that he gave his assent.'[17] But consent in this case merely indicated agreement not to parade his views too openly. What the Arch-duke felt in private is made crystal clear in a letter he wrote to Aehrenthal while attending German army manoeuvres in August:

I have just been talking to the Chief of General Staff and I would like to be sure that Your Excellency is fully aware of my opinion on the matter.

If an annexation is considered absolutely necessary, then I can only agree to it if the two provinces are declared a 'Land' of the empire; in other words that both are made a part of the Monarchy.

If Hungary should lay claim to the territories in the name of St Stephen's crown (which will, of course, happen in any case) the demand should in no case be conceded, even if it means abandoning the annexation and leaving things as they are . . .

In general, I am completely against all such displays of strength, in view of our depressing domestic circumstances. In my opinion only a powerful, united state can allow itself to indulge in such actions . . .

However, should the crown's advisers decide that annexation is absolutely called for, then I am against mobilization and think we should just increase our military readiness, which can be done quite well without consulting Parliament.[18]

The Archduke's apprehensions grew as the international tension mounted. Isvolsky, increasingly frustrated and furious as he found no support in either Paris or London for his side of the Buchlau bargain – the opening up of the Straits – fell back on trying to thwart Aehrenthal by having the whole annexation problem brought before a conference of the original 1878 signatory powers. For this idea he found Anglo-French sympathy, only to be told in Berlin that Germany was backing Austria's unyielding stand: no conference about compensation unless the annexation were recognized in advance.

This diplomatic deadlock was made more serious by mounting war fever in the Balkans. The sabre-rattling and agitation from Serbia and Montenegro grew so loud that in December 1908, General Conrad – who made no secret of his own desire to smash Serbia in a preventive war while he thought the military chances were still favourable[19] – pushed through with the Emperor the so-called 'brown mobilization' of Austrian forces on the southern frontier. This involved a reinforcement of the army there in two stages by a total of twenty-nine infantry battalions and one cavalry squadron. For the moment, the Archduke's arguments against general mobilization had prevailed, but he was having a hard time keeping Conrad, his own protégé, on the leash. As he wrote to Brosch in another typical exposition of his philosophy:

> Please restrain Conrad for me. He should stop all this agitating for war. Of course it would be splendid, and is very tempting, to throw these Serbs and Montenegrins into the frying-pan. But what use are such cheap laurels to us if we then face such an escalation through general complications in Europe that we could find ourselves having to fight on two or three fronts, something we could not manage?[20]

In the middle of February, when the crisis was at its height, the Archduke went off with his family for one of his frequent winter visits to St Moritz. It is possible that he wanted to distance himself from the so-called 'war party' in Vienna.[21] It is equally likely that he was determined that nothing short of war would get in the way of his precious domestic routine. Whatever the reason, letters exchanged between him and Conrad during this period make it clear that, if war came, Franz Ferdinand was determined to fill his expected role in the limelight as Commander-in-Chief of the imperial forces. Though he never joined the war party, the Archduke did not want to be left behind should it carry the day.

Thus when, on 1 March 1909, Conrad wrote to him in St Moritz saying that Aehrenthal was opposing the Archduke's appointment 'because it was hardly suitable for Your Highness, as heir to the throne, to command operations against Serbia and Montenegro',[22] Franz Ferdinand promptly left his family behind to enjoy the delights of the Engadin and caught the next train back to Vienna. He arrived there on the evening of 3 March, and immediately summoned Conrad to report to him at the Belvedere. There was a lively but inconclusive discussion on the command problem lasting one and a half hours, to be followed by an even livelier session between the two men on 20 March, during which, according to Conrad, the Archduke produced the following outburst: 'When I become Commander-in-Chief, I shall do as I please. Woe betide any who stand in my way; I'll have them all shot.'[23]

Had the crisis got much worse, the Emperor would have been forced to nominate his field commander for 'Kriegsfall B' (as the Monarchy's secret war plan for war in the Balkans was – not very subtly – named). But, as things turned out, uncle and nephew were to be spared from hostilities by a sudden breakthrough on the diplomatic front.

From the very start of the affair, Germany had been appalled by the prospect of being dragged into a conflagration by her impulsive Austrian ally, acting without even properly consulting Berlin. On 14 March, the German government offered Russia a way out for them all: Austria would invite the great powers to sanction the annexation, provided Russia agreed beforehand, if requested by Vienna, not to make difficulties. Everybody's face was saved by this ingenious compromise. Austria came out best by getting international agreement for her *coup de main* (the Young Turks had been bought off already in February by a large cash compensation); the Entente powers could feel that the sanctity of treaties had been nominally preserved; and Russia, who came out by far the worst, at least had the consolation of being asked by Aehrenthal to give her formal blessing to a situation she was anyway incapable of altering.

It still proved to be a very taut, tight finish. Russia, pressed hard by Chancellor Bülow, grudgingly accepted the German proposal on 22 March and England, France and Italy – only too glad to get this tiresome crisis behind them – rapidly followed suit. But that still left Serbia on the warpath, and it needed the strongest pressure from all sides to push her off it. From St Petersburg came urgent warnings that, however good the cause, this was simply not the moment to have a pan-Slav showdown with Austria in the Balkans (a decision reached by the Tsar's Ministerial Council on 17 March that Russia was in no state militarily to take up arms for Serbia showed that the warnings were not insincere).

In Vienna on 29 March, the Habsburg Monarchy again

bared its yellowing teeth by putting five of its fifteen army corps on a full war footing. This measure, which still fell short of full mobilization, nonetheless satisfied Conrad that he had at last won the day. He felt bitterly disappointed – and the Archduke greatly relieved – when, forty-eight hours later, Serbia formally gave way. 'In deference to the advice of the great powers,' her declaration read, 'Serbia undertakes to renounce the attitude of protest and opposition which she has adopted since last autumn with regard to the annexation.'[24] At that, the Austrian and Serbian reinforcements facing each other along the Bosnian frontiers were stood down and all Europe breathed again.

The military crisis may have died down; but its political tremors reverberated far and wide. Aehrenthal's superficial triumph, for which he was subsequently made a count, turned out to be a disaster, both for his own country and for Europe as a whole. On the diplomatic front, Austria had done herself an injury comparable with the self-inflicted wound caused by her neutral stand in the Crimean War. This time, however, the damage sprang not from being too cautious but from being too rash. Like a hitherto staid old man who suddenly embarks on a display of virility, the Habsburg Monarchy had provoked more dismay than admiration.

Within the Triple Alliance, Italy, who had been reduced to the role of a mere bystander in the whole affair, nursed not only wounded pride but also growing jealousy at Austria's 'forward policy' in the Balkans, an area where Rome had ambitions of its own.* More serious for Austria was the anger of her prime partner, Germany, at the way the annexation had been handled. The Emperor William, who heard the news on a hunting trip at Rominten, took days to calm down. 'So I am the last of all in Europe to be told anything at all,' he exploded.

Though Franz Ferdinand was not prepared to lift a finger to soothe Italian susceptibilities, he was ready to move mountains

---

* One by-product of the annexation crisis was the so-called Racconigi Pact of October 1909 between Italy and Russia whereby, in great secrecy, the two powers agreed to coordinate any moves in south-east Europe – despite the fact that they belonged to opposing political camps.

to restore good relations with Berlin, and, above all, with the German Emperor. As the crisis moved towards a settlement, he assured the German embassy in Vienna of his 'unending gratitude' to William II for his support, adding, 'I will never forget what your most gracious master has done for us. You know how close I am to him and how deeply I revere him.'[25] And while the crisis was still at its height, the Archduke had been able to indulge in some of his hunting-lodge diplomacy when William II was his guest for the stag-shooting at Eckartsau. The Emperor, describing the occasion in a letter to Chancellor Bülow in Berlin, tells how the Archduke had repeatedly thanked Germany for her 'loyal help' over the annexation and had tried to coordinate their future policy in the Balkans. (He had also proved a wonderful host, personally supervising the sporting arrangements to such good effect that his august guest shot no fewer than sixty-five stag.)[26] Such effusions of gratitude were later to prompt the Emperor William – never one to miss out on a heroic pose – to describe Germany as standing by Austria 'like a knight in shining armour', a phrase which gave the totally erroneous impression that Berlin had been the prime mover in the annexation affair.

In the Entente camp, France and England were appalled, as Germany had been, by the unpredictable impulsiveness of Austria's action. For these two powers, the Habsburg Monarchy was valid only so long as it worked to preserve stability in the Danube basin and the Balkans. That, after all, was its historic role and one which it had jeopardized by the annexation.* Russia, the third member of the entente, took a different and far more drastic view. For her, the annexation had not merely upset a delicate balance. It had tilted the Balkan scales directly against her own vital interests in the area, inflicting in the process a national humiliation which she vowed to revenge.[27]

Isvolsky, who was eventually demoted and sent as ambassador to Paris, worked with an almost demented fury from the

---

* The annexation crisis had done nothing to diminish the Archduke's old mistrust of the English. 'As usual, England's behaviour has been infamous,' he wrote to a friend on 6 January 1909.

French capital to bring Austria down; so demented indeed that, when war was declared between the rival alliances in 1914, he screamed with delight, '*C'est ma guerre! C'est ma guerre!*' The claim was ludicrous but also significant. The closest that Austria and Russia had ever got was the ill-fated plotting of their foreign ministers at Buchlau. When the plot collapsed for Isvolsky and his Tsar, the rift between the two countries grew wider than ever. For Franz Ferdinand, the annexation crisis had meant the end of his dream of reconciliation to bridge the gap between Europe's opposing pacts. Difficult enough to achieve even before 1908, it became an impossibility afterwards.

Finally, there were the doleful consequences in the Balkans themselves. There, the two 'lost provinces' became the focal point of all pan-Slav ambitions. Indeed, for those in Belgrade and St Petersburg who yearned for a 'Greater Serbia', they came to play the same emotional and geographical role as did the provinces of Alsace and Lorraine in the long conflict at the other end of Europe between France and Germany. Russia repeatedly assured her smaller Slav brethren that they only had to wait until the army of the Tsar was reorganized and ready before revenge would be taken on the double-headed Habsburg eagle which preyed upon their lands. And until that day came – and in preparation for it – Serbian agitation against the Dual Monarchy was to be stepped up. The deeper the Austrian police in Bosnia-Herzegovina drove this subversion underground, the more violent and fanatical it became. In this way, the crisis of 1908 led, by a clear if zigzag route, to the catastrophe of 1914.

CHAPTER TEN

———⊗———

Climbing Up

IT IS TIME to leave the Monarchy's domestic and foreign problems and return to the Archduke's private worries, and above all his struggle to place his wife on the highest pedestal he could find. 1909, which saw the annexation crisis end in an outward victory for his country, was also something of an *annus mirabilis* on this personal front. Their own list of triumphs for the year began in July when the couple paid their postponed visit to Rumania* as the guests of King Carol and Queen Elisabeth.

As simply another contact between the two courts of Vienna and Bucharest, the occasion was understandable enough. King Carol was a Hohenzollern Prince and his wife a German Princess of Wied. Moreover, Rumania had been allied to the Dual Monarchy ever since 1883 when the two countries signed their secret defensive treaty against Russia, a pact which had been renewed at intervals ever since. For Franz Ferdinand, King Carol had an additional special value – as a partner in the process of cutting the Magyars down to size, for Rumania coveted the lovely border province of Transylvania, held under the Dual Monarchy as part of the Hungarian lands of St Stephen. But however natural and congenial the background, this journey still marked a personal breakthrough for Sophie. As the Archduke's secretary (who went with them on the trip) wrote:

For Princess Hohenberg, this visit to a royal court meant

---

* It was originally planned for the summer of 1908, but had been put off due to Sophie's last pregnancy. This ended tragically with the birth of a stillborn son after Sophie had been ill with influenza.

something of a baptism of fire ... Even if more or less forced into it by the invitation, Franz Joseph had nonetheless given his permission, for the very first time, for the former Countess Chotek to accompany her husband abroad to represent the Emperor himself at purely formal ceremonies.[1]

The trip turned out to be more of a long-delayed official honeymoon than any test of endurance, thanks largely to the warm personal relations already established between the two royal couples and the refreshingly easy lifestyle of the Rumanian court. The guests set out for Rumania straight from a cruise along the Dalmatian coast, and, apart from certain incidents in transit, the holiday spirit never seemed to be lost.

Franz Ferdinand must have been purring with delight from the very beginning at the reception prepared for his wife, who was treated for the first time in her life as though she were a born archduchess and a future empress and not a morganatic consort. On the railway station at the frontier town of Predeal, for example, the full panoply of royal protocol was spread out to greet them when their train pulled in at four o'clock in the afternoon of 10 July. The reception party was headed by the Rumanian Crown Prince Ferdinand, who was accompanied by (and this was the significant point for Sophie) the Crown Princess Marie.[2] The line of politicians waiting on the platform was led not by the Foreign Minister – which would have been perfectly adequate for visitors of this level – but by the Prime Minister himself, Bratianu. And when they arrived, just over an hour later, at their destination, Sinaia, it was not just the old King (who, in his early years, had signed that treaty of 1883) who was waiting to welcome them, but also Queen Elisabeth. This was tantamount to regarding Sophie herself as being of royal blood – a potent piece of flattery.

The next few days at Pelesch Castle, in the lovely mountains of Sinaia, were, the Archduke often declared afterwards, among the happiest memories of his married life. They were a mixture of the formal and the informal, each made equally agreeable for the guests. Among the formal occasions was the gala dinner given on the evening of their arrival in the great Turkish-style salon of the castle. The company at table, the toasts exchanged during the banquet and the decorations exchanged beforehand – all were of a scale and style normally reserved for hospitality towards reigning sovereigns; and Sophie was indeed placed at the right hand of the Rumanian king. Montenuovo and the protocol pin-pricks of the Vienna court must have seemed a million miles away instead of a few hundred upstream on the same Danube.

The informality of King Carol's court was also a world removed from the fusty clockwork regime of the Hofburg. Typical of this was a most unorthodox 'tea house' which Queen Elisabeth had had constructed in the castle park. This consisted of a square wooden structure, richly decorated inside, which was anchored thirty feet up from the ground to four pine trees, so that the only access was through a hole in the floor reached by a rope ladder. Franz Ferdinand and his wife, who were climbing up another ladder of their own, were soon to pay visits to more important courts than this. But never again was their treatment to be quite so regal or so relaxed.

Predictably, the only shadows on the visit were those cast by Hungary, who viewed this journey of her greatest political enemy to the court of her greatest territorial rival with the deepest distrust. While in Sinaia, the Archduke had made a point of receiving a delegation, of Rumanians born in the Hungarian half of the Monarchy but expelled because of their 'treasonable' views. It was headed by Aurel Popovici, the author of the plan to reform the empire along federalist lines which had caught the Archduke's eye when it had been published three years before. Popovici's book, *The United States of Greater Austria*, was banned in Hungary and he himself faced a prison sentence in a Hungarian jail if he returned there. To accept a loyal address from such a man while on foreign soil was a highly provocative act on Franz Ferdinand's part, especially as student hotheads were already using his visit as the occasion to try and tear down Hungarian flags. Back in Budapest, the Magyars reacted accordingly. The newspapers erupted with angry articles and a group of extremist deputies tried (unsuccessfully) to convene an emergency session of parliament to protest at the goings-on in Sinaia.

Then there was the tricky question of the journey home, for the main railway to Vienna ran unavoidably through Hungary. There had been problems already on the outward trip. At one point along the Hungarian stretch of the line someone had hurled quite a hefty stone (in the public report it was described as 'the size of a man's fist') against the windows of the archducal dining-car, which fortunately was empty at the time. No official reception of any sort awaited the heir to the throne when the train then made a brief evening stop at Budapest station (though this was quite clearly at his request). A crowd of sightseers had, however, gathered on the platform to catch a glimpse of the famous couple, and these onlookers were highly offended when the Archduke, after one quick glance out, withdrew from sight behind closed curtains.

Clearly, things had to be handled differently on the journey back, where there would be an afternoon wait of thirty-five minutes in the Hungarian capital. (The Archduke's special coaches were nearly always attached to the end of regular express trains and so were subject to the normal timetables.) The problem was met by the Archduke taking his wife, in an ordinary hired carriage, for half an hour's drive around the main streets of Budapest during the interval. He also addressed some flattering words, in the best Hungarian he could muster, to the senior railway official sent to greet him. Was the top man of the iron road ill, or was it deliberate that only the *deputy* chief of the Hungarian Railways, one Johann Marx, had been selected for this honour? One could never be sure about such matters, whenever and wherever the Archduke and his Magyars came together. They were always fencing with each other.

The second great triumph of the year was, of course, Sophie's elevation to the rank of Duchess, which was announced on 4 October. It is conceivable that the Emperor had decided this entirely off his own bat. Sophie had not only proved herself a model wife and mother for more than nine years but had also demonstrated on the visit to the Rumanian court that she was now quite capable of conducting herself regally – a far cry indeed from the picture of the retiring domestic mouse which Franz Ferdinand had presented to his uncle when battling for permission to marry. It is more likely that the Emperor was influenced, in part at least, by constant pressure from the Archduke and his small but influential band of champions to do something more about Sophie's rank. The imminence of another foreign visit which the couple were due to make, and which we shall come to in a moment, may also have played its part. In any case, her upward path had already been smoothed, if one can use that word to describe the tortuous 'promotion', by the Emperor four years earlier, in an official letter to his nephew. This bestowed upon all members of the house of Hohenberg, who had hitherto only been entitled to the predicative 'Princely Grace', the right to be called 'Serene Highness' instead. Sophie was thus moved one notch forward in the protocol racket. She would henceforth rank 'immediately *before* the lady of the palace fulfilling the role of Count Marshallin'.[3] The lady who was fulfilling that function in 1905 must have been furious; and so too, presumably, was the Archduchess Isabella.

But though doubtless of profound import to the jealous little world inside the walls of the Hofburg, this remained little more than a play with words. Elevation to the rank of duchess was a very different matter. This carried to the real world outside instant connotations of royalty, for nowhere in the German lands was there a duke who had not once reigned over a kingdom of his own. To be a duchess looked and sounded like palaces rather than mere castles. This was just as well, for the Archduke and his wife were now heading for the most pompously self-conscious palace in all Europe.

It was natural that Berlin should be the first major capital they should visit together. In the six years that had passed since Chancellor Bülow had prevailed upon his royal master to pay homage to Sophie, the German Emperor had often exchanged shooting invitations with Franz Ferdinand and his wife, or met the Archduke at army manoeuvres, while the personal correspondence between the two men had grown steadily more frequent and more cordial. Germany's decisive role in settling the annexation crisis in the spring of 1909 had drawn Emperor and Archduke even closer – with the former combining an air of bombast and false modesty over the affair. As he wrote to his 'Dear Franzi' that Easter, 'It was a real joy for me to be able to act as your good second and . . . to show the world that when the two imperial powers stand together, Europe simply has to listen to them.' There followed compliments to the Archduke on the 'prompt and exact functioning of the Austrian military machine', and the warmest personal greetings for his wife.[4] Clearly, it was time to complete this affectionate triangular relationship by introducing Sophie to the Empress Viktoria Augusta. On the evening of 10 November 1909 the great moment arrived when the Archduke and his wife left Vienna by special train for Berlin. They travelled with a very small suite and there was no formal ceremony of departure. Only the director of the north-west station and sundry other railway officials were assembled to bid the heir to the throne and his newly-created Duchess farewell.[5]

It was a very different picture when they arrived at Berlin's Anhalter station at quarter to one the following afternoon. Sophie found that she was within a whisker of being treated – as in Rumania – like royalty to royalty born. That whisker was, however, clearly visible. The male turnout on the carpeted platform was everything that could be expected. It was led by the Emperor himself, who embraced the Archduke warmly on both cheeks and then kissed the hand of his wife. The new German Chancellor, Bethmann-Hollweg,* was there, dolled up as a Major of Dragoons (it was typical, incidentally, of Prussia's standards of value that the head of government should prefer the uniform of a relatively junior officer to the frock coat and top hat of the empire's leading politician); so was the Foreign Office Secretary of State, Herr von Schoen. There were diplomats aplenty and the usual garnishings of military bands and guards of honour. But to greet Sophie the court had sent Princess Eitel Friedrich, the wife not of the German Crown Prince, but of his

---

* Bülow had resigned on 17 July of that year.

younger brother, and it was she who presided over the ladies' side of the programme from now on. However, at a 'family' level, Sophie was placed on equal terms with the German Empress at the dinner given in the 'Neues Palais' that evening. Protocol problems were ingeniously avoided by placing the two royal couples by themselves at one table, with the other guests scattered among smaller separate tables.

After this, Sophie had to be looked after separately because, early on 12 November, her husband left with the Emperor for the imperial shooting lodge at Lesslingen. The main purpose of the hunting expedition was drastically to reduce the local population of fallow deer which, to simplify matters, were driven out of the forest towards the guns between wattle screens erected on the flanks to prevent the animals breaking out to left or right. In one hour the Archduke, who had been allotted the prime position, had killed 125 bucks, and was to bring his personal bag over the two days to a total of 360 deer and wild boar. This *Trieb mit Lappen*, as it was called, was typical of the style of shooting not just in the Dual Monarchy, but elsewhere on the continent in his day, wherever the enormous reserves of wild game made it possible. As host or as guest of honour, the Archduke, when handling a rifle, rarely missed. The arithmetic of his personal tally followed as a matter of course.

After almost primeval performances like these in the forests, an evening spent purely in playing bridge would have seemed rather tame. But Lesslingen and that irrepressible extrovert William II rose to the challenge between them. The castle boasted a very special drinking goblet fashioned by the host's ancestor, King Frederick William III. It consisted of the crown of a giant stag's antlers with a silver cup set in a hollowed-out space in the centre. Every guest, on his first appearance at a Lesslingen shoot, had to drain the cup dry of champagne without spilling a drop – no easy matter as the face had to be jammed between the forks of the antler and then the lips lowered before the cup could be reached. One by one the newcomers went through the ritual, to the accompaniment of loud guffaws and lively airs played by the regimental band of the 16th Uhlans which was on parade in the gallery. It was a very Teutonic evening; but like the visit as a whole, it marked a further stage in the growing influence of Emperor William on the heir to the Austrian throne as well as the growing status of the Archduke and his wife as European figures.

Within the Monarchy, however, that same battle for status had to be fought every inch of the way, and some of the protocol skirmishes were still being lost. To the bitter end, for example, the barriers stayed up against the couple appearing together in public in Vienna, even on informal occasions. When the Archduke submitted a modest request that his wife might be allowed to accompany him to performances at ordinary, as opposed to state, theatres (and the submission itself must have been written with a grinding of teeth), he received in reply the following ornately bland refusal, transmitted by Prince Montenuovo:

> His Imperial and Royal Apostolic Majesty has determined thus in respect of a most humble request as to whether it would be proper to go to theatres which do not possess royal boxes: in proper company, highest gentlemen may visit such theatres, but it is graciously pointed out that this All-Highest ruling does not apply to highest ladies.[6]

It was within the armed forces, over which Franz Ferdinand was gaining steadily increasing influence, that he was able to project Sophie more and more as the consort of the empire's future ruler and wartime Commander-in-Chief. True, he had failed to get his uncle's permission to take her with him to the military celebrations held in August 1909 in the Tyrol, which marked the hundredth anniversary of the epic victory of Andreas Hofer's peasant army over a Napoleonic force. But this, as the Emperor had pointed out in an almost apologetic reply,[7] was a very formal occasion, full of those ceremonies which would only create awkward problems. As if to sweeten the pill, Franz Joseph had added, in a rare written expression of cordiality, 'But you know that your wife belongs to our family circle and I take great pleasure in seeing her in close family contact with us.'

Six months later, however, the Emperor had a gratifying

New Year's present for the couple. His Military Chancery decreed that, with effect from 1 January 1910, the army should present arms in front of the Duchess, who would also now be allowed to attend military ceremonials and act as patroness of regimental colours.[8] This was a major step forward. The composers of the day, as usual wind-vanes of public favour, were quick to fall into line. Within three years, no fewer than eleven of them had written special tunes in Sophie's honour.[9] The most distinguished contributor was Karl Michael Ziehrer, creator of many popular Viennese operettas and waltzes who was also (from 1907 until the collapse of the Monarchy in 1918) Director of Music at Court Balls. That New Year's decision brought more than waltz dedications. It made it possible for Sophie to accompany her husband without any questioning whenever he inspected a regiment or launched a new warship. It was also to enable her to go with him to the manoeuvres at Sarajevo.

Preliminary tremors of that 1914 earthquake were felt throughout the twelve-month period from October 1912 to October 1913, when the continent was convulsed by the two Balkan Wars. As in 1908, the crisis was brought about by a scramble to wrest from the feeble grasp of the expiring Ottoman Empire the last of her titular possessions in south-east Europe. This time, only the smaller powers did the actual looting, falling to begin with upon their common Turkish prey and then upon each other, squabbling over the spoils. But the great powers were again involved by proxy; again, the shadow of an armed confrontation between Austria and Russia loomed up; and again Franz Ferdinand, after an indecisive start, did all in his power to head it off.

The course of these violent, treacherous little conflicts, which only needs outlining here, shows why the Balkans were the despair, and the nightmare, of the European continent. The first wave of fighting was led by the mountain kingdom of Montenegro, which on 8 October 1912 declared war on its suzerain, the Ottoman Empire. Ten days later, Serbia, Greece and Bulgaria all joined in the fray. The Turkish army crumpled like a rotten oak tree under the storm. The Bulgarians marched south right up to the fortresses guarding Constantinople; Greek forces moved east to seize the key Mediterranean port of Salonika; the Serbs swept south-west along the Vardar valley and reached the Adriatic, the sea outlet they had long coveted, by occupying the northern part of Albania.

It was this last thrust which preoccupied Vienna. 'Greater Serbia', which the Monarchy had naïvely hoped to curb by the annexation of Bosnia and Herzegovina in 1908, was now on the march with a vengeance. If Montenegro agreed to merge with Serbia, as was being rumoured, the two annexed provinces would themselves be ringed off to the south. Above all, the Serbs had to be pulled back from the Adriatic coast, which made any encirclement complete. This could only be done by the creation of some form of independent Albanian state, presiding over a coastline of its own. As Italy immediately fell in with this solution (if only with the long-term aim of swallowing up Albania herself one day),* that left only German assurances to be secured. This the Archduke helped to assure by another of his favourite exercises in hunting-lodge diplomacy. He went in November to Springe, just south of Hanover, for a few days' shooting with the German Emperor and came back with a firm pledge of support for Austria's stand over the crisis.[10] The government in Berlin was already inclined in the same direction but William II's personal blessing was nonetheless a valuable reinforcement.

On his return to Vienna, the Archduke was able to make a much more decisive personal intervention, this time on the military front. The Dual Monarchy had already mobilized its four army corps which faced Serbia in the south, and also (as a precaution against any Russian move to help the Serbs) the three army corps which were stationed in the north-eastern province of Galizia; but Franz Ferdinand was still worried that if it should come to war, the military machine needed more resolute hands at the controls. He tackled Franz Joseph direct with the plea to reinstate Conrad, who had resigned as Chief-of-Staff the year

---

* An aim realized for a few years by Mussolini with the Italian invasion of Easter 1939.

before after a long and bitter squabble with the Foreign Minister, Aehrenthal. The Emperor finally agreed, albeit insisting that the Archduke's latest protégé as War Minister, General von Auffenberg, should be replaced as well. On 12 December 1912, Conrad moved back into the job he was to hold, in peace and war, for the next five years.[11]

The fact that Franz Ferdinand had been personally responsible for bringing the headstrong Conrad, an outspoken champion of the 'preventive war' against the Serbs, back to his old post at this crucial juncture was used to justify the charge that the Archduke was himself itching for blood. The allegation, as will be seen, was false. Conrad's reappointment was merely insurance against the risk of a political solution failing, as well as a move in the game of political blackmail itself. It carried with it, as Franz Ferdinand realized, the added burden for him of fighting down a war-party which would henceforth be strengthened by Conrad's powerful voice.

That challenge was to reach its climax in the new year. In the last weeks of the old, peace was, for the time being, preserved by a compromise reached over the Albanian question by the London Conference of Ambassadors on 16 December. At the suggestion of the British Foreign Secretary, Sir Edward Grey, it was agreed that an independent Albania should be established, but with boundaries to be defined later. Nobody was enchanted by the solution; but the Austrians came out best and, by the same token, the Serbs, denied the precious window on the Adriatic, came out worst, though holding on to their other gains.

Satisfaction around the green baize table of diplomacy was not, however, good enough for Conrad. Within forty-eight hours of resuming his duties as Chief-of-Staff he was bombarding the Archduke with arguments for settling the Monarchy's account with Serbia on the battlefield instead. He returned to the charge with another long memorandum sent to the Belvedere on 30 December. Two short extracts give its pungent flavour: 'The cause of the trouble is the suddenly increased strength of Serbia; it is this which must therefore be broken and then all our other worries are removed. The situation has developed into a trial of strength between the Monarchy and Serbia. We must face the trial . . .'[12]

Throughout January 1913, Conrad hammered even louder at the door, presenting the Emperor with a memorandum which urged an immediate attack on Serbia and Montenegro and pressing the same line in two separate audiences at the Belvedere. Conrad seemed puzzled himself as to what was going on in Franz Ferdinand's mind. 'I was never certain,' he wrote of this period, 'whether, deep down, the Archduke had plumped for military action or not. He discussed everything which bore on such action . . . but did not seem to me to be really inclined towards it in his heart.'[13]

The General had caught only the tail-end of Franz Ferdinand's true feelings. These came out fully at a private dinner party given for his brother-in-law, Duke Albrecht of Württemberg, in Vienna at the end of January. When the table talk turned to Conrad's crusade for a preventive war, the Archduke exclaimed:

> Let's even suppose that nobody else interferes and we are left to settle the reckoning with Serbia by ourselves: what would we get out of it? Just one more pile of thieves, murderers and rascals, plus a few plum trees. In other words, more rubbish acquired at the cost of so many soldiers and a few billion crowns in money. And even this optimistic arrangement – namely that no-one would try to prevent us – seems to be more than unlikely.[14]

These little states, he argued, should be allowed to fight out their own battles.

That was precisely what happened when, on 30 June 1913, Bulgaria, resentful that one of her partners in the 1912 campaign had seized too much of Macedonia for herself, suddenly attacked Serbia and tried to grab the disputed border province back. But 'Foxy' Ferdinand of Bulgaria – since 1908 the self-styled 'Tsar' of an independent kingdom – had sadly miscalculated his chances. Greece, who had a score of her own to settle with him, came in on Serbia's side. So did Rumania, who had taken no part in the 1912 fighting and had therefore come out of the imbroglio so far with empty hands. Even the Ottoman Empire joined forces with some of the little vultures who had been preying on it, and attacked Bulgaria from the south.

Within six weeks, the second Balkan war ended when Ferdinand was forced to sue for peace. At the treaty of Bucharest he not only lost a large slice of the conquests gained from Turkey the year before, but was also obliged to yield up some of his own territory – the northern border strip of the Dobrudja – to Rumania, whose troops were sitting there.

If, of all the participants, Bulgaria ended up, next to Turkey, as the loser of these two wars, Serbia, despite being frustrated over Albania, emerged as the clearest winner. Her territory and population had been nearly doubled, and both her fighting morale and her enthusiasm for the pan-Slav crusade had leapt ten-fold. It was not just the Belgrade government which breathed fire and brimstone against Vienna. The call for a day of reckoning with the Dual Monarchy, cost what it might, was taken up ever more stridently by Serb students, and a secret society of Serbian army officers was now planning for that day in earnest. This was to prove a lethal combination.

It was the effervescence of the Serbs and the continuing unrest in the nascent kingdom of Albania* which produced the last scare of the long Balkan crisis. In October, fighting broke out on the Albanian–Serbian frontier, with atrocities by troops on both sides. The Serbs mobilized again, crossed the border and once more laid claim to a large slice of Albanian territory. Count Berchtold – whom we last encountered as Austrian Ambassador to St Petersburg and the owner of Buchlau Castle – was now Foreign Minister in Vienna. He had so far played a pathetically vacillating role in the 1912–13 drama, being alternately bellicose and pacific. At first, he seemed just as wobbly in the face of this new flare-up. There were long ministerial discussions on 3 and 13 October. Conrad, as ever, argued for war. Count Tisza, the formidable Magyar nobleman who had become Hungarian

---

* After much debate between the great powers as to who should be its monarch, yet another German princeling was imported into the Balkans when, in 1914, William Prince of Wied was made ruler (*Mrbet*) of Albania.

Prime Minister four months before, was for attempting a peaceful way out, at least to start with.[15] Berchtold hedged his bets at both sessions, but then suddenly, in the early morning hours of 18 October, slammed in an ultimatum to Belgrade to withdraw its troops from Albanian soil within the next eight days or face dire consequences. One week later, with only a day to go, Serbia complied, and the tangled twelve-month crisis in the Balkans was over at last.

This was certainly a victory for Berchtold, who had astounded everyone in Europe, and not just the Serbs, by this uncharacteristic show of energy. In addition to being astonished, Austria's principal ally was also extremely irritated. Throughout the summer, the German government had been urging caution on Vienna.[16] Now, once more, as in 1908, the Austrians had dived head-first into the Balkan maelstrom without even consulting Berlin. The worst of it all, however, was still to come. Having got away once with a bullying ultimatum to Serbia in 1913, Berchtold was to try it on again, with disastrous consequences, in the summer of 1914.

For Franz Ferdinand there was only one cause for regret over the year-long muddle of the Balkan wars. Vienna's links with King Carol's Rumania, which the Archduke had himself tried so hard to build up, had come under severe strain.

Once the fighting started, and with it the wrangle over the corpse of Turkey-in-Europe, relations grew steadily worse, as Vienna was blamed for favouring Bulgaria and neglecting Rumania in that unseemly squabble for the spoils. Indeed, by the end of the year, nationalist feeling among the Rumanian people was running so high that Russia felt able to launch a promising campaign to lure Rumania out of the Austro-German orbit altogether. It all went very much against the grain for King Carol, who had spent more than thirty years of his reign trying to seal a friendship with Austria. But, as he glumly confessed to Austrian diplomats in December 1913, he could now no longer guarantee that if it ever came to war between the big powers, Rumania could stand by the pledges of support she had given the Dual Monarchy in the secret treaty of 1883 and renewed at intervals ever since. At this, General Conrad ordered staff plans to be drawn up for 'Case Ru.' – a war against Rumania. It seemed a world away from the happy, intimate days which the Archduke and his wife had spent at Sinaia only four years before.

Despite this threat to one of Franz Ferdinand's cherished aims, on the personal plane the long crisis of 1912–13 had brought him nothing but increased prestige. He had secured the reinstatement of Conrad as Chief-of-Staff in case of war, but, having covered that possibility, he prevailed against this strong-willed General's warring tendencies in the clash over policies which followed. It had, for example, been largely the Archduke's doing and against Conrad's wishes that, in March 1913, the Austro-Hungarian forces in Galizia were stood down from a full mobilization footing in order to minimize the dangers of a clash with Russia.

Yet though Franz Ferdinand again came down emphatically against the 'war party', it would be wrong to regard him as a compulsive peacemaker, like his young nephew Charles, who was eventually to take the Habsburg throne in his place. The underlying reason why he strove for peace in 1913, as in 1908, was that he knew the Dual Monarchy was not yet ready for war. Two private utterances made within hours of each other at the height of the crisis reveal clearly enough the roots of his thinking.

On 26 February, when he was having one of his periodic debates with Conrad about the Albanian crisis, the General questioned whether it was worth while, in terms of the Monarchy's prestige and vital interests in the Balkans, adopting a pacific line. The Archduke replied, '... rest assured, later, when our internal political situation is better than it is now – then, yes!'[17] And the same day, when discussing the position with a German diplomat in Vienna, he remarked, 'Before everything else, we must establish order inside the Dual Monarchy. Only after that can we pursue a strong foreign policy.'[18] In short, Franz Ferdinand's efforts for peace were more pragmatic than moralistic. They came from the head rather than the heart.

In 1913, as in 1909, a year of political crisis was rounded off with personal triumphs for the Archduke and his wife. For the Archduke himself, though not for Sophie, there had been a most gratifying public occasion in the last days of the Balkan tumult. One hundred years before, between 16 and 19 October 1813, the combined forces of Austria, Prussia, Russia and Sweden had driven Napoleon's army back into the gates of Leipzig and then shattered it, after storming the city. The French troops who survived retreated westwards across the Rhine, and Napoleon's hold on the German lands was broken for good.

For the centenary of this so-called 'Battle of the Nations', great celebrations had been devised. Large official delegations had been invited from all the powers who had taken part in the victory and Franz Ferdinand, as heir to the Habsburg throne and Inspector-General of its armed forces, headed the deputation from the Dual Monarchy.

Though King Frederick Augustus of Saxony did the honours by meeting the Archduke at Leipzig station, it was soon clear that the Emperor William had devised the various ceremonies – and especially the unveiling on 18 October of a special monument – so that they would redound to the greater glory of Prussia in general and of himself as King of Prussia in particular. This irritated the Archduke, and with reason, for quite apart from the share Austrian troops had taken in the common victory, it was an Austrian Field-Marshal, Prince Karl Schwarzenberg, who had commanded the allied armies.

It is this irritation which provides such scanty excuse as can be found for the public outburst of bad temper of which he was guilty that same evening.[19] After a huge dinner for four hundred and fifty guests had broken up, the Emperor William summoned General Conrad and asked him to present the senior officers of the Austrian delegation, some of whom were unknown to him. Conrad hurried away to round them up but had barely begun when the Archduke pounced upon him, and, having heard what the General was doing, barked out for all around to hear, 'That is for me to do. Are you the Army Commander? I will not allow this.' In vain did poor Conrad explain, once more, that he was only carrying out the German Emperor's orders. The Archduke brushed him aside and proceeded with the presentations himself. Conrad had been so humiliated in front of his own and allied officers (his opposite number in Germany, General von Moltke, immediately came over to commiserate with him) that he was tempted to offer his resignation on the spot. It took days for him to calm down when back in Vienna and see the Serbian crisis through to the end. The Leipzig celebrations had shown the Archduke at his worst.

It was a very different story all round the following month. November 1913 brought the crowning success of Franz Ferdinand's campaign to launch Sophie on the international stage: an invitation from the King and Queen of England to be their guests at Windsor. The visits to the courts of Rumania and Germany had each been milestones in their way. But the Court of St James had always been the Archduke's ultimate goal in this dynastic progression, not only because it stood in the opposite camp to the Triple Alliance (and was therefore much more difficult to break into), but also because the London of his day was, quite simply, the centre of Europe. Once Sophie had been received there, she could afford to face her treatment by any other capital – including Vienna – with a certain equanimity. That the Archduke realized this is shown by the relentless pressure he had exerted to get the invitation issued, the principal victim of that pressure being the Austrian Ambassador to London since 1904, Count Albert Mensdorff-Pouilly-Dietrichstein.

Even the resounding international flavour of the envoy's full name (given here for the only time) does not reveal his greatest personal value to the Archduke in this matter. Mensdorff was a second cousin to King Edward VII, who shared with him a common great-grandfather in Prince Francis Frederick of Saxe-Saalfeld-Coburg. He was therefore unique even among the large and glittering diplomatic corps of pre-1914 London in that he could operate at court as one of the family – however distant. Indeed, when the monarchs of England wrote to him, the words 'dear cousin' would nearly always appear somewhere at the beginning and end of the letters. Despite all this Count Mensdorff had to sweat blood – if that is not too crude an expression for such a fastidious figure – to consummate the Archduke's ambition.

With Edward VII himself, Franz Ferdinand seems to have made no personal contact of note. He had attended the King's postponed coronation on 9 August 1902* and the new monarch had duly elected him 'Knight Companion of My most Noble Order of the Garter ... as a public testimony of my cordial friendship and esteem.'[20] But the 'friendship' referred to remained purely formal. We know from the writings of the influential *Times* correspondent of the period, Henry Wickham Steed,† what the King felt about the Archduke's morganatic marriage, which was that reality would have to be faced, and Sophie recognized as Empress, after Franz Joseph's death.[22] In other words, he was coolly pragmatic; the warmth which Edward VII undoubtedly felt for the Vienna court was concentrated (after Crown Prince Rudolph's death) on the old Emperor himself.

It was different with the King's son and heir. George Prince of Wales and Franz Ferdinand were not only closer to each other in temperament and tastes (both somewhat introverted, for example, both very absorbed in domestic life and both passionate devotees of shooting); they were also given more opportunity to meet, and not simply at coronations or funerals. Prince George visited Vienna in April of 1904 and, as his diary records, he spent all morning on the twentieth leaving cards 'on all the archdukes and archduchesses and finished by paying a visit to Franz Ferdinand and his wife Princess Hohenberg'. (The Prince went on feelingly to write, 'Everybody most kind and nice, but my goodness, this Court is stiff and they are frightened of the Emperor.')[22]

Just over two years later, on 31 May 1906, the two Heirs-

---

* It had been planned for 26 June 1901 but postponed within a few days of the event, when the King went down with acute appendicitis.
† Steed was *Times* correspondent in Rome from 1897 to 1902 and in Vienna from 1902 to 1913. At the outbreak of war he became the paper's Foreign Editor.

Apparent met again when both attended the wedding in Madrid of King Alfonso XIII to Princess Ena of Battenberg. Neither was likely to forget that occasion for the rest of his life. As the state carriage bearing the newly-married couple from the church of Los Gerominos headed for the royal palace, an anarchist hurled a bomb at it, and though the King and his bride of a few minutes both escaped unhurt, others near the carriage were killed and some of the blood was spattered on the bridal gown.

When, therefore, Prince George became King of England at the death of his father fifteen minutes before midnight on 6 May 1910, Franz Ferdinand was one of the first to send him a telegram and to receive, two days later, a warm personal reply.[23] Immediately, the Archduke set to work to try and get Sophie included in the royal guest list for King Edward's funeral. Woefully, Mensdorff's diary takes up the story.

On 12 May (sitting in the Ritz Hotel, whence he had removed while the embassy at 18 Belgrave Square was being redecorated) he writes, 'The Archduke has the unhappy idea of bringing his wife with him. The idea is that she puts up incognito in a hotel and then, after all the ceremonies are over, stays on a few days with him, still incognito.'[24]

Whatever faint hopes Franz Ferdinand may have had of this highly unorthodox arrangement being acceptable were dashed by a leak in the Vienna press about Sophie attending the funeral, with the erroneous conclusion that clearance had already been given from London. This was duly reported by the British embassy to the Foreign Office, and Mensdorff, in a letter sent to the Archduke, tells what happened next:

> Queen Mary was immediately informed, and she pointed out ... that it would be impossible to ignore the presence of Her Highness, even if this was incognito. And since, moreover, the Queen has had to refuse the visit of many other princesses who are closely related to her, she would be in a very difficult situation if she were to receive other ladies.[25]

Franz Ferdinand persisted, in a manner somewhat unbecoming to the heir to the Habsburg throne as well as extremely embarrassing to its London envoy. He suggested to Mensdorff that Sophie should arrive 'under the strictest possible incognito', and that she should not simply come under another name but arrive at a different time from her husband, with her presence in London 'not even being mentioned'. An unhappy Mensdorff tried this on Sir Charles Hardinge, then just ending a four-year term as Permanent Secretary at the Foreign Office before climbing even higher up the ladder as Viceroy of India. Hardinge turned the idea down flat on King George's behalf as being plainly impracticable.

Mensdorff's diary tells the end of the story: 'I telephoned this to Aehrenthal and got the reply that the Duchess will *not* come. Naturally, the Archduke is furious. Constant telegrams from him, Rumerskirch [the head of Franz Ferdinand's private office] and the Ministry. Some people just don't have the talent to approach things practically and simply.'[26] By way of consolation, Mensdorff was able to report that the Archduke, as heir to the throne of a great power, would be accorded 'the first rank after the kings' at the funeral ceremonies.

And so it was when the 'uncle of Europe' came to be buried on 20 May 1910. No fewer than nine sovereigns led that last glittering procession up the steep road winding along the grey flanks of Windsor Castle. And immediately after the third row of monarchs (the King of Bulgaria, the King of Denmark and the boy-King Manuel of Portugal) came Franz Ferdinand and the Hereditary Prince of the Ottoman Empire, walking on either side of the King of the Belgians. The massed ranks of Imperial, Royal, Grand-Ducal and Serene Highnesses from Prussia, Russia, Saxony, Teck, Hesse, Saxe-Coburg and the rest all marched behind him. Still, he was not entirely happy, if only because the insufferable 'Foxy Ferdinand' of Bulgaria, whom he could not abide (in common with most of European royalty), was placed right in front of him as 'Tsar' of Bulgaria. But had he been alive to plan the procession himself, the monarch they were burying, who had been the master of royal etiquette, could not have ordered it otherwise. At Windsor, as at the Hofburg, there were certain iron bands of protocol which could not be bent.

That Franz Ferdinand was irked by the whole occasion –

despite the impeccable treatment accorded to him personally –
is shown by his own report on the funeral ceremonies, written on
his return to Vienna.[27] His anger that Sophie could not be with
him increased the irritation which the 'arrogant English' had
always tended to arouse in him ever since his lengthy experience
with them at close quarters in India (where, of course, they were
always at their worst). The result was a bad-tempered verdict
full of sarcasm and not free from extraordinary errors. The
Bulgarian King, his favourite target, was described as 'a totally
false and unreliable creature who cut a particularly pathetic
figure in London' as well as 'looking like a pig when on his
horse'. The Presidents of France and the United States were
dismissed as 'the two Republicans, Pichou and Roosevelt, who
distinguished themselves by an exceptional lack of any courtly
manners', with President Roosevelt even being labelled as
'cheeky'. As for the Crown Prince of Serbia, he looked just like a
'bad gypsy'.

His hosts came in for strong criticism because of the length
of the funeral ceremony (which lasted from nine in the morning
to six in the evening and was, admittedly, arduous). The final
stage, in St George's Chapel Windsor, aroused his particular
ire because there were no chairs and everyone had to stand
throughout. 'But, after all, what better can one expect from the
English?' he added; a curious comment, considering that the
English were renowned for designing the most comfortable
armchairs in the world.

He was even drawn, very imprudently, into poking fun at
certain details of the funeral procession. He evidently believed,
for example, that the organizers had made a frightful blunder by
fixing the late King's riding boots back to front in the horse's
stirrups. A simple enquiry would have instructed him that any
English sovereign buried in military style – or, for that matter,
any former army commander – was always borne thus to his
grave, to symbolize that his days in the saddle were over.
Altogether, this report does not show the Archduke at his best,
and one can only assume that he penned it with the frustration
over Sophie in his mind. Certainly, his whole view of England

and the English was to be transformed once that frustration was ended.

Mensdorff had wound up his apologetic reports to the Belvedere that month by assuring the Archduke of George V's warmest sympathy, and the envoy added his hope that it would soon be possible 'to work out another plan' for the Duchess's visit. Two years later, the happiest possible solution presented itself, with blossoms, not coffins, as the pretext. In May 1912, the Horticultural Society of England staged their first international flower show. What could be more natural than for the Archduke to attend, not as the heir to an empire, but as the squire of Konopischt, whose rose gardens were already achieving a certain reputation even outside the Monarchy? And, since he was coming as a garden-lover and travelling, strictly incognito, as the Count of Artstetten, what could be more reasonable than that his wife should travel with him? And so, from the windows of a suite of rooms at the Ritz Hotel in Piccadilly, Sophie looked out on London at last that month. They stayed for fourteen days, making several trips to well-known country houses* as well as to the exhibition. More important, thanks to Mensdorff's preparatory labours, the first breakthrough to the Court of St James took place – lunch on 23 May at Buckingham Palace with King George and Queen Mary and the Queen Mother, Alexandra. Recording the occasion in his diary, the King commented that his guests were 'both charming and made themselves very pleasant.'[28]

'*C'est le premier pas qui coute.*' Once Sophie had been received (and approved of) as Countess of Artstetten, it was not a difficult matter to invite her, privately though no longer incognito, as the Duchess of Hohenberg. Most appropriately, this vital family crusade, which had been initiated through a gardening exhibition, was now advanced by the Archduke's shotgun. One of the great houses he and Sophie had visited in May 1912 had been Welbeck Abbey, where the Duke of Portland had asked him to come and shoot the following

* Most were arranged by Sophie's niece, Countess Elisabeth Baillet-Latour, who lived for most of the year in England.

autumn. This gave Mensdorff the lead he wanted. On 19 July 1913 the Austrian envoy was able to report to the Belvedere that when, 'yesterday', he had mentioned to George V that the Archduke and his Duchess intended to come for a week's shooting at Welbeck at the end of November, the King had promptly suggested that the couple should stay at Windsor Castle for a shoot the week before. As if to emphasize that they were both really welcome, Mensdorff continued, 'The King spoke in front of me with the Queen about the invitation ... and Her Majesty repeated it also from her side in the warmest terms.'[29]

Mensdorff ended his report with the formal (and, in the circumstances, almost facetious) expression of hope that the Archduke would find it possible to accept. His letter reached Franz Ferdinand on a seaside family holiday at Blankenberge on the Belgian coast. A seven-page reply despatched from them immediately gave Mensdorff any assurance he may have needed. The 'gracious and friendly invitation' was accepted 'with the greatest joy'. Mensdorff was instructed to tell the King and Queen 'in the warmest possible words' how 'quite exceptionally enchanted' the Archduke and his wife felt over the invitation. Franz Ferdinand brushed aside the fact that their stay would only be a private one by stressing how pleasant such occasions were, in contrast to formal visits with their 'terrible banquets and toasts.'[30]

A week later Mensdorff, recording this triumph in his diary, added, in rather squashed-up French, '*Allons tout mieux*'. And indeed, the five-day Windsor visit, which duly took place from 17 to 21 November 1913, was to exceed everybody's expectations. It must have been a huge relief for the Archduke and his wife, though they again stayed at the Ritz Hotel, to emerge at last from under the blanket of their 1912 'incognito'. It also made things much easier for their long-suffering London ambassador, who was now able to give a proper dinner party at the embassy for his august guests on the weekend of their arrival. 'Twenty-eight persons ... and we danced a little, including the Archduke, so that it wasn't stiff,' Mensdorff wrote.[31] On the afternoon of

Monday the seventeenth, they all went down by train to Windsor, where King George was waiting at the station, in morning coat and top hat, to greet them. (Some commentators in Vienna, looking for any 'evidence' of a slight against Sophie, made much of Queen Mary's absence on the platform; in fact, it was perfectly normal for the Queen to await her royal guests in the castle, especially if these were not themselves crowned heads.)

As we have seen, shooting was one of the main passions of Franz Ferdinand's life. Much had been heard in England of his prowess, and here he was to demonstrate it, in the hallowed grounds of Windsor, with the King of England as his host, and the Queen and his own wife among the interested spectators. There are some appallingly inaccurate accounts of the occasion in existence. This, for example, is how his private secretary, Nikitsch, sets the scene:

At our [Austrian] shoots ... we can reckon, given our plentiful reserves of wild birds, that ten guns will collect a day's bag of one and a half thousand pheasants on average. But in England, on the other hand, even with twenty guns, the day's results don't add up to much more than a hundred head ... Long before the shoot begins, they collect the pheasants together ... and then, on the day, release them one at a time behind a tall forest. The result [at Windsor] was that the birds, in order to fly away, had to clear the tree tops and then flew on ... over the heads of the guns more than thirty yards up.

Now the Archduke had only equipped himself with shotguns, which, with us, would be the obvious choice for a shoot like this. As a result, at the end of the first day, he had only brought down one single pheasant, and that probably due to a fluke. For that matter, even the best of the English shots present, who had had years of practice at this technique and were all using bullet-firing rifles, could only achieve a maximum of some thirty to forty birds killed at the best.

But on the second day Franz Ferdinand equipped himself with the necessary weapons and was able to show himself once more as an exceptional marksman, and hold his own with the English sportsmen.[32]

Almost every fact and figure given in that account is totally wrong. The King, who throughout his life kept a meticulous game book, records in his diary that on the first day, Tuesday the eighteenth, despite a strong wind and pouring rain in the afternoon, 'we got over a thousand pheasants and four hundred and fifty ducks'. On the Wednesday, when it was fine and bright, the bag was over seventeen hundred pheasants; on the Thursday, it was 'about a thousand'; and on Friday's concluding shoot, despite 'an awful day, blowing and pouring with rain, a regular deluge in the afternoon', they still managed to kill 'over eight hundred pheasants and nearly four hundred ducks'.[33] Moreover, the number of guns out on each day was not twenty but precisely five, including the Archduke and the King.

So much for Nikitsch's statistics. His statement that the wily English shot at driven game with rifles and that the Archduke only got going after he had followed their example is too ludicrous even to merit rebuttal – though, in fact, a rifle was the one weapon with which Franz Ferdinand might have astounded his hosts, even against birds on the wing. The truth was that the Archduke needed time to adjust himself to the rocketing pheasants of Windsor, which, because of the way the drives were sited, flew consistently higher and faster than anything he was accustomed to at home. The King put it quite fairly. 'The Archduke shot quite well,' he wrote of the first day, 'but he uses sixteen bores and light charges.'[34]

There was a little international politics as well as a lot of shooting during the Windsor visit. Other guests who came for part or all of the five days included Lords Lansdowne, Rosebery and Salisbury and the Foreign Secretary, Sir Edward Grey, with whom the thorny problem of Albania was discussed. But the crux of it all, from the Archduke's point of view, was to launch himself and Sophie, both as man and wife and as future Emperor and consort, at the most coveted of European levels, and to hope for a good impact there. In this they succeeded more than they were ever to realize during the brief time now remaining to them. The Archduke's messages of gratitude despatched after the visit in French tell little in themselves: thank you letters, especially between royalty, follow a formal pattern which stifles sentiment. Mensdorff, who went on with Franz Ferdinand and his wife to Welbeck Abbey for a week's 'superb shooting' with the Duke of Portland, gives a more spontaneously enthusiastic account of the '*Erzherzog sejour in Windsor*'. 'The Archduke,' he wrote, 'had a great personal success, but just as much the Duchess ... The contact with their Majesties was as warm and friendly as one could imagine and they were all *entzückt* [enchanted] with one another ...'[35]

The visit to Welbeck, where Mensdorff wrote those lines, marked another stage in the Archduke's rapidly growing enthusiasm for England and all things English. Windsor had been something of a test of nerves, however triumphantly mastered. At Welbeck he could afford to relax and be expansive. His host, the sixth Duke, was already a good friend, and, grand though the house was, Sophie could have no complexes about its hostess. Duchess Winifred was the only daughter of a Mr and Mrs Dallas-Yorke of Walmsgate. They were an admirable family, without doubt, but untitled – what, in Austrian terms, would be classed as *gut-bürgerlich*, and not a patch, therefore, on the aristocratic Choteks.

In his memoirs, the Duke gives the following account of Franz Ferdinand's shooting:

> On his first day out, the Archduke found some of the high-flying pheasants rather more than he could manage; but on the two following days he proved himself to be quite first-class, and certainly the equal of most of my friends. I am convinced that, given enough practice in this country, he would have been equal to any of our best shots.[36]

It sounded like a repeat performance of Windsor, though with much more gratifying results towards the end.*

The shooting at Welbeck also produced, among the excellent sport, an alarming incident which nearly cost the Archduke his life. There was deep snow on the ground, and after a rise of

---

* The daughter of Count van der Straten, one of the nine guns in the party, has preserved the game card her father was given. On the three days, 25–7 November, 6480 head were shot, mainly comprising 6332 pheasants.

pheasants one of the loaders tripped and fell, discharging both
barrels of the gun he was carrying. The shot whistled past within
a few feet of the host and his guest of honour. 'I have often
wondered,' pondered the Duke in later years, 'whether the Great
War might not have been averted, or at least postponed, had the
Archduke met his death then ...'[37]

But the short-range pellets missed, and the sport went on,
and everyone parted on the happiest terms when the week was
over with a return invitation to Konopischt being issued and
accepted. The Archduke had again displayed that charm and
human warmth which he was always capable of displaying when
at ease in a small private circle, and Sophie had been at her
serene best. They left for London (and home) leaving golden
reputations behind them.

The most impressive tributes to them arising from the
England visit – impressive because never intended for their eyes
– were two penned by Queen Mary in letters to her Aunt
Augusta, the Duchess of Mecklenburg-Strelitz. On 20 November, while the Windsor visit was still in progress, she wrote:

> The Archduke is most amiable, delighted with everything and
> very appreciative of the beauties of this place, which of course
> appeals to me. He is making an excellent impression and is
> enjoying the informality of the visit. The Duchess is very nice,
> agreeable, and quite easy to get on with, very tactful, which
> makes the position easier ...
>
> In the Waterloo Gallery the Archduke was delighted at
> seeing portraits of his two Great-Grandfathers, Kaiser Franz
> and Archduke Karl and we could scarcely drag him away. I
> was amused as I always feel the same when I see any of the
> 'ancestors'' pictures in a Palace abroad ...[38]

A week later, after her guests had departed, Queen Mary
wrote in particular about Sophie:

> The Archduke was formerly very anti-English but that is
> quite changed now, and *her* influence has been and is good,
> they say, in every way. All the people staying with us who had
> known *him* before said how much he had changed for the
> better and that he was most enthusiastic over his visit to us
> and to England ...[39]

A Windsor Castle menu for 19 November 1913, preserved among the Hohenberg private papers, shows a dinner which began with 'Consommé Britannia' and ended with 'Charlotte Viennoise'. Whether the Archduke's visit would have led him, when Emperor, to make a political reality out of that menu and break the fatal mould of European alliances with a pro-English approach is one of the countless speculative 'ifs' which surround his life and death. Morsey, his newly-acquired secretary, almost certainly shot over the target when he wrote of the Windsor visit, 'In 1913 the Archduke sought to play a mediating role between England and Germany, analogous to that which the Emperor William tried to take, also in vain, in Venice in 1914 between Italy and Austria.'[40]

On the other hand, the then Archduchess Zita, who saw a lot of her 'Onkel Franzi' during the last months of his life, was sure that the Archduke now wanted not merely a revival of the 'Three Emperors' League' to link Russia up again with Austria and Germany, but was also keen on having 'the greatest possible participation of England' in this new great powers' alignment.[41]

Just as the Emperor William's calculated wooing of Sophie on a Vienna railway platform ten years earlier had turned the Austro-German alliance into a close family affair for Franz Ferdinand, so the five days at Windsor with his wife had blown away, like a summer cloud, his mistrust of 'perfide Albion'. His wife probably never realized that their marriage was becoming such a political factor. All she was sure about, and very happy about, when they celebrated Christmas of 1913 was that this had been the year when she had finally 'arrived'. Even her former mistress, the ever-resentful Archduchess Isabella, had never been entertained by the King and Queen of England.

CHAPTER ELEVEN

———— ⌘ ————

Two Paths to Sarajevo

THE PROMISE OF the old year stretched forwards into the first months of the new. At the Vienna Court Ball in February 1914 – which, as things turned out, was the last ever to be held – the Emperor asked Sophie to come and sit next to him for a while. It was a gesture both trivial and momentous which reflected her newly-won prestige and further enhanced it.[1] The following month brought more dividends from that hard-won trip to England. The Portlands came to Konopischt, and plans were even made to receive King George and Queen Mary at Blühnbach, the Archduke's favourite autumn retreat, in September.[2] For the first time in France Joseph's reign (now well into its seventh decade), a real family link seemed to be developing between the Catholic court of Vienna and the Protestant court of St James.

There was further evidence too of the Archduke's already close relationship with that other powerful Protestant monarch, the Emperor William. The German ruler had recently added to his agreeable annual travel routine a cruise in late March to Corfu; and, in 1914, he decided to combine the journey with an intensive exercise in inter-allied diplomacy. In particular, he was at pains to consolidate the somewhat shaky position of both Rumania and Italy inside the Central Powers' Alliance. In both cases that meant securing greater goodwill towards these two uncertain partners on the part of Austria-Hungary. On his way from Berlin to Venice, he had stopped off in Vienna, where he secured from Count Tisza, the strong and statesmanlike figure who was now Prime Minister of Hungary, promises of better treatment for the large Rumanian minority living in the Hungarian half of the Dual Monarchy. If carried out, such pledges would have gone a long way towards keeping a resentful Rumania out of Russia's clutches.

In Venice, the German Emperor met with King Viktor Emmanuel III and put into operation the first stage of a scheme designed to bring the Italian monarch and the anti-Italian Franz Ferdinand together at last. He invited the King to attend the German army manoeuvres that autumn, having already decided to ask the Archduke as well. Then the Emperor boarded the royal yacht *Hohenzollern* and, with a naval escort massive enough to match that substantial vessel, set sail across the bay for the lovely seaside castle of Miramare, just outside Trieste. Here, on 27 March, the Archduke and his family were awaiting him.

Franz Ferdinand had dressed for the occasion as a Grand Admiral of the German navy, an attire in which he looked and felt somewhat awkward – as indeed did most Austrians when obliged to exchange their own comfortable naval or military garb for the uniforms of their principal ally. 'It doesn't matter,' he assured one of his aides as they prepared for the arrival of the German flotilla, 'the German Emperor is always dressed up himself in the worst possible taste.'[3] The Archduke must have been in very good spirits to allow such banter – even if affectionately meant – to cross his lips, and the talks at Miramare did nothing to dissipate that mood.[4]

Franz Ferdinand, as expected, had his reservations both over Hungarian assurances concerning their Rumanian subjects and over Italy's worth and loyalty to the common alliance. But when William II spoke of the need for a stronger centralist policy within the Dual Monarchy, based on its German-speaking core, he was talking the Archduke's language. The compliments distributed all round by the Emperor when he inspected the dreadnought *Viribus Unitis* – pride of the Austrian navy and apple of Franz Ferdinand's eye – ended the one-day visit on a note as radiant as Miramare's spring sunshine.

But the first shadow had just been cast in a very different

setting. On this same date, two Bosnian-Serb students, sitting on
a park bench next to the present-day Palace Hotel in Belgrade,
shook hands on a solemn pledge to kill the heir to the Austrian
throne in Sarajevo.[5] Their names were Gavrilo Princip and
Nedeljko Cabrinović, and though many young Slavs had dreamt
of such an exploit before them, and though other recruits soon
joined their own band of conspirators, these two were the only
ones who, when the test came, matched their fiery words with
deeds.

The path which led to that park bench was long and dark. It
began, for all South Slavs, with the legend of Kosovo, on the day
– 28 June 1389 – which had been followed by the long night of
Turkish rule. Sultan Murad and his Ottoman army had crushed
the Serbian forces of Prince Lazar, but though both commanders died on the battlefield only the Serb is known to have died in
battle. The Sultan was said to have met his end at the hands of
one of Prince Lazar's nobles, Milos Obilić, who somehow
managed to penetrate the Turkish lines and stab Murad to death
in his own tent. 28 June was St Vitus's Day, or Vidov-Dan, and
throughout the five centuries of corrupt and oppressive rule
which followed, the legend of what happened on that day,
commemorated in countless folklore poems and songs, became a
symbol of all Serbian struggles for freedom.

Assassination thus stood at the cradle of Serb nationalism
and was never to move far away from it. When, in 1908, Austria-
Hungary converted its military occupation of Bosnia and
Herzegovina into sovereign possession, the daggers were sharp-
ened against the Habsburgs and their servants. As we have seen,
the creation of the Serbian *Narodna Obrana* or National Defence
dates almost from the hour of the Austrian annexation. More
violent and more secret organizations were soon to sprout up
underneath its shade.

Any South Slav hothead could, by now, draw much
additional comfort and inspiration from the fact that assassinations – especially of royalty and heads of states – were fast
becoming the stock-in-trade of political extremists. In 1881, both
Tsar Alexander II and President Garfield of the United States

had been murdered. A year later, a plot was uncovered to assassinate the Emperor Franz Joseph in Trieste. The monarch had escaped, only slightly wounded, from one murder attempt on the ramparts of Vienna thirty years before, and was to survive many later conspiracies which were either abandoned by the plotters or discovered in time by the police. In 1898, his wife, the Empress Elisabeth, had fallen under the dagger of the Italian anarchist on the shores of Lake Geneva. Two years after that, Europe was shaken by another regicide when King Umberto of Italy – for long an assassin's target – was murdered at Monza. And, though it was hardly an episode the Serbs would boast about (though many would not have felt exactly shamed by it) the bloodiest example of all royal killings – worse even than the murder of the King and Crown Prince of Portugal five years later – was one which had been enacted in their own capital.

On the night of 11 June 1903, the ancient and lethal feud between the Obrenović and Karageorgovich families for the crown of Serbia was finally settled in favour of the latter. The unpopular King Alexander and his even more detested wife Draga (a humble engineer's widow who became a corrupt and scheming virago once she reached the steps of the throne) met a spectacularly gruesome end which sent a shudder through all the courts of the continent. A group of twenty-eight 'patriotic' officers surrounded the Royal Palace in Belgrade with their military units, forced an entrance by dynamiting the doors, and, after two hours of black comedy hide and seek through the salons and corridors, found the King and Queen hiding in a clothes closet, she attired only in a silk petticoat, white stays and one yellow stocking. The assassins first emptied their revolvers into the luckless couple, then hacked their bodies about with sabres and ended by hurling the mutilated corpses out into the garden through the palace windows. For good measure, the assassins also shot down the Queen's brothers (one of whom she was scheming to make heir to the throne) and finished off a long night's work by killing several ministers. Among the leading conspirators – severely wounded by the palace guards early on in this somewhat chaotic enterprise – was a young army captain,

Dragutin Dimitrijević. Unhappily for Franz Ferdinand, he became far more practised in his trade in the decade ahead.*

Such, then, was the hothouse atmosphere of intrigue and violence which enveloped the radical students of 1914 as they sat for hours at the little marble-topped tables of their Belgrade *Kafanas*, ordering one cup of coffee and then endless glasses of water, and all the while brooding over the Habsburg 'tyranny' in the annexed provinces and how best to shake it off. These cafés served as social and political clubs, and it was to one of them, the 'Golden Sturgeon', that at Easter time the letter addressed to Cabrinović arrived which was to set the cataclysm in motion. It had been posted to him by a Bosnian friend from Zenica (in a successful attempt to avoid Austrian police censorship) and contained simply a newspaper cutting announcing the forthcoming visit of the Archduke Franz Ferdinand to Sarajevo to attend the summer manoeuvres. No message was enclosed beyond the one word 'Greetings', and none was needed.

Cabrinović, a swarthy nineteen-year-old who sported a toothbrush moustache to suggest manhood, was a born drifter. He had, however, been drifting steadily in one direction for the previous five years – ever closer to anarchism. A native of Sarajevo, where his father, rumoured to be an informer for the Austrian police, kept a seedy café, he had fallen foul of the authorities several times for printing subversive pamphlets and arranging protest strikes during the Balkan Wars of 1912–13. He had no clear-cut political ideas beyond a vague dream of restoring the great medieval Serbian kingdom of King Dusan, a dream haunted by a fierce hatred of all things Habsburg and especially, it seems, of the heir to the Austrian throne in person. Indeed, in October of 1913, when his wanderings had taken him for a while to the Adriatic resort of Abbazia, he had already declared his intention of one day assassinating the Archduke.[6] He was the classic psychological product of that old Obilić legend as perpetuated among the South Slavs by the *Goslars* or

---

*Even in 1903, the Belgrade regicide had uncomfortable undertones for the Archduke. The scandalized court in Vienna was convinced that King Alexander's unsuitable marriage was the real reason for his death.

popular ballad singers – light in argument but very strong on passion, mindless yet single-minded.

Princip, to whom Cabrinović showed the letter when the two met for lunch at another favourite café haunt of Belgrade students, the 'Garland of Acorns', was only six months older than his friend but was already far more composed and mature. He was one of nine children of a peasant family who had been settled for centuries in the rocky and isolated valley of Grahavo Polje in Western Bosnia. Their original name – fittingly enough for the only Princip ever to achieve immortality – had been 'Ceka', or 'he who waits in ambush'. Gavrilo's father, Petar, was respected both as a pious man who never missed a church festival and as a conscientious servant of the Austrian empire who never failed in his duties as the local postman, carrying up to sixty pounds of mail around on his back when the winter snow blocked the valley for his horse-wagon. Gavrilo inherited none of his father's piety (indeed, he openly confessed to atheism) but had all his father's stolid dedication – though directed to destroying the Habsburgs, not serving them.

The turning-point in his life, and in Cabrinović's, came amidst the upheavals of the Balkan wars. At the beginning of 1912, Princip, then at school in Sarajevo, was expelled for taking part in violent anti-Austrian demonstrations in the city. He set off on foot for Belgrade where, in the coffee house, he made contact with the *Narodna Obrana* movement. Through them, he volunteered for service with the *Comitadjis*, those fanatical bands of irregulars who had been operating against the Turkish army long before Serbia formally went to war with the Ottoman Empire. His fate was to end up, close to the Turkish border, before one Major Vojislav Tankosić who was busy grouping his *Comitadji* forces for battle. Tankosić was a fierce disciplinarian, who chose only the pick of Serbian youth and then drove them to the limit in training (he was said to have ordered some of his volunteers to dive forty-five feet off a railway bridge into the swirling River Sava, just to test their obedience). He took one look at this slightly built seventeen-year-old with the deceptively gentle blue eyes and waved him impatiently away. Seething with humiliation, Princip trekked back to Belgrade. Not for him the military glory of avenging the shame of Kossovo by marching against the Turks, wearing the crossed bandoliers and the skull and crossbones badges of the *Comitadjis*. All that was left to prove himself their equal was to find personal glory in some private act of revenge. The handshake on the park-bench seemed predestined.

It had been preceded by fifteen months of confused plotting, conducted mainly in Belgrade and Sarajevo but ranging as far afield as Toulouse in southern France, where at least one secret meeting of the conspirators was held – though the exact date and the names of those attending are both in dispute. Out of it all two things had crystallized by the beginning of 1914: the choice of Franz Ferdinand as the target and the emergence of a trusted core of plotters from whom the actual assassins would be selected. Thus, when the two conspirators on the park bench decided that they needed to co-opt a third, their choice immediately fell upon Trifko Grabez, Princip's roommate in Belgrade.

Grabez was yet another student refugee from Bosnia, though he had left for somewhat different reasons: in the autumn term of 1912, he had punched Professor Trubelka, his teacher at Tuzla High School, in the face, and was expelled and given fourteen days in prison for the offence. On his arrival in Belgrade, Grabez seems to have had no political inclinations to go with his violent temper; but, over the months, Princip supplied these for him, and the two had indeed been debating all manner of murder plots long before the fateful Easter of 1914. Though a second *troika* of young assassins* was to join them as a support group in Sarajevo, it is with these three – Princip, Cabrinović and Grabez – that we are mainly concerned.

The trio had decided exactly whom they wanted to kill, and roughly when and where. The problem now facing the young

---

* Vaso Cubrilović, Cvijetko Popović and Muhamed Mehmedbasić. The last-named was the son of a prosperous Turkish smallholder in Herzegovina who, despite his Moslem background, had become a fanatical supporter of 'Greater Serbia'. Most of the 612,000 Mohammedans in the annexed provinces tended to support the Austrians.

desperadoes was how to get hold of the necessary instruments of murder and how to be trained to use them. The only organization they and their fellow conspirators were all linked up with, *Mlada Bosna*, or Bosnian Youth, could not help them here. This was essentially a cult movement which had sprung up at the start of the twentieth century among young students, school-teachers, apprentices and the like, with Mazzini, the Italian revolutionary, as its hero and the writings of Russian anarchists, such as Kropotkin, as its spiritual fodder. True, one of the movement's founders, Bogdan Zerajić, had proved himself capable of fiery deeds as well as fiery words, though the deeds were enacted in that glorious muddle which seems inseparable from the South Slav tradition. Zerajić originally intended to kill Emperor Franz Joseph when the Austrian monarch visited Mostar, the Herzegovinian capital, in June 1910, two years after the annexation. But he changed his mind for no apparent reason at the last minute, when his august quarry was only a few paces away from him, and, returning to Sarajevo, marked down the Austrian Governor, General Varesanin, as his victim instead. Even this went wrong. On 15 June 1910, after firing five times at the General, Zerajić then blew out his own brains with the sixth bullet, in the quite mistaken belief that his prey was dead. In fact the only shot which found its mark was the one with which he killed himself. The irrational switch of targets, the grim farce of his unnecessary suicide, the botched murder attempt itself – all this made Zerajić more and not less of a sacred model for his followers, as his story reflected so well those premonitions of doom and martyrdom which darkened all their dreams of glory. But there was one vital respect in which the Belgrade trio of would-be assassins fell short of their hero: they did not possess even one bullet between them, let alone anything to fire it with. It was this search for weapons which quickly sucked them into a vortex from which there was no escape, even had they wished it.

The trio turned initially to yet another of the Bosnian emigrés kicking his heels in the Belgrade coffee houses, one Milan Ciganović, who was a much admired figure among the Young Bosnian café habitués of the capital. Ciganović had succeeded where Princip had ignominiously failed, by enlisting as a *Comitadji* fighter in 1912 and actually winning a gold medal for bravery in skirmishes with the Turks. He had other souvenirs from those Balkan wars too: a collection of primitive bombs which he kept in a wooden chest at the lodging house where Princip also lived. This was clearly the man to provide the weapons and, after a few days delay, Ciganović duly obliged. He had spoken on their behalf, he told them, to an unnamed *gospodin* (or gentleman) and six bombs (better than those in his own hoard) as well as four revolvers would be duly provided for the murder plot. They would also be given use of the Serbian underground travel route by which good anti-Habsburg patriots were smuggled in and out of Bosnia across a frontier closely guarded by the Austrian army and police.

Without at first knowing it – and perhaps never realizing it to the full – the three students had now become pawns in the hands of the really dangerous terrorists of Belgrade. The *gospodin* who had been consulted was Major Tankosić, the Serbian army officer who had rejected Princip for his élite band of young guerillas two years before. And the man whom Tankosić had had to approach in turn was none other than Dragutin Dimitrijević, the regicide of 1903, now a staff colonel and head of the Serbian military intelligence department. Both men were leading figures in the Serbian secret society 'Union or Death', commonly known as the 'Black Hand', which had been formed in 1911 out of impatience with the feebleness of the existing Greater Serbia movement.

The 'Black Hand' was like something straight off the stage of a Grand Guignol theatre. Its members – mostly regular officers, civil servants, university professors, legal officials and the like, and Serbs one and all – were inducted in a darkened room where, over a crucifix, a dagger and a revolver, they swore their readiness to make any sacrifice, 'by the Sun that warms me, by the Earth that nourishes me, by the blood of my ancestors, on my honour and on my life'. Revolutionary activity to create a Greater Serbia by any means 'in all lands inhabited by the Serbs' was the organization's prime aim.[7]

Whether the authors of all these theatricals had ever got down themselves to anything practical in the three years of their society's existence is a moot point. What is clear is that in April 1914 they had found three young fanatics to do their work for them. The burly Colonel Dimitrijević (or 'Apis' as he was nicknamed, after the Egyptian word for a bull) kept in the background throughout. But Major Tankosić did receive one member of the trio once the preparations were complete, just to assure himself – as with those volunteers he had ordered to leap off a railway bridge – that they were really up to the mark. There was, after all, much more to this operation than a ducking in the River Sava.

Princip, still smarting under his humiliation on the Turkish border two years before, refused to see the Major himself and sent Grabez along instead.[8] Yet, ironically, it was the rejected volunteer of 1912 who was now by far the most promising candidate. It was not simply that Princip had showed himself the best marksman of the three at the target practice organized by Ciganović in Belgrade's Kosutnjak park (six hits out of ten shots aimed at an oak tree from two hundred paces); he was also psychologically the more impressive of the two, for his quiet, almost gentle earnestness carried much more conviction as a potential assassin than the moodiness and voluble bragging of the others.

After nearly two months of training and planning, they were ready. They had money for the dangerous journey and cyanide capsules to break and swallow after the deed was done. The murder weapons (handed over in yet another Belgrade café) they carried on their bodies, the Browning revolvers and ammunition stuffed into their pockets and the six bombs tied, two to each man, around their waists. On the morning of 28 May they left Belgrade by steamer, heading upstream along the Sava. Their first destination was Sabac, a small town some fifty miles due west of the capital, where the river turns abruptly north. Here, according to a plan Grabez had worked out in Belgrade with Major Tankosić's own men, they were to leave the boat and head for the Bosnian border on foot.

In this last week of May, while the Archduke's assassins were setting out on their journey to kill him, his loyal subjects in Sarajevo were planning, down to the last detail, how to make his visit a smooth success. On 21 May, for example, his office in the Belvedere received the following telegraphic enquiry: 'Request to be informed the weight of His Imperial Highness, also length of stirrups he uses and whether saddle and bridle will be sent on here from Vienna.'[9] The heir to the throne would need horses for the manoeuvres, and everything had to be arranged for his maximum comfort.

That telegram (promptly answered the next day with the information that, for example, the Archduke weighed exactly $83\frac{1}{2}$ kilos) was among the last finishing touches to a project that had been many months in the making. The 1914 summer manoeuvres in Bosnia, with Franz Ferdinand in attendance, are mentioned as far back as September 1913 when General Conrad, already informed by the Archduke of the plan, discussed arrangements briefly with General Potiorek, the Governor and Military Commander in Sarajevo, who was visiting Vienna.[10] As Inspector-General of the empire's armed forces, the Archduke was expected to attend major manoeuvres; indeed, he would normally have insisted on being present. In this case, there was an additional reason to look forward to the event. Sophie, now 'cleared' by the Emperor to be accorded full honours at military ceremonials, was to come with him on this journey to the Monarchy's most sensitive provinces.

Yet, as the summer approached, Franz Ferdinand was filled with an unaccountable reluctance to go. To some extent this might be explained by the near-certainty of the anti-Habsburg political demonstrations that awaited him in the newly-annexed territories. Moreover, the subversive literature recently circulated in Bosnia-Herzegovina had included some highly offensive personal invective. One series of pamphlets distributed in the Orthodox parishes of the countryside described poor Sophie, for example, as 'a monstrous Bohemian whore' who had to be killed off. It ended, 'Down with the Este dog and the filthy Bohemian sow!'[11] Whether he ever knew about that particular onslaught against his beloved wife or not, the Archduke can have been under no illusions that they would not be universally welcomed in the two provinces. Curiously enough, the possibility of a hostile reception weighed heavier than the menace of physical danger. His dynasty had long since come to terms with assassination threats. Sullen crowds were always intolerable.

Then there was the matter of Franz Ferdinand's health. Certain areas which lay along his proposed route were known to be infested with malaria. Sarajevo, like its twin capital of Mostar, lies in a mountain bowl which becomes oppressively humid and hot in midsummer. The Archduke, who was suffering more and more from asthma as the years went by, was apprehensive on this score too. When the day for his scheduled departure drew near, he decided to tackle the Emperor in person and try to have the trip cancelled altogether. His niece, the then Archduchess Zita, cannot recall the exact date of this fateful audience* but remembers hearing what had happened:

> The Archduke used the excuse of the great heat in Bosnia as a reason for getting out of attending the manoeuvres. Normally, he always prevailed with the old Emperor when deciding his travels, even on such important political matters as going to Rome or not. But on this occasion, and over such a relatively routine trip, he failed. While leaving the final decision to him, the Emperor made it quite clear that he desired the Archduke to go; such a wish, especially on a military matter, amounted to an order. Looking back, it was amazing that this Sarajevo journey should have been the one occasion when he didn't get his own way.[12]

That was, in fact, but one link in the long chain of chance, coincidence and mishap which was eventually to bring Gavrilo Princip and Franz Ferdinand face to face.

The eight days and nights which it took the three plotters to reach Sarajevo were filled with other fortuitous happenings and lucky escapes – any one of which incidents, had it gone the other

---

* The only audience between royal uncle and nephew actually reported during this period was on 7 June 1914, when the Emperor received the Archduke for forty-five minutes from 7.45 to 8.30 a.m.

way, could have prevented the murder. Austrian spies were active, even in Serbia, and any Serbian official not in the terrorist underground would have arrested the trio on sight had their arrival been discovered. Once across the closely-watched frontier and inside Bosnia, they would feel the full weight of Austrian police pressure. It was all a question of how efficient the secret 'tunnel' would turn out to be.

The omens were reassuring. At Sabac, Princip sought out his first prearranged contact, Captain Rade Popović, a Serbian army officer with a special intelligence assignment in the border area, and who worked, therefore, directly under 'Apis' in Belgrade. Once he had tracked him down (the captain was enjoying a game of cards at the 'Amerika' café), Princip handed him a card bearing simply the initials M.C. The captain nodded; they were the initials of Melan Ciganović, who had acted as the · go-between in Belgrade, and served in Sabac as a password.*

After some discussion about possible routes it was decided to make the crossing into Bosnia at the town of Loznica, forty miles to the south-west, where the River Drina formed the frontier. The captain gave them a note to his colleague there – 'Take care of these men and get them across wherever you think best' – and even arranged for reduced fares on the short train journey between the two towns. This was achieved by turning the trio into bogus customs officials, with Princip as the 'sergeant-in-charge'. The Apis 'tunnel' seemed to be working like a dream and the relieved trio spent the night at a local hotel. Their weapons and ammunition they hid in a stove, which, they reasoned, was the one place which would never be disturbed at midsummer.

At Loznica there was some delay as their new guide, Captain Jovan Prvanović, wanted to confer with his frontier customs sergeants before picking the safest route. To avoid suspicion, the three students went off to the nearby spa of Koviljaca for the day, where they behaved like ordinary holidaymakers. Cabrinović,

---

* The frontier captain had just returned from a visit to Belgrade, where he had doubtless been briefed personally by Major Tankosić about the mission.

who had alarmed his companions once already by gossiping with a Serbian gendarme on the steamer, now frightened them out of their lives. He ran into a former *Comitadji* comrade from the Balkan Wars who spotted his bombs and asked him what they were for. Only with difficulty did they drag their garrulous comrade away in time.

Now, at Koviljaca, there was more trouble over the postcards they decided to send. Princip used his one message as a further exercise in deception, writing to a cousin in Belgrade that he was on his way to a monastery to prepare for an examination. But Cabrinović could not resist some final flourishes of vainglory. He sent off half a dozen cards to various men and women friends in Trieste, Sarajevo and other Austrian cities, plastering some of them with heroic lines from Serbian folk-poems. Clearly, his comrades decided, they would be safer without this irrepressible chatterbox, so, when they returned that evening to Losnica, it was arranged that the trio should split up. A somewhat offended Cabrinović was persuaded to hand over his weapons to the others and then, equipped with a false pass, was sent forward on his own to be smuggled across the frontier by the 'tunnel' operators. He was to make straight for Tuzla, a town some fifty miles inside Bosnia, where his comrades would join him.

The journey which took Princip and Grabez across the border was much more complicated and hazardous. The whole of 31 May they spent on Isakovica Ada, a tiny willow-strewn island in the middle of the Drina River. Sergeant Gribić, the Serbian customs sergeant in charge of this part of their journey, used the island, which belonged to Serbia, as an intelligence-gathering centre, and for this purpose had opened up a cut-price plum-brandy bar to lure the peasants across from the Bosnian bank. Two of these were now allotted to the students to smuggle them safely onto Bosnian soil. As Princip and Grabez were merrily indulging in revolver practice when their guides arrived on the island, they had to be confided in, if only to the extent of being told that 'something great' was afoot.

The cat was let completely out of the bag when on 2 June,

'And then our children! They are my whole pride and joy. I sit with them all day long in amazement that I can love them so much.'

The German Emperor William on one of his many shooting visits to Konopischt (castle in background).

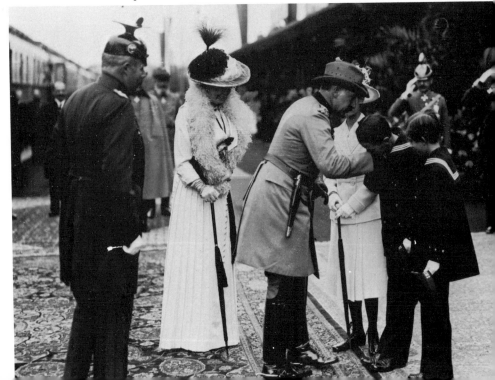

The German Emperor being greeted by the Archduke's children on his last visit to Konopischt, 12-13 June 1914. A fortnight later the fond parents (left) were dead.

Zur Nachricht.

Die Telegramme müssen deutlich geschrieben sein und in der Adresse alle jene Angaben enthalten, welche nötig sind, um den Adressaten schnell und sicher auffinden zu können. Wenn der Wohnort desselben keine Haupt- oder bedeutendere Stadt ist, so muß in der Adresse auch das Land, in welchem dieser Ort liegt, angeführt werden.

Dem Sprachgebrauche zuwiderlaufende Zusammenziehungen sind unstatthaft.

Für Nachteile, welche durch Verlust, Verstümmelung oder Verspätung der Depeschen entstehen können, übernimmt die Telegraphenverwaltung keine wie immer geartete Verantwortlichkeit.

Telegramm. Brzojavka.

TELEGRAMM

Raum
zum
Aufkleben der Marken.

Prinzessin Sophie Hohenberg
Schloss Chlumetz

Glücklich in Ilidža angekommen. Habe Mami
sehr wohl gefunden. Hier ist es sehr schön und
angenehm. Wir haben eine herrliche Wohnung. Wetter
sehr angenehme. Gute Nacht, umarme Dich
und die Geschwister innigst
Papi

The last message the Archduke sent his thirteen-year-old daughter from Sarajevo.
It ends: 'I embrace you and your brothers most tenderly.'

The Archduke and Sophie walking down the steps of Sarajevo Town Hall minutes
before their assassination on 28 June 1914.

The sarcophagi of Franz Ferdinand and Sophie in the crypt of the family castle at Artstetten: 'A cheerful place where I can hear the birds sing.'

Artstetten Castle, just north of the Danube. It is still in the family today and now houses a permanent 'Franz Ferdinand Museum'.

having evaded the Austrian frontier guards, the party of four reached their next contact at a village called Priboj, roughly halfway to the Tuzla rendezvous. To get there from the border they had marched, virtually non-stop, for twenty-one hours through forests and ploughed fields, and arrived exhausted with the weight of weapons and soaked to the skin by an overnight thunderstorm. Perhaps it was this exhaustion which caused Princip to drop his guard, for the only time.

The 'tunnel' operator at Priboj was the village schoolteacher, Veljko Cubrilović. He took one look at the heavy sack into which the lethal cargo had now been stowed and put the disconcerting question, 'Tell me, are these weapons for the visit of the Heir-Apparent?'[13] Princip hesitated a moment and then replied, 'Yes, they are. We are going to Sarajevo to assassinate him.' Cubrilović was so excited that he confided the great secret to two village peasants in whose house they all rested and ate supper that night. They proved trustworthy, and were indeed to end on the Austrian gallows for keeping their mouths shut. But things at Priboj could so easily have gone the other way.

The contact man at Tuzla, Misko Jovanović, was a figure of some local importance – an Orthodox Church Council member, a director of the Serbian bank and the owner of the town's first cinema. It was an imposing façade behind which to conduct subversive activities. But even his aplomb was disturbed when the two guides who had shepherded the students all the way from the river Drina – and who had now gone into Tuzla ahead of them – woke him up early in the morning and deposited six bombs and four revolvers on his kitchen table.

Princip, whom he met a few hours later in the town reading-room, was worried about taking the weapons on the final stage of the journey and begged Jovanović to hide them until he could arrange for their collection. The cinema proprietor agreed – a decision which was to lead him also to the gallows – and a code-sign was arranged. Whoever came to Tuzla to collect the weapons would identify himself by producing a packet of 'Stephanie' cigarettes. That settled, Princip and Grabez met up in a café with Cabrinović (who had arrived in Tuzla two days before) and the three then boarded the night train for Sarajevo, travelling in separate compartments.

It was just as well that they had shed their weapons. Cabrinović, who seemed to attract danger as surely as a steel mast draws lightning, found himself sitting next to a Bosnian police agent who knew his father. As things turned out, the agent's suspicions were not aroused, although they talked at length about the impending royal visit. Indeed, it was the police detective who first revealed to Cabrinović the exact date, 28 June, of the Archduke's arrival in Sarajevo. Unlike those other remiss Bosnian subjects of the Emperor, the police agent did not have to face the gallows afterwards. But he must have had some very awkward explaining to do.

On 4 June 1914, therefore, all three assassins were safely in Sarajevo, where each took up different lodgings and tried to live as normal and inconspicuous a life as possible during the waiting weeks ahead. Princip went to stay with the mother of a close friend and fellow-conspirator, Danilo Ilić. Ilić, a twenty-four-year-old native of Sarajevo, had been drawn into the whirlpool of Bosnian terrorism along a familiar life-path. First, a poverty-stricken childhood as the son of a cobbler who had died before the boy entered school; then, as no steady work could be found once school was over, an aimless odd-job existence ranging from railway porter to *souffleur* with a wandering circus; next, a year or two as a schoolteacher, after securing a state grant for the training course; then a volunteer for the *Comitadjis* in the Balkan Wars; and finally, the attempt to project all that nationalist fervour into peacetime by writing freelance articles for radical newspapers and translating the works of Russian anarchists.

Ilić had known Princip for five years and had been involved in those chaotic months of plotting which preceded Princip's clear-cut decision to murder the Archduke at Sarajevo. He was in no way responsible for that decision as pro-Serbian apologists (anxious to transfer the blame for the deed from Belgrade) tried to make out in later years. Indeed, he had just heard about it in a letter from Princip himself. But, though he was to have second thoughts about the wisdom of the assassination as the day drew near, it was Ilić who, from now on, supervised all the local preparations. It was he, for example, who, at Princip's suggestion, recruited the second *troika* of assassins as reinforcements or stand-bys for the main group. And it was Ilić who carried out the most vital task of all – collecting the murder weapons from Tuzla.

This tricky operation was yet another example of how luck stayed on the conspirators' side and how easily the plot could have blown up in their faces. Ilić arrived in Tuzla on 14 June and identified himself to Jovanović, the keeper of the weapons, in the agreed manner, by producing a packet of 'Stephanie' cigarettes. The cinema proprietor had already packed the bombs and revolvers into a black sugar box wrapped round with newspapers and tied up with string. They decided to make the hand-over not there and then at Tuzla but the next day in the waiting room of the railway junction at Doboj, which is a few stops to the west on the Sarajevo line. This arrangement led to a muddle which would have been hilarious had not the peace of the world hung on the outcome. Jovanović got to Doboj on time with the early morning train but Ilić overslept and had to catch the next connection. Jovanović, not finding his man in the waiting room, simply dumped the lethal sugar box there and left it, covered by his raincoat, while he went to search. When he returned, still without Ilić, the box – which could so easily have been stolen, taken by mistake or knocked over and broken open – was still there, so he removed it next to a tailor's shop. Here, at last, the two conspirators met up and the transfer was made.

By the next day, 15 June, Ilić had brought the sugar box, without further problem, to his mother's house in Sarajevo, where its contents were unpacked and stowed away in a small wooden chest under Princip's bed. The underground tunnel of Colonel Apis – operated all along the route, be it noted, by Serbian army officers or customs officials and their agents – had thus delivered its three most important passengers with their baggage safely to their destination. But there had been at least half a dozen moments when that tunnel might easily have caved in over their heads.

While the assassins were collecting the murder weapons down in Bosnia, at the other end of the empire, in Bohemia, the victim was staging what was to be his *grande finale* as squire of his beloved Konopischt. His roses were the main reason why this particular date had been picked. He had owned the castle for nearly thirty years and for twenty of those he had kept an army of men and a bevy of experts hard at it to produce perfection in the gardens. Now, there seemed nothing more that knowledge and labour could do. The creation was finished, ready to be admired by the world at large; and so the Archduke decided to break with all precedent and allow the public into the park for two days, from 15 to 17 June. Konopischt was to have what later generations of landowners would have called its first 'open day'. (It was a great success, with special trains bringing thousands of curious sightseers, dolled out in their best summer finery, to the tiny local station of Beneschau and with no fewer than five hundred gendarmes drafted into the castle grounds to make sure that they behaved themselves.)

Before that, however, the Archduke wanted the castle very much to himself to receive the Emperor William. Because this Konopischt meeting of 12 to 13 June, the last between the two men, came within a fortnight of the Sarajevo murders and the catastrophe which followed, a great web of fantasy was spun around it, mainly to serve the purposes of political propaganda. The Serbs tried to shake some of Franz Ferdinand's blood off their hands by claiming that, walking his carpet of roses, he had plotted war against them with the German ruler. And in 1916, when that war was in mid-course, Henry Wickham Steed of the *Times*, one of England's most influential pan-Slav champions, produced his own, far more dramatic version of the 'Pact of Konopischt'.

According to Steed, the Emperor William II had not only outlined a scheme to provoke war and secure a lightning victory against France and Russia (with England staying neutral); he had also unfolded a master-plan for the Europe which would follow. The Austrian lands, including Trieste, would be incorporated as a separate state into the Hohenzollern empire, though ruled over by an Austrian archduke. In return, Franz Ferdinand himself was to be made sovereign of an enlarged Poland, stretching from the Baltic to the Black Sea, which would pass to Max, his elder son, after his death. The younger son, Ernst, would be given an equally brilliant inheritance as King of a third new realm, to be made up of Hungary, Bohemia, Serbia, Dalmatia and even Salonika on the Aegean.[14] This legend of Emperor and Archduke distributing new crowns amidst the rose-bushes was repeated, thanks to the serious reputation of its creator, by many later writers, especially in France. It has been systematically demolished already.* However, as it traduces the Archduke in the last political act of his life, and as new evidence to reject the fairytale is available, there is no harm in elaborating on the demolition work.

One of the things which gave the legend credibility was the unusual nature of the Emperor's suite. He had with him Baron von Treutler, the same official who had accompanied him on previous travels such as the 1913 trip to Italy and Miramare, and whose presence therefore meant that current diplomatic questions would again be under review. But also in the suite was Grand Admiral Alfred von Tirpitz, the creator of the powerful German navy, whose appearance caused much head-scratching even at the time. 'The ravishing aroma which rises out of the flowerbeds has suddenly taken on the smell of gunpowder,' was how Vienna's leading paper put it in an editorial.[15] Had a war council really been intended, the Emperor would surely have brought along a general, and probably his Chief-of-Staff, von Moltke, instead of an unaccompanied admiral.

Still, what *was* Tirpitz doing at Konopischt? The Archduke's secretary, Baron von Morsey, who helped prepare the visit, gives the answer. It was not merely that Franz Ferdinand, as a naval enthusiast, was curious to meet the famous Tirpitz, whom he did not know. Tirpitz was himself equally curious to see Konopischt. The Admiral shared another passion with the Archduke. He was also a great gardener, and with a

* Notably by Fay, Vol. II, pp. 37–41.

special interest in roses.[16] To make sure that he was not disappointed, Herr Umlauft, the supervisor of the gardens (his name appropriately translates into 'running around'), had helped nature along by sprinkling the flowerbeds for hours on end with lukewarm water.

Punctually at 9 a.m. on 12 June, the imperial train pulled into Beneschau, where the Archduke, clad as an officer of the 10th Prussian Uhlans, was waiting with his whole family to greet the Emperor. The Emperor was clearly in high spirits. 'Well, children, here we are again,' he called out as the train stopped. His two smooth-haired dachshunds, 'Wadl' and 'Hexl', put a temporary damper on this jovial mood when they reached the park. Once out of the car they shot off on a private hunt of their own, to return soon afterwards proudly lugging a dead pheasant between them. Unfortunately, it was a golden pheasant, reared very much for show and not for shooting. Indeed, it was the only one the Archduke possessed and the only game bird in Konopischt which had nothing to fear from him. Ironically, the Emperor was dressed in his self-designed hunting uniform: long green jacket, high leather boots with spurs and the Order of St Hubert dangling from his neck.

As for the talks, the Emperor and Archduke, according to Morsey, had only one hour alone. (This does not count, of course, their frequent excursions together by car.) The secretary's description of the general discussions accords closely with the factual account given by von Treutler in his official reports back to Berlin, reports which were written before any crisis, let alone war, had broken out. The main topics were those which had already preoccupied the two royal friends at Miramare, namely the various strains on their four-power alliance. Could Italy be relied upon? Was Hungary a pillar of strength or a source of weakness? What sort of a man was Tisza, her present Prime Minister? Could he be persuaded to adopt more liberal policies towards his large Rumanian minority in Transylvania, ensuring the loyalty of Rumania herself, the fourth and most restive member of the alliance? And, as at Miramare, the Emperor and the Archduke, so far from agreeing to carve up Europe afresh, had to agree to differ over most of these questions which they could not resolve in their own part of the continent.

As usual when Franz Ferdinand was politicizing, Hungary occupied the centre of the stage. That country, he assured the Emperor, was nothing better than the playground of a few families. 'The name of the man at the top is immaterial. Every Hungarian strives more or less openly to gain advantages for his country – at the expense of Austria and to the detriment of the Monarchy as a whole.'[17] The Emperor tried in vain to commend Tisza as an unusually gifted statesman whose qualities ought to be made use of. To the Archduke, though he did not say it in so many words, this was just another example of Berlin viewing the Habsburg empire through Magyar spectacles.

But these were differences of view that both men expected to be aired, and they cast no shadow over two amicable and enjoyable days. It must have been a particularly proud and happy time for the *chatelaine* herself. This was the most prestigious gathering that Konopischt had seen, and she played to the full her proper role of hostess. It was the Emperor who gave her his arm when the main party of twenty-six went into dinner. She sat, then as throughout, at his right hand. Her sister Henriette and several other relatives were prominent among the Bohemian nobility distributed elsewhere around the table.[18]

Nobody could have imagined that this glittering climax was also to be the end. Indeed, the Archduke and his wife were given fresh grounds to look confidently to the future, for it was very probably here at Konopischt that a particularly brilliant prospect was held out for their elder son. Conceivably, it was this which, duly amplified and distorted, gave rise to the Wickham Steed legend. The then Archduchess Zita recalls:

The German Emperor wanted to get on the closest possible terms with Franz Ferdinand as heir to the throne and this largely explained his treatment of Sophie. But there was another bait. Just before the war, the Emperor floated the idea of making the Archduke's elder son, Prince Max Hohenberg, Duke of Lorraine. This was a title he himself had held since the province, together with Alsace, was taken from the French after the 1840 war. But Lorraine was pre-eminently a Habsburg title, for of course the dynasty had been called Habsburg-Lothringen ever since the marriage of the Empress Maria Theresa to the then Duke in the eighteenth century. Franz Ferdinand and his wife were naturally enchanted by the idea. In this way, their son, who in accordance with the marriage pact of 1900 could never become an archduke of Austria, might nonetheless carry one of the proudest of the Habsburg names for himself and his heirs. But with the death of Franz Ferdinand, the German Emperor lost all interest in the idea. It no longer had any political value for him as the sons were no longer in the game. So when, in 1916, the Archduchess Maria Theresa wrote to William II trying to revive the plan, he didn't even reply.[19]

All that seemed, and was, far away from Konopischt in mid-June 1914. On Saturday evening, the thirteenth, there was a splendid last dinner in the castle. The nine-course menu, arranged by Sophie, included saddle of lamb, crayfish à la Parisienne, chickens on spit, asparagus hollandaise and strawberries (all from the farms and gardens of the estate). The military band music, selected by the Archduke, included the march 'Hohenzollern Glory' and a *pot-pourri* of the German Emperor's favourite hunting songs. Then, at half-past nine, everyone, including the three children of the house, gathered in the hall to bid the exalted guest goodbye.

When the Archduke, who accompanied him to the station, watched the six carriages and two locomotives of the imperial train puff away from Beneschau shortly before midnight, it was in the firm belief that he would be welcoming William II again at Konopischt for shooting in the autumn. There were already rumours that this might somehow be combined with the invitation to King George V, so that the Archduke's 'shooting-box diplomacy' might achieve its greatest triumph, a meeting between the English and German sovereigns. The English visit had already been reported as a fixed event in the Vienna papers of 4 June. The same issues carried details of the large-scale Bosnian manoeuvres to be held later that month 'in the region of

Sarajevo–Konjica'. For the first time, the Archduke's travel programme from 24 to 27 June was also published in full.

Franz Ferdinand stayed a day or two longer at Konopischt, first to receive on 14 June the Austrian Foreign Minister Count Berchtold and brief him on the talks, and then to watch the crowds streaming between the rose-beds when the gates were opened on the fifteenth. The last days in Bohemia were serene, untroubled ones. On the nineteenth he went for a day's pigeon-shooting on the Namiest estate of Count Haugwitz. On the twentieth, he moved with his wife and children to his second property at Chlumetz, in south-eastern Bohemia, to spend a long family weekend there before embarking on the journey south. That Sunday he went out with his elder son Max and Baron Morsey on an inspection of the woods. They would belong one day to his younger son Ernst, he told Morsey, and, in order to preserve them for him in good condition, he had shot out the deer and stags completely. 'Here, the father has prevailed over the hunter.' But the hunter did have something to do, even at Chlumetz on a Sunday. As they were sitting in the car, a cat appeared on the meadow. The Archduke took aim with the pistol he always kept handy, and steadying his arm on the back seat, killed it with one bullet.[20] It was the last shot he was to fire in his life; not the most rousing of conclusions.

On the twenty-fourth, the parents said goodbye to their children – promising a reunion in Chlumetz in a week's time – and the journey began. The Archduke and his wife were to return to the Belvedere together, where their routes would separate. She would go by train via Budapest and Brod to Bad Ilidze, a little spa just south of Sarajevo where a suite of rooms (including one specially converted into a chapel) had been got ready for the royal couple at the Hotel Bosna. He would go by train to Trieste, thence, on board the *Viribus Unitis*, down the Adriatic to Metkovic and from there by rail again up the Narenta valley through Mostar to rejoin his wife.

There were one or two minor mishaps on the journey, each provoking some sardonically macabre comments from the Archduke. At the very beginning, for example, in Chlumetz station, it was discovered that one of the four axles of his private saloon-car had run hot, and the carriage had to be abandoned for an ordinary first-class compartment in the Vienna express. He is normally quoted as saying simply, 'Well, well, this journey is getting off to a really promising start.' But to his equerry Baron Morsey he was much more dramatic. 'You see,' he exclaimed, 'that's the way it starts. At first the carriage running hot, then a murder attempt in Sarajevo, and finally, if all that doesn't get anywhere, an explosion on board the *Viribus!*'[21]

When he and his suite arrived at Vienna's South Railway Station at 9 p.m. that evening to catch the Trieste-bound express, another problem was reported. The electric light had failed in the saloon car which had been mobilized to replace the defective carriage left behind in Bohemia. There was nothing for it but to use candles instead. As he took leave of the aide who had been detailed to accompany his wife on her journey to Ilidze, the Archduke quipped, 'What do you say to the lighting? Like in a grave, isn't it?'

· Incidents like these were later read by the superstitious as supernatural portents of the disaster to come and the Archduke's reactions taken to mean that he himself sensed some peril ahead. What should one make of this? He was a resolute man and, as such, shared that phlegmatic approach to assassination, a mixture of philosophical acceptance and religious faith, adopted by all his royal contemporaries who were not physical cowards. There were always assassination threats being reported to, or discovered by, the Austrian police, and Bosnia in 1914 had been no exception. Ten years later, as part of the protracted propaganda debate over 'war guilt', the claim was made that, six days before the Archduke started on his journey south, the Serbian envoy in Vienna, Joca Jovanović, acting on instructions from Belgrade, had warned the Austrian Finance Minister, Herr von Bilinski, that danger awaited Franz Ferdinand in Sarajevo. The Archduke never seems to have received this vague message (if indeed it was ever delivered in that form); and even if he had, nothing short of precise names and facts would have given him pause. His general attitude to the ever-present threat to his life was summed up in a remark he made when one of his most trusted advisers had pointed to the need for security precautions if he were to take a short-cut across Italian territory while staying at Miramare in the spring of 1914. 'Precautions? Safeguards by the Director of Police? To me, that's all rubbish . . . We are at all times in God's hands. Look, some rogue could have a go at me now, coming out of that brushwood. Worry and caution paralyse life. To be afraid is always a dangerous business in itself.'[22]

Yet, though it was never recorded in any of the contemporary accounts of his suite, there had been one extraordinary outburst of his which did show that – whether afraid of the Sarajevo journey or not – he somehow sensed that it would prove a journey to disaster. It was made before the young couple who were soon to succeed him on the steps of the throne. The future Empress Zita relates:

> At the beginning of May 1914, my husband and I were in Vienna and Uncle Franz rang up one evening, asking us come over to the Belvedere for supper. It was just a small family meal, with ourselves as the only guests. Everything passed off normally – indeed quite gaily – until after supper, when the Duchess went to take the children up to bed. After his wife had left the room, the Archduke suddenly turned to my husband and said, 'I have something to say but I must say it quickly as I don't want your aunt to hear anything of this. I know I shall soon be murdered. In this desk are papers which concern you. When it happens, take them, they are for you.'

When the nephew protested that this must, surely, be a joke, his uncle assured him that, on the contrary, he was in deadly earnest. After all, Franz Ferdinand added, 'The crypt in Artstetten is now finished.' At that moment, Sophie reappeared. The young couple did their best to resume normal conversation.[23]

Yet, despite this clear premonition of death before starting out and the macabre moments on the first stages of the journey, the Archduke was in the best possible spirits when, shortly before 8.30 a.m. on the morning of 25 June, he arrived at Mostar for the first formal ceremonies of the tour. Major Kamodina, in a

flowery speech, welcomed him to the Herzegovinian capital
(which, at that early hour, had not yet begun to stew in its heat-
bowl of mountains). He assured him of the 'unshakeable faith
and loyalty' of the people and wished him 'a long and happy life'
– sentiments which did not seem at all inappropriate on the day.

The Archduke was benevolence itself. He knew that an aunt
by marriage of the town governor, Baron Manuel von Pawel-
Rammingen, had been born Princess Frederike of Hanover, so
did not forget to enquire after the health of the royal relative.
And his reply to the Major ended with one painfully-rehearsed
sentence in Serbo-Croat, which brought delighted roars from
the crowd. Then on to Bad Ilidze, which he reached in the early
afternoon, for a joyful reunion with his wife. One of his first acts
was to send a telegram to his other Sophie, the thirteen-year-old
little princess left behind at Chlumetz: 'Safely arrived in Ilidze.
Found Mama very well. Very beautiful and pleasant here. We
have splendid quarters. Weather very nice. Good night, fond
embraces to you and your brothers.'[24] It was the last message
she was ever to receive from him.

As for his assassins, the principal trio had all lain low since
their arrival in Sarajevo, but they had been far from idle.
Cabrinović, for example, had made several discreet reconnais-
sance trips to Bad Ilidze, the final one on 20 June, the day the
Archduke arrived at Chlumetz for the farewell weekend with his
family. As usual, Cabrinović had chattered too much to all and
sundry, but no suspicions were aroused. Grabez based himself at
Pale, a village fifteen miles south-east of Sarajevo, but came into
the capital several times to be briefed by Princip on the
preparations. Princip discussed plan after plan with Ilić, and
worked at anything during the daytime to pay his board. In an
attempt to appear natural, he spent most of his evenings in wine
shops, though, until then, he had never tasted a glass in the
whole of his austere young life. (The true 'Young Bosnian' was
so fired with pure political passion that he often abjured sexual
pleasures as well as alcohol, in sacrifice to his ideals.)

Then, on the day of the Archduke's arrival, a strange chance
brought killer and victim together. The suites of rooms at the

Hotel Bosna had been lavishly furnished by one Elias Kabiljo, who kept a large oriental store in the Bas Carsija, the old Turkish market of Sarajevo. At five o'clock on the afternoon of the twenty-fifth, having barely settled in to the hotel, Franz Ferdinand suggested to his wife that as he would be on manoeuvres for the next two days they should take a drive and visit the merchant. (This was, presumably, his insatiable collector's enthusiasm at work.) This they did, making several purchases as a cheering crowd gathered outside. One person in that crowd who was not cheering was Gavrilo Princip, who just happened to be passing at the time. He had his pistol with him but did not use it. The reason he gave to his friends at the Semiz wine shop that evening was that there was a policeman just behind him. The reason he gave to his Austrian interrogators a week later was that he was afraid of hitting the Duchess of Hohenberg had he fired into the congested shop. Whatever the motive, it gave the Archduke and his wife another three days to live.

CHAPTER TWELVE

Two Pistol Shots

BY THE EARLY AFTERNOON of Saturday 27 June, the manoeuvres of the 14th and 16th Army Corps in the inhospitable mountains west of Sarajevo* were over. The weather had been mixed – rain and even snow storms on the first day, giving way to some sunshine on the second – yet the Archduke had certainly escaped that overpowering clammy heat he had been fearful of for his asthma. Instead, his aide commented, they might have been back in the bracing air of his native Styria.[1]

As the mock-battle between the 'Blue' and the 'Red' armies also went off well (the troops concerned had twice been fully mobilized over the past six years, in 1908 and again in 1912–13, and were therefore fully trained) the Archduke had every reason to be in good spirits. He displayed this in ironic circumstances when a solitary civilian suddenly leapt out of a thicket towards the uniformed figures of the general staff officers and pointed a long black tube at the heir to the throne. A gendarme officer promptly grabbed the intruder by the neck as a potential assassin. The Archduke, recognizing the man, roared with laughter. 'But that's the court photographer,' he called out. 'Let him go. He's only doing his job, and we all have to live.'[2]

Back in Ilidze, he despatched a brief report to the Emperor (who was by now in his favourite summer retreat at Bad Ischl) praising the high morale and military efficiency of the troops.

---

* The mere fact that they were staged, according to plans decided on many months previously, in this area, well away from the Serbian border, disposes of the allegations made later in Belgrade that Austria was, in reality, preparing to invade.

The telegram ended, 'Tomorrow I visit Sarajevo, and leave in the evening.' In fact, that programme came within a hair's breadth of being changed as, once again, chance nudged him towards his fate.

An early but elaborate dinner was served in the Hotel Bosna for forty guests. General Conrad (who had attended the manoeuvres as an observer) then took his leave of the Archduke, saying he wanted to set off straight away to inspect the garrison at Karlowitz. The General's staff and several other officials of the main party left with him. This prompted Baron Rumerskirch, the head of Franz Ferdinand's household, to suggest after dinner that they should all follow suit and wind up the visit there and then, as the main object of the trip had, after all, been satisfactorily concluded.

Rumerskirch's mind was not on assassinations; but he was still worried about the danger of hostile demonstrations, a concern which had caused him to argue against the journey in Vienna in the first place.[3] The question was debated at length in the Archduke's presence. Other voices spoke up in Rumerskirch's favour, and there was a moment when it seemed Franz Ferdinand himself was won over.

The programme for the twenty-eighth was something of an anticlimax: routine inspections of army camps; visits to museums; the inevitable call on the Town Hall with its predictable address of welcome. Sophie had anyway spent most of the previous two days seeing the Great Mosque, the famous carpet factory and all the other sights of the city, as well as visiting schools of the principal religious denominations, where money had been distributed from the Archduke's private purse. The Bosnian capital could not complain of being ignored. Both she and her husband were already counting the hours to get back to Bohemia, collect the children and then move on to Blühnbach, where they planned to stay for the rest of the summer. So far from being perturbed at the thought of overturning an official programme, the Archduke always rather relished the confusion which sudden upsets created around him.[4] The dies seemed to be cast for immediate departure.

However, the officers of General Potiorek's staff were reluctant to lose their exalted guests a day early, now that their own military proceedings were safely concluded. Lieutenant-Colonel Erik von Merizzi, the General's adjutant, was particularly persuasive, arguing that the Archduke's premature departure would give deep offence, especially to the loyal Monarchist elements of the population.[5] That argument finally carried the day. The debate had done nothing to dampen everybody's spirits. Indeed, the company then sat up over their cognac until after midnight, with the Archduke still in his most jovial of moods.

While this was going on in Bad Ilidze, the assassins in Sarajevo were completing their preparations, quite unaware that they had nearly been deprived of their prey altogether. Ilić, as technical organizer, distributed weapons on the afternoon and evening of the twenty-seventh to the locally-recruited reinforcements – the Moslem Mehmedbasić, and two Sarajevo students still in their teens, Cubrilović and Popović. Once again, coffee houses were used as meeting places. The students, from whom not much was anyway expected, had never handled a bomb or a pistol in their lives, and there was no opportunity for training now. Ilić merely told them that with the bombs you just unscrewed the fuse-cap, counted up to ten, and then threw them at the target. As for the pistols, all he had time for was to explain about the safety catch as he handed the weapons over ready-loaded with their seven bullets. Each student was also given his poison dose, with even briefer instructions as to use.

The teenagers ran off as though they had been given exciting new toys to play with, and promptly told various student friends in the town that they were going 'to attack someone tomorrow and had bombs and pistols for the job'.[6] They even offered to let their comrades feel the weapons in their pockets to prove they were not joking. Their chatter escaped the ears of the police, who, it transpired later, had not even bothered to place any surveillance on well-known troublemakers like Princip, despite the fact that he had solemnly registered his Sarajevo address with them as early as 15 June.

Princip and his two companions from Belgrade behaved on that same Saturday like the relatively mature conspirators they were. To minimize the risks, Princip and Ilić arranged to hand out the arms only a couple of hours before the attack. For once, a coffee house was not to be used. Instead, the Vlajnić pastry shop in Cumurja street was selected as an innocent-looking rendez-vous and Cabrinović and Grabez were told to be there at eight o'clock on the Sunday morning. That night they all paid separate pilgrimages to the Kosovo cemetery of Sarajevo, where Zerajić, hero of the bungled assassination attempt of 1910, was buried. Princip was the last to visit the shrine. He walked there on his way home from the Semiz wine shop shortly before midnight and laid some flowers on the grave. Once safely back in his lodgings, he completed his mental preparation for the deed by reading from the works of Russian anarchists. Then he went to sleep over the reduced hoard of weapons under his bed.[7]

Sunday 28 June dawned a brilliantly sunny day. While the Archduke and his wife were kneeling at mass in their private chapel at the Hotel Bosna, their young murderers were in the confectionery shop making final arrangements to despatch him. To the end, Cabrinović remained his theatrically convivial self. Before slipping into the back room for his bomb and pistol, he calmly consumed three cakes and afterwards persuaded a friend whom he ran into outside to come with him to have their photos taken. Though the photographer, one Josef Schrei, promised the finished pictures in an hour's time, that seemed, even to the casual Cabrinović, to be cutting things too fine. Instead of calling back, he asked the man to post some copies to various relatives and friends at addresses scattered between Belgrade and Trieste. The picture taken that morning·has survived. Though the pistol is well tucked away out of sight, it is just possible to discern the bulge in the jacket made by the bomb which the sitter was calmly concealing.

The actual plan of attack had been worked out by Ilić and Princip once full details of the Archduke's programme, together with timings, had been published in the local press. It was simple, almost naïve in conception, suggesting that though the officers of the 'Black Hand' back in Belgrade had been happy enough to arm and train their three young volunteers and smuggle them through to Sarajevo, once there they were left to their own devices without the benefit of any general staff advice.

The Bosnian capital is bisected by the Miljacka river, a stream some twenty-five yards wide whose course – slow and sluggish in midsummer – is spanned by half a dozen bridges. Only on one bank, the side of the old Turkish town with its new Austrian additions, does a through road run, and it was along this, then called the Appel Quay, that the Archduke's motor procession would travel on its way to the Town Hall, which is opposite the far bridge. The six armed fanatics had spaced themselves out between three bridges lower down the route – a total distance of less than four hundred yards – with four of them clustered around the Cumurja Bridge, which was the first the Archduke would have to pass on entering the town proper. All three of the Sarajevo students were posted here, with the unarmed Ilić as observer. In case they all failed, one of the

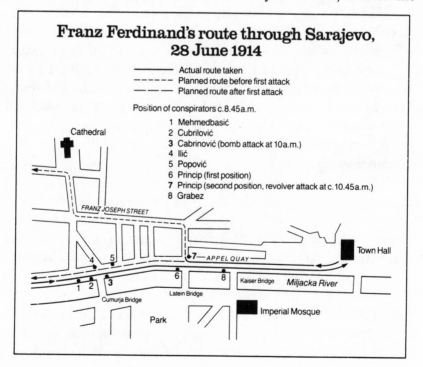

Franz Ferdinand's route through Sarajevo, 28 June 1914

——————— Actual route taken
– – – – – – Planned route before first attack
— — — — Planned route after first attack

Position of conspirators c. 8.45 a.m.

1 Mehmedbasić
2 Cubrilović
3 Cabrinović (bomb attack at 10 a.m.)
4 Ilić
5 Popović
6 Princip (first position)
7 Princip (second position, revolver attack at c. 10.45 a.m.)
8 Grabez

Cathedral

FRANZ JOSEPH STREET

Town Hall

7—APPEL QUAY

6   8

Kaiser Bridge *Miljacka River*

4 5   3

1 2

Latein Bridge

Cumurja Bridge

Park

Imperial Mosque

'serious' assassins, Cabrinović, was also stationed close to them. Princip and Grabez took up their positions by themselves close to the Latein and Kaiser Bridges respectively, which were the next two along the route.

At that time of the day, the sun would be striking the river and the embankment which ran along it. This meant that the crowds were concentrated in the shade of the houses on the opposite side, leaving the embankment pavement very sparsely filled. Despite this, all but one of the armed youths – and all three of the main group – were posted on the embankment side, where they were hideously conspicuous.

Perhaps Ilić had not thought about the weather at all. Perhaps he had, and concluded it would be better if the bulk of his men were free from the constraint of crowds and policemen. Perhaps he thought that the shallow river and the park on the far bank offered even better chances of escape than the maze of alleyways in the old town. But then, none of them was supposed to escape.

Had all six fanatics lived up to their word, six pistols would have been emptied that morning, six bombs hurled and six doses of cyanide swallowed. This was, after all, the 525th anniversary of Vidov-Dan and to any Bosnian extremist the Archduke was the twentieth-century reincarnation of the hated Sultan Murad. He was also far easier to get at. Yet it was a much less resolute story when, at about 10.20 a.m. (the programme was running twenty minutes late), the convoy of cars approached the Cumurja Bridge.

There were seven vehicles to start with, spaced some fifty yards apart. In the first rode officers of the Sarajevo police. They had booted out Franz Ferdinand's private detectives when the convoy was loaded up at the garrison barracks and grabbed the places for themselves. The second car carried the Town Mayor, Curcić, and his party. The Archduke and his wife travelled in the third, the famous six-seater open 'Double Phaeton' which belonged to Count Franz Harrach. The owner sat in front next to the chauffeur, one Leopold Loyka (who was about to induce a world war almost single-handed). Behind, with his back to

Harrach on a collapsible seat, was the Military Governor, General Potiorek; he in turn faced the Archduke and Sophie, who were side by side on the main passenger seat. The four cars behind carried the Archduke's suite, members of the Governor's staff, and, for some reason, the head of the Fiat works in Vienna, Herr Adolf Egger, for whom this must have been a very proud day.

The Archduke was resplendent in his full dress uniform as a General of Cavalry: light blue tunic, dark trousers with red stripes and, waving from his helmet, that unmistakable symbol of a Habsburg field commander, a spray of green peacock's feathers. Sophie also had feathers on her broad-brimmed hat – in her case those of an ostrich – and was clad underneath in a white silken dress.

Cabrinović had reached his place by the Cumurja Bridge well before time and, true to form, had passed the time of day 'talking' by signs and gestures to a well-known town figure, the deaf and dumb boy Moritz Alkalaj. Then there was a hum and bustle in the crowd and the procession was seen approaching. One of Sarajevo's police detectives (the city had 150 in all) happened to walk past at this moment. 'Which is the Archduke's car?' Cabrinović asked. 'The third,' replied the detective, and kept his eyes excitedly glued on the oncoming cars instead of, as instructed, on the bystanders. Once again, the police had actually helped Cabrinović.

When he saw that the convoy was driving past without any of the three Sarajevo conspirators around him so much as lifting a finger (their excuses, made later, were either that they had been hemmed in by gendarmes or that they 'felt pity for the Duchess'), Cabrinović tried to do the job for them. He pulled his bomb from inside his jacket, knocked the detonator off by banging it against an iron tramway mast and hurled it straight at the green feathers. An eyewitness standing on the pavement opposite was to testify that at first he had thought Cabrinović was just knocking out a pipe, which had seemed a most disrespectful thing to do in the royal presence.

But the would-be assassin, who intended far more than

disrespect, got his timing all wrong. Either he had simply forgotten to count up to ten before throwing – as he had been taught in Belgrade – or, more likely, he allowed the convoy to get too close to him. The bomb missed the brilliant green feathers by a few inches and then bounced off the hood of the car, which was folded down at the back, to land spluttering in the gutter. Some witnesses said that the Archduke raised his hand as though to ward the flying object off, but without making contact. The bomb smoked on for another eight or nine seconds and exploded just as the fourth car in the procession was passing over it.

Splinters flew in all directions. Windows and street lanterns were blown in; the wooden shutters of a nearby shop were smashed to pieces; and a hole a foot square and six inches deep blasted in the granite paving stones of the road. Some twenty people in the crowd were wounded, yet, in the car itself, only one passenger was badly hurt. This was the Governor's adjutant, Lieutenant-Colonel von Merizzi, the officer who had been largely responsible, in the discussion at the Hotel Bosna the night before, for ensuring that they were all driving down the Appel Quay this Sunday morning. He received a gash in the back of the hand, and, after first-aid bandaging at a doctor's surgery which was almost opposite the wrecked vehicle, was driven off to the garrison hospital for further treatment.

As for the conspirators around the bridge, they scattered like the bomb splinters – and almost as speedily. Cabrinović, who later testified that he just had time to see the Archduke 'turning his cold and piercing eyes at me', leapt over the embankment wall into the river where he tried to wash down his cyanide powder with a draught from the muddy Miljacka. Neither the cyanide powder, most of which he spilled in his excitement, nor (given Sarajevo's sanitary system) the almost equally lethal water from the river had any effect, then or later. He was overpowered within seconds by enraged bystanders and agitated gendarmes.

The other three would-be assassins, instead of hurling their bombs and firing their bullets into the disorganized convoy – which had halted briefly to evacuate the shattered fourth car and redistribute its unwounded passengers among the vehicles behind – simply took to their heels and fled. To complete the tableau, the little deaf and dumb boy who had been gesticulating with Cabrinovic until seconds before the attack scuttled away like a frightened rabbit over the bridge, in case the police should think he had anything to do with it.

One bomb which missed its target but caused total panic among all the locally-recruited conspirators; a failed suicide attempt and an arrest. Such was the net result of the action so far. It looked as though the Young Bosnian Sarajevo fiasco of 1910 was going to be repeated. The time was nearly 10.30 a.m.

The fact that things turned out to be very different was due to Princip. Yet it was only due to the wildest and most unpredictable chance of this whole chain of coincidence that he was given his opportunity. Standing against the embankment wall of the Latein Bridge, nearly 150 yards further down the route, he heard the explosion but had no idea what its effect had been, nor, at first, who had caused it. Then he saw Cabrinović being collared in the river and led away. The thought flashed across his mind to run back down the embankment, kill his colleague to preserve the secrecy of the plot, and then commit suicide himself.

While these ideas were flashing through his mind, the reassembled centre and rear of the convoy, which had moved off at high speed, sped past both Princip and Grabez on the way to the Town Hall before they had time to act. These two last hopes of the murder plot must have noted, from the brilliant green plumes waving above the blue uniform, as well as by the stately woman alongside, which was the Archduke's car. They would also have seen something else, an officer standing up on the running board opposite the steering wheel (the car had a right-hand drive). It was Count Harrach, who had left his seat next to the chauffeur and taken up his precarious perch in order to shield the Archduke with his body from any further mischief.

The scene which now unfolded at the Town Hall was like something out of a black farce. The Mayor had not halted his car at the Cumurja Bridge because, though he had heard the explosion, he had taken it to be just another salvo of greeting from the so-called 'Yellow Bastion' where the ceremonial artillery was positioned. He had thus driven on ahead and, surrounded by the leading civic and religious dignitaries of the capital, was now awaiting the royal couple on the broad steps outside as though nothing untoward had happened. The luckless fellow even plunged into his original speech of welcome: 'Your imperial and royal Highness, our hearts are transported with happiness by your gracious visit . . .' He only realized something was sadly amiss when the Archduke interrupted him: 'Mr Mayor, we come to Sarajevo for a visit and get a bomb thrown at us. It's scandalous! Right, now carry on with your speech.'

After that, protocol was hollowly observed. The Mayor completed the loyal address unamended, and the Archduke gave his prepared response. He altered it only at the end where he declared that the people's joy 'over the failure of the attack' was but another proof of their loyalty and devotion to the crown.

What had to be decided was whether and how, after the demonstration already offered, that loyalty and devotion should be further put to the test. The grave error was now made – no matter where it was decided to proceed next – not to reinforce the streets with every soldier and officer of the law who could be roped in at short notice. The twenty thousand men who had been stood down from manoeuvres the day before could be ruled out as immediate reinforcements. They were still out in the field and it would have taken the rest of the day to fetch them in. There was, however, a force of some two hundred and fifty men readily available in the town. This, for some unaccountable reason, was not called upon, though at least an officer on the Governor's staff, Major Höger, claimed later to have urged that the streets must be cleared by the military before the Archduke moved another step outside.

The Archduke himself seemed to have been perfectly calm, though in one of his grimly sarcastic moods. 'It looks to me as though we might still get a few more pot shots today,' he was quoted as saying, and the sentence quite fits him. So does his other reported observation that the bomb-thrower, instead of

248

being punished, would, 'in true Austrian style, be given a high-decoration and perhaps finish up as a Privy Councillor'.[8]

It was Franz Ferdinand's own sense of obligation as Inspector-General of the armed forces which decided the next move. Whatever happened, he announced, he would visit Merizzi in the garrison hospital, for the officer had, after all, been wounded on his behalf. He sent his secretary to the upper floor of the Town Hall, where Sophie was receiving the Turkish ladies of the town, with instructions to return with her to Bad Ilidze with a separate vehicle. But when Baron Morsey appeared upstairs, already carrying the Duchess's mantle for the journey, he was met with a firm refusal: 'So long as the Archduke is showing himself in public I shall not leave his side.'[9] With that, Sophie had sealed her own fate.

An unholy muddle now arose. The royal couple descended the broad steps of the Town Hall again between the deeply-bowing rows of dignitaries and climbed back into their old positions in Count Harrach's car. As before, General Potiorek took up his place opposite them on the fold-up seat and, as before, the Count himself mounted the running board on the left hand side of the vehicle to give the Archduke some protection. The old programme, which had involved turning right at the Latein Bridge on the return journey for a brief detour around the town to visit the museum, was scrapped. Instead, the convoy was to drive straight back along the embankment without leaving the Appel Quay, stopping only at the military hospital, which lay on the outskirts of the capital, on the way to the Hotel Bosna and home.

The Mayor and the Chief of Police, Dr Gerde, were to lead off in their car and the Archduke's chauffeur was to be told to follow them. Colonel Bardolff, the head of the Archduke's Military Chancery, was heard to instruct Dr Gerde precisely about the revised route, and the police chief was heard to acknowledge the instructions – albeit somewhat cursorily – while he was hurrying on ahead down the Town Hall steps.

Whether the police chief had not heard properly, or misunderstood, or failed in turn to instruct his own driver, is not clear. At all events, he and Mayor Curcić were the immediate cause of the disaster. The convoy passed the Kaiser Bridge without incident on the return journey, despite the fact that Grabez, armed with his bomb and his fully-loaded Browning pistol, was still standing there,* but then slowed down on reaching the Latein Bridge, where it proceeded to turn right up the Franz-Joseph Street into the town, as laid down in the original programme. Chauffeur Loyka, who was simply follow-ing the car in front, started to do the same. General Potiorek belatedly came to his senses and shouted at the driver not to follow the police car but to reverse back on to the Appel Quay. It was while he was fumbling with the gears, mounted in those days on the outside running board, and while the vehicle itself was as good as stationary for a few seconds that, from the crowd massed only a few feet away on the pavement, the shots rang out.

How Princip came to be in any position to fire those shots is the most unlikely of all the extraordinary tales of that day. Though it seemed too much to expect that after the bomb incident the procession would stick to the return route announc-ed in the papers, Princip had nonetheless left his position by the river wall, crossed the road and posted himself at the corner of the road junction opposite. Even so, he would have had no clear field of fire at the Archduke had Count Harrach, who was thinking only of a possible attack from the embankment, not been standing on the left or offside running board, giving the Archduke no protection from the right. And Princip would not have got a shot off at all had a detective standing just behind him been able to grapple with him in time. As it was, the detective was kneed in the groin by a Young Bosnian enthusiast, Simon Pusara, as he was trying to knock Princip's arm down, and the assassin found himself gazing at the Duchess with the Archduke an open target at her side.

He claimed later that he had felt a moment's hesitation at firing into a car with a woman in it, which may well have been

* Grabez was full of lame excuses all round afterwards. He had not, he said, wished to use the bomb which he was 'only carrying for Ilić'. He wanted to use the pistol, but the safety catch was on.

true. His other claim – that he turned his head aside as he pulled the trigger – is certainly true, for it was confirmed by eyewitnesses around him. In other words, Princip was not even looking at his victims as he struck first the Duchess, with a bullet in the abdomen, and then with his second bullet hit the Archduke in the neck. The slight kickback from the first shot would by itself have raised the barrel slightly for the second, and thus done the assassin's aiming for him.

The most authoritative – and most graphic – description of what happened next is that given by Count Harrach. He takes up the story from the moment the car hastily backed out of the Franz-Joseph Street again and then made straight across the Latein Bridge for the other side of the river and the safety of the Konak, the old palace of Sarajevo's Turkish governors.

As the car quickly reversed, a thin stream of blood spurted from His Highness's mouth onto my right cheek. As I was pulling out my handkerchief to wipe the blood away from his mouth, the Duchess cried out to him, 'In Heaven's name, what has happened to you?' And at that she slid off the seat and lay on the floor of the car, with her face between his knees. I had no idea that she too was hit and thought she had simply fainted with fright. Then I heard His Imperial Highness say, 'Sopherl, Sopherl, don't die. Stay alive for the children!'* At that, I seized the Archduke by the collar of his uniform, to stop his head dropping forward and asked him if he was in great pain. He answered me quite distinctly, 'It's nothing!' His face began to twist somewhat but he went on repeating, six or seven times, ever more faintly as he gradually lost consciousness, 'It's nothing!' Then, after a short pause, there was a violent choking sound caused by the bleeding. It stopped as we reached the Konak.[10]

---

* Many years later, Harrach's account was questioned by medical analysts, who claimed that the bullet which severed the Archduke's neck artery and damaged the surrounding area would have instantly rendered him incapable of speech of any sort. Diagnosis is not infallible, however, and many patients have astounded their doctors by behaving against the rule-book and living on when they ought, by rights, to be dead. The words quoted by Harrach (who was within inches of the Archduke's lips as he supported the dying man's head) ring true enough. More 'famous last words' of history were actually spoken than invented.

Some doctors ran after the car (it was five minutes to the old Turkish palace); others hurried there from the hospital. But neither the Archduke nor his wife, who were taken up to the first floor and laid on beds, regained consciousness. About a quarter of an hour later, they died, within minutes and within inches of one another.

It was a South Slav assassin – within minutes in police custody, bleeding and battered from sabre cuts and blows – who pulled the trigger to kill the heir to the Austrian throne and his wife. But the real murderer had been Austrian *Schlamperei*, that talent for happy-go-lucky muddle which, all his life, had infuriated the Archduke about his fellow-countrymen. It had always been the despair of the dynasty. Now, in a way that not even he could have predicted, it was leading to the end of that dynasty, and of much else beside.

CHAPTER THIRTEEN

———— ⬡ ————

Requiem

AS THE DEAD COUPLE were taken to the upstairs rooms of the Konak to be embalmed and laid out – he with his secretary's crucifix pressed between his white-gloved hands, she with the bouquet of flowers presented half an hour before by the Moslem ladies of Sarajevo placed close to her head – the Archduke's suite started on the appalling task of communicating the news. The tables which had been set in the Konak for a formal lunch in the victims' honour were swept clear and turned into work desks, the flowers taken upstairs to the death room. Everyone was called in from Ilidze to help in the task. Telephone and telegraph lines were commandeered in an attempt (vain, as it turned out)* to stop any reports reaching the outside world before all the official messages had been transmitted.

The first to be told was, of course, the Emperor, though no-one in Sarajevo presumed to get in touch with the eighty-four-year-old demigod in person. Instead, Baron Rumerskirch rang his opposite number, Prince Montenuovo, in Vienna, and the Prince in turn rang the Emperor's adjutant, Count Paar, at the imperial villa in Bad Ischl. That faithful old courtier, who had had to bear so many tragic family messages to his master over the years, was now, at about 11.30 a.m. on the morning of 28 June, charged with the task yet again.

The Count is quoted (though only at second-hand and not by the most reliable of narrators)[1] as watching the Emperor

———————————
* One coded message reached Colonel Dimitrievich in Belgrade within the hour. It read, 'Both horses well sold.'

'slump in his desk-chair as though struck by an electric current' when given the news. Then, after pacing agitatedly up and down the room, he is said to have regained his customary composure and pronounced the following verdict: 'The All-Mighty cannot be defied with impunity. A divine will has re-established that order of things which I, alas, was not able to preserve.' The composure may well have been customary, but not those words, which sound far too contrived and flowery to have come from Franz Joseph's lips. Whatever the sovereign said, he was almost certainly more shocked than grief-stricken. His nephew had never found a way into that closely-barricaded old heart. But after fourteen years, the Emperor had quite come to accept the marriage of 1900, which had turned out to be such an exceptionally happy one. Moreover, he had developed a growing respect for the Archduke's capabilities, especially in the military field, and a growing fondness for his wife.

Years later, the story was spread about – quoting supposed outbursts from the lips of Princess Stephanie, the Emperor's widowed daughter-in-law – that Franz Joseph had in fact connived at his nephew's murder by deliberately sending him to face known dangers.[2] It is hard to discern what can have been behind such a *canard* – except, perhaps, that the conspirators' secret sign at Tuzla had been a packet of 'Stephanie' cigarettes. Franz Joseph may have become something of a bigoted and blinkered bureaucrat in his old age but he remained, to his death, the Christian *grand seigneur* of old Europe. To accuse him, in effect, of conspiring to murder his own heir makes wilful mockery of a character who always lived by God in heaven and by the book of dynastic rules on earth. The shock that Sunday midday in the imperial villa may be taken as perfectly genuine. So was the fashion in which the Emperor mastered it. After lunching alone – a very rare happening when at Ischl – he returned to his desk and worked away until nightfall.

The next priority in the royal family was Archduke Charles, the twenty-six-year-old prince who, at his uncle's murder, had just become the new heir to the Habsburg throne. He was spending that weekend with his family at Reichenau, their quiet country home near the Semmering Pass, some thirty miles south-west of Vienna. We have an authoritative first-hand account of the scene here. His wife relates:

> It was midday, and beautiful summer weather, and we were having lunch outside in our little garden house ...
>
> Suddenly there was a pause in the serving of the meal ... For minutes on end, no more food appeared. Then a servant came out, carrying, instead of the next course, a telegram in his hand which he handed to the Archduke ... My husband opened it, and looked at the signature first. 'Rumerskirch,' he said, 'That's odd. Why him? He's with Uncle Franz!'
>
> Then he began to read out the brief message. The exact words I forget. But it was something like, 'Deeply regret to report that His Imperial Highness and the Duchess were both assassinated here today.'
>
> For a moment, the Archduke went as white as a sheet in the sun. Then he stood up without a word ... and went back into the house.[3]

Well might the young Archduke have gone pale. In June 1914, he and his wife were counting on a relatively tranquil family life for another twenty-five years or more until, in the late thirties or early forties, the Emperor Franz would have followed the Emperor Franz Joseph to the grave, and the heavy Habsburg crown would be his to carry. He would have gone paler still had he known what was in fact in store over that span.

While Rumerskirch was passing the official message to Vienna, Baron Morsey, as the Archduke's personal secretary, had to deal with the family of the dead couple. He and Countess Lanyus telegraphed all Sophie's brothers, sisters and other principal relatives. One of the brothers was handed the message while at the racecourse in Karlsbad and was reported to have fainted clean away.[4] But what should be done about the three children, waiting excitedly at Chlumetz for their parents' return? Morsey decided on the following telegram, addressed to their tutor there, Dr Stanowsky: 'Please tell our poor dear children as gently as possible that the exalted personages have fallen victims to the brutal hands of a murderer.'[5] It speaks volumes for the awe which the Habsburg dynasty inspired in its devoted servants that, even in a message like this, the grief-stricken Baron could not bring himself to use the simple word 'parents' when addressing himself to the orphaned children of his late employers.

Nearly seventy years after the event, Franz Ferdinand's daughter described how, as a thirteen-year-old child, she and her two brothers received that message at Chlumetz:

> We were awaiting our parents' return, and had even thought out a little 'tableau' which we could enact for a welcome. Then, while we were at lunch on the Sunday, Monsignor Stanowsky, the tutor to my brothers, was called away from the table to the telephone. He came back completely shaken but said nothing, and we thought it was bad news about his mother, who was very ill at the time. He immediately rang up our aunt Henriette, my mother's sister, in Prague, and asked her to come to Chlumetz immediately. She arrived that afternoon and told us, more or less straightaway, that there had been an attack on our parents and that they were both injured. We were shattered and begged to be allowed to go to them. Instead, we were taken to the village church in Chlumetz to pray for them. Still we had no idea how dreadful the news really was.*
>
> They let us sleep – as well as we could – overnight, and then, early the next morning, we were told the dreadful truth. Dr Stanowsky told my two brothers and my uncle, Count Wuthenau, the husband of my mother's favourite sister, who had also arrived at Chlumetz, broke the news as gently as he possibly could to me. The anguish was indescribable, and also the feeling of total bewilderment. All our lives, we had known nothing but love and total security. Now, suddenly, we simply couldn't imagine what was to become of us.[6]

In Vienna, where the Emperor had hurried (joined at Hietzing station by Archduke Charles, who then drove with him in an open carriage the few hundred yards to Schönbrunn Palace), there was also a feeling of stunned dismay. Even the normally

---

* Baron Morsey had managed to reach Countess Henriette Chotek on the phone and had told her that there would be a service for the victims at 5.30 that afternoon in Sarajevo. It was he who suggested that the children should be taken to pray at that same moment in Chlumetz.

unemotional Franz Joseph was, for once, overcome by it. The Archduchess Zita has described how, when they were all alone at last in the palace and the servants had withdrawn, the old ruler suddenly lost his composure and burst into tears in front of them. It was then – and not, as so often reported, on first hearing the news of the assassination – that he uttered those oft-quoted words, '*Mir bleibt nichts erspart*' ('I am spared nothing').[7]

In imperial Schönbrunn, however, unlike at Chlumetz, the dead man had his appointed successor – the Archduke Charles, who had just made his first brief public appearance at the Emperor's side as the new heir to the throne. But though there was no doubt whatsoever as to how Franz Ferdinand should be succeeded, there was much uncertainty and discussion as to how he should be buried. Should this, as befitted his rank and international status, be made a full ceremonial event, with the crowned heads of Europe in attendance? Or should it be restricted, as far as was feasible, to an act of Habsburg family mourning?

The German Emperor was the key figure in deciding whether the funeral should be turned into a European event. He was both the closest and most powerful royal friend the dead man had possessed and, above and beyond that, was the ruler of Austria's principal ally. With all this in mind, he had been the first foreign sovereign to whom Baron Rumerskirch had sent the news of the tragedy from Sarajevo. It had reached him in somewhat laborious fashion on the afternoon of 28 June at Kiel, where he was attending the annual international regatta. There seems to have been some problem in telegraphic communication with the royal yacht that day, for on getting the message, Admiral von Müller, the head of the German Naval Bureau, set off from shore in the pinnace *Hulda* and shouted its contents over a loud-hailer to the *Hohenzollern*. Instantly, William II ordered the regatta to be broken off – which must have caused him a slight twinge of regret, as his own yacht, the *Meteor*, was leading its nearest English rival by fifteen minutes in the race in progress at the time.[8] All vessels then lowered their flags to half-mast and, as Franz Ferdinand had held an admiral's rank in the

German navy, the Austro-Hungarian battle flag was hoisted up halfway to meet them on every German warship. It all augured for the maximum in pomp and ceremony to come.

First expectations in Vienna were, indeed, that every European dynasty would be attending the Archduke's last rites, mostly in the person of their crowned heads. The presence of the German Emperor would, for example, almost automatically involve the Kings of Saxony, Bavaria and Württemberg, each of whom had close family ties with the house of Habsburg. King George V, linked by friendship if not by blood with the Archduke was, it was confidently stated on 30 June, sending Prince Arthur of Connaught as his representative. The King of the Belgians, on the other hand, was reported in Brussels to be coming in person.

Yet there were complications, even on the protocol side. The venerable King Carol of Rumania would gladly have come to bid farewell to his good friend; but what of Austria's other ally, Italy? The dead man's hostility to Rome had been so notorious, and his boycott of the Italian royal house itself so obdurate, that it was unthinkable that King Victor Emmanuel would come to Vienna, and by no means certain that he would even send the Crown Prince. Then there were possible complications with Russia to be considered. St Petersburg could not complain, like Rome, of Franz Ferdinand's antagonism; quite the reverse. Yet Russia was the great protector of the Slavs in general and the patron of 'Greater Serbia' in particular. As a harsh confrontation between Vienna and Belgrade was the very minimum now to be expected in the wake of the Sarajevo murders, how comfortable would the Tsar feel at the Archduke's funeral – especially with the acrid smell of bombs in the air?

Security was, undoubtedly, an additional problem. As so often, one spectacular political assassination had spawned threats and rumours of many others. Clearly, something had gone very wrong with the police precautions down in Bosnia. Could the Austrians be relied upon – indeed, did they trust themselves – to safeguard against another and even graver catastrophe in the streets of their own capital? Several of the rulers expected in Vienna had, after all, either seen their predecessors murdered, or survived similar attacks themselves, or both. In the crisis-laden atmosphere of those last days of June, both the Austrian security chiefs and their potential royal charges had every reason to be apprehensive.

Finally, there was the very genuine problem of Franz Joseph's health. The eighty-four-year-old Emperor had gone down on 20 April with another of his severe bronchial attacks. It had been bad enough for regular medical bulletins to be published and for a train to be kept ready under steam for the next ten days at Beneschau station, in case the Emperor's life should be in danger and his heir, who was at Konopischt, be needed speedily in Vienna. On 1 May, the sovereign's condition improved; yet it was not until 23 May that his private physician, Dr Kerzl, issued the last bulletin.[9] News of the illness had even prompted Ciganović, the go-between for the assassination weapons, to comment in Belgrade at the time that these would not now be needed after all, as the heir to the throne would never, in those circumstances, be journeying to Bosnia.

Unfortunately for the Archduke, his uncle recovered in time for him to attend the manoeuvres. Nonetheless, when the question of the funeral was being debated, the Emperor had been restored to health for little over a month. He had barely reached his summer retreat when the news from Sarajevo had forced him to hurry back to Vienna again, and the old man's personal yearning can only have been to return to the peace of his beloved Ischl as soon as he could. This, in turn, was only possible if the funeral ceremonies in Vienna were reduced to a decent minimum and the fatiguing business of entertaining at least half a dozen fellow sovereigns avoided altogether.

The claim has often been made that the decision to restrict the Vienna ceremonies to a one-day domestic affair was prompted by a desire to spite the Archduke and his wife even at their graveside. The factors listed above show that the allegation does not hold much water. Even if this decision was not unwelcome to his enemies, they were probably not its principal inspiration. The question which does remain to be answered is whether that minimum of ceremony accorded in Vienna was, in fact, decent enough.

Certainly, the dead man would have had little to complain about over his removal back to the capital, travelling along precisely the same route he had taken the week before. On the evening of the twenty-ninth, as the embalmed bodies were loaded on the train for the journey down to the coast, the same artillery that had saluted his entry into Sarajevo now sounded salvos of farewell. Although the train travelled by night, silent crowds gathered at every station down the Narenta valley to watch it pass. At every station, army regiments stood in salute – the *Deutschmeister* at Konjica, for example, and the 6th Hussars at Mostar.

As for the Austro-Hungarian navy, it had honoured its late Admiral and patron by summoning every warship available in the Adriatic to await him off Metkovic with the *Viribus Unitis*. Franz Ferdinand's prize battleship fired a twenty-one gun salute as the coffins were placed under a baldachin on the quarter deck, covered with war-flags and flowers. The column of ironclads then steered slowly north across a calm sea. It kept as close inshore as the draught of the big vessels allowed and, from each island and mainland port, little armadas of black-pennanted ships, everything from coastal steamers to sailing dinghies, set out to meet it. At Makarska, the bishop gave his blessing from the beach as choirs from the Croat communities – stubborn friends of a dynasty which had hitherto done little for them – sang songs of mourning. From Spalato, then from Pola, Brioni, Pirano and Parenzo, more artillery salutes puffed and echoed out from the shores as the convoy steamed past. Even Trieste, not exactly famous for its pro-Habsburg sympathies, paid full honours when the *Viribus Unitis* dropped anchor there on the evening of 1 July.[10]

It was in Vienna, where the coffins arrived by express train at 10 p.m. the following night, that the equivocation and the arguments began. Few Habsburg princes had led such a controversial life as Franz Ferdinand. None rounded it off with such a controversial funeral.

The accusation was made – especially by members of the Archduke's staff and by highly excitable friends of his such as Count Sternberg – that, in one final display of spite against the dead man and his wife, the Hofburg had accorded them only a 'third-class burial'.* Inevitably, Prince Montenuovo is made the prime villain of the piece, with the old Emperor exonerated as having been too weary to offer any resistance to the detailed arrangements laid before him on his return from Bad Ischl. We are thus presented with a scenario whereby Franz Ferdinand conducts, as it were from under his coffin lid, one last battle by proxy with his old rival. The truth, as the Archduke's own family have come to admit, and as neutral testimony confirms, was somewhat different.

The Court Chamberlain certainly never went one inch out of his way to pay more than the basic tributes prescribed. Moreover, his hostility to Sophie as an 'intruder' to the charmed Habsburg circle was fully demonstrated in one or two petty gestures (though *not* those which have been most commonly reported). Yet that same protocol which so often restricted the Archduke and his wife while they were alive ensured them the essential ceremonial required in death – given the fact that the decision had been taken to exclude foreign royalty and restrict the actual proceedings to the absolute minimum in time.

The old Emperor himself – so often portrayed as the passive tool of his Court Chamberlain in the matter – is the best witness of this. Many years later, the then Archduchess Zita described how, when the funeral arrangements were being made, some of Franz Ferdinand's circle had approached her husband, as the new heir to the throne, to intervene personally with the Emperor to order a 'proper burial', especially with regard to Sophie. At this, the Emperor replied to his young great-nephew, 'A proper burial? What do people want? The Duchess is being buried as my own Empress was – and she too was murdered!'[11]

The parallel may have been somewhat exaggerated. How-

---

* The phrase *Begräbnis dritte Klasse* crops up repeatedly in the final pages of Morsey's diary and Count Sternberg wrote frequent philippics on the theme in later years. (See, for example, his article in the Vienna monthly *Tagesfragen* for July 1919.)

ever, one only has to study the six-page official 'Ceremonial for
the Reception, Lying-in-State, Blessing and Transmission of
the bodies of his late Imperial and Royal Highness the Archduke
Franz Ferdinand of Austria-Este and of Her Highness Sophie,
Duchess of Hohenberg' (both names, incidentally, printed in
type of exactly the same size) to realize that, whatever his
personal inclinations may have been, the Court Chamberlain
had to apply certain standard procedures for an archducal
funeral as long as the bodies were in Vienna and therefore under
his charge. There was no other way for All-Highest remains to
be despatched, though, as we shall see, once inside the precincts
of the Hofburg itself, the distinction between All-Highest and
Highest had to be drawn.

It had been decided, after forty-eight hours of consultation
between the Hofburg and other principal courts of Europe, that
the crowned heads, or their heirs, who might otherwise have
been present would all be represented instead by their ambassadors in Vienna. At 6 p.m. on 3 July, within an hour of the last
ceremony being completed in the capital, the British envoy, Sir
Maurice de Bunsen, sat down at his residence in the Metternich-
gasse and penned a twelve-page report on the funeral for his
sovereign, King George V. As the Ambassador was not exactly
a novice in matters of protocol, his eyewitness account may be
taken as authoritative as well as objective. The only fault he
could find in the arrangements from beginning to end was the
choice of the small Hofburg chapel for the service itself, 'instead
of ... a church capable of holding a much greater number of
people'. He specifically discounts stories put about by the
Archduke's circle that the Emperor William had deliberately
stayed away 'because of the insufficient funeral honours bestowed on his friend'. He continues, 'It is natural that the
Emperor should be spared as much as possible and, as regards
ceremonial, I am assured that the ancient custom has been
observed.'[12]

Sir Maurice pronounced himself moved most of all by the
cortège which met the coffins at the West Railway Station at
10 p.m. on the night of 2 July and conducted them through the

darkened streets past the Belvedere Palace itself to the chapel of the Hofburg, where they were locked up overnight. The spectacle was, clearly, both eerie and impressive. Two grooms bearing lanterns led the procession. Then came a detachment of cavalry, followed in turn by the court carriages for the chamberlains, aides and adjutants, Baron Rumerskirch travelling side by side with Prince Montenuovo. Two more grooms with lanterns then preceded the coffins themselves, which were flanked on one side by twelve guardsmen with halberds and on the other by twelve dismounted cavalrymen with drawn swords. Then came more bobbing lanterns, followed by a four-seater court carriage for the suite of the Archduke and precisely the same conveyance for the suite of his wife. More cavalry brought up the rear and a long file of soldiers marched on either flank of the entire procession. Nothing could be objected to here, nor in the scene at the lovely old Schweizerhof of the Hofburg where – to the music of the choir singing the 'Miserere' – the coffins were laid to rest overnight side by side in the chapel, escorted by archers, life-guards and, 'on each side, four boys of noble birth, each carrying burning wax candles'.

There was much grumbling on the following morning because the chapel was only opened for four hours, from 8 a.m. to noon, for members of the public to pay their last respects. Certainly, as on all such occasions, thousands more were eager to file past, despite the fact that the Archduke was far from being a national idol. But, again, everything flowed from the decision to compress all the proceedings in Vienna to a timespan of twenty-four hours precisely. This decision was at least partly influenced by the fact that the burial itself would be quite separate and private, for, in accordance with the dead man's explicit wishes, he was not to be housed with his ancestors in the dynasty's musty and crowded crypt underneath the Capuchin Church. ('I would never have any peace lying there,' he is said to have exclaimed. 'Just imagine it, with the electric trams rattling past overhead all the time!')[13] The fifteen-minute service which followed that afternoon had to demonstrate that man and wife could not expect to be equal in death before the Habsburg family altar because they had never been equal in life – one belonging to that family and the other not. Montenuovo was doubtless very content that the distinction should be displayed. But content or not, it is hard to see how, even had he so wished, he could have eliminated all symbolism of a morganatic union in this most solemn and sacred of all ceremonies. Thus, though Sophie's casket was no less ornate than her husband's, it was smaller in size and set some eighteen inches lower on its stand. The two coffins rested side by side on a dais draped with a cloth of gold, surrounded by nearly a hundred long wax candles, set in batteries of candelabras, and with a black baldachin swaying overhead. On Franz Ferdinand's casket lay his Prince's crown, his Archduke's hat and his General's helmet and sword, with his orders and medals pinned to large velvet cushions in front. A similar cushion laid against Sophie's coffin carried but one decoration, her Order of the Star Cross, awarded as far back as January 1889. Her coffin lid was equally bare – just the black fan and white gloves which symbolized a noblewoman, as well as a lady-in-waiting. Their presence here was not necessarily, therefore, an offensive token of Sophie's former station.

The entire royal family, headed by the Emperor in his white Field-Marshal's uniform, were in attendance as the Archbishop of Vienna, Cardinal Piffl, conducted the brief service. 'At 4.15 it was all over,' wrote de Bunsen, who had been striving to identify the various archduchesses under their heavy veils. 'There was some very fine singing, without accompaniment. It was a deeply and painfully interesting occasion . . .'

The three children were not at the ceremony. They were admitted three hours later by themselves for a reunion with their parents so tragically different from the one they had expected. That good angel of the Hofburg, their step-grandmother Archduchess Maria Theresa, had greeted them on their arrival in Vienna, and Franz Ferdinand's greatest champion in the press world, the *Reichspost*, had organized a touching reception for them. Schoolchildren, brought out to line the entire route from the Franz Joseph Station to the Belvedere, stood in silent sympathy as the carriage bearing the three orphans passed by.

The Court Chamberlain cannot be reproached for taking no hand in this. The children were not of the Habsburg family and they were therefore no concern of his.

However, Montenuovo could be, and indeed was, sharply criticized for his handling of the proceedings after the Hofburg ceremony. The route lay to the West Railway Station and though there was nothing wrong with the procession itself (which was an elaborate version of the previous day's cortège) so far as this went, the trouble was that it did not go far enough.

The dead man had not only been heir to the throne. He had also been Inspector-General of all the armed forces of the Dual Monarchy and its presumed Commander-in-Chief in time of war. Yet apart from the small troop detachments which formed a standard component of the cortège, almost the only uniformed personnel appointed to follow their Generalissimo on his last journey through the capital were those court officials and former members of his suite who happened to hold military rank. In fact, representatives of every branch of the army – right down to that Voluntary Motorized Corps which had provided most of the privately-owned vehicles in the Sarajevo convoy – ought to have marched behind him. So, by rights, ought officers and men of every regiment he had served in or commanded. (The 7th Uhlans had been confidently polishing themselves up for the occasion, only to be kept in their barracks at Stockerau. Ironically, they were called to Vienna two days later, for the funeral of an ordnance general.)[14] Above all, perhaps, the navy should have been called on to honour the Admiral who had helped create the Monarchy's modernized fleet.

Montenuovo's reply to his critics would most probably have been that as there was no precedent for the funeral of an archducal Inspector-General and his wife the case was not covered by protocol, and what was not covered by protocol was not within the Court Chamberlain's ken. He could also, with some justice, have pointed a finger at the Minister of War, General Krobatkin, whose proper province this was. Certainly the General, who had hurried back to Vienna on 29 June specifically to organize the military honours, seems to have confined himself to the routine practice of lining the funeral route with troops.

But, in the true Austrian tradition of emotional improvization, what had been officially ignored was spontaneously put right. Prince Ernst Rüdiger Starhemberg – a man with an emphatic mind of his own, as later history was to show* – led a last-minute revolt against Montenuovo's niggardly closing ceremony. As a result, not only all the archdukes, led by the new heir, Archduke Charles, followed by the coffins from the Hofburg, but also the heads of most of the Monarchy's oldest families and many members of its Officers' Corps. This was, perhaps, the best tribute of all.

Once the Western Railway Station was reached at about 10.30 p.m. that evening, Montenuovo was able to ring the curtain down with a vengeance. As the coffins were loaded on to the waiting train, he turned to Janaczek, that faithful amanuensis of Franz Ferdinand's who had been bustling about all the time in the background, and remarked, 'Now my job is done. From here on, it's your private affair.'[15]

The private affair he was referring to was the burial at Artstetten. Franz Ferdinand had started on the construction of a family crypt here following the tragedy of his last, stillborn child in 1908. His quip about wanting to avoid the Capuchin Church in Vienna because of the tramway rattling overhead was not, of course, the real story. It was to him inconceivable that, even as the Emperor he counted on becoming, he could ever allow himself to be buried without a place for his beloved Sophie at his side. Yet in the Capuchin Church that was problematical as she was not a member of the royal house and could never become one, whatever decrees he passed. The same applied with added force to his children, formally excluded by his oath of 1900 from all rights of succession. So he had long since decided on Artstetten for his own last resting-place, and it was to Pöchlarn, the little station two miles south of the castle on the opposite bank of the Danube, that the special train was now heading.

* In the post-war Republic which survived as the Austrian rump of the Monarchy he became leader of the Fascist-style patriotic Heimwehr movement.

It would have been an elementary courtesy, if not a moral duty, for Montenuovo to have extended all the help he could a mere sixty miles upstream from the capital – more particularly as the new heir to the throne and his Archduchess, accompanied by all the other archdukes, were representing the Emperor at this final act. But on the railway platform of Vienna, where the family took over, the Court Chamberlain cut off the last shred of official aid like snipping off some thin golden ribbon. There were some undignified moments as a result, with the weather adding considerably to the difficulties.

The train pulled into Pöchlarn at 2 a.m. Almost as the wheels stopped, a violent midsummer thunderstorm broke out over the Danube. The original plan, which was to bless the coffins in the open square in front of the station, had to be abandoned. The army and ex-servicemen's units already on parade there (alongside the inescapable fire brigade) were hastily stood down in the deluge and transferred to the shelter of the covered platforms. As for the religious ceremony, there was no alternative to holding this in the hall of the station ticket-office, hastily transformed into something resembling a chapel with candlesticks and wreaths brought from the train.

Dawn began to break and, storm or no storm, the river had to be crossed to reach the castle in time for the burial ceremony. The coffins were loaded on to two ordinary black hearses supplied by the Vienna Municipality and the illustrious mourners piled into hired taxis to drive down to the ferry. The crossing of the swollen river under thunder and lightning was a nightmare. At one point in midstream, the lead horses of the funeral coaches took such fright at a thunderclap that they nearly plunged off the huge raft altogether and into the torrent, taking the coffins with them. But once safely on the other shore, all danger and turmoil seemed to die away. The weather cleared and Artstetten was reached without further incident.

Hundreds more funeral guests arrived by special trains from Vienna to attend the final service, held in the chapel of the castle at 11 a.m. that morning. They included, apart from Sophie's many relatives, Prince Starhemberg and most of the aristocratic mourners he had assembled in Vienna the night before. There would doubtless have been an even bigger collection of great names present had not an official court requiem been held in the Vienna Hofburg, timed to coincide exactly with the family ceremony at Artstetten. This was not necessarily one last act of spite on the Court Chamberlain's part, as the Archduke's followers suggested. It could also be interpreted as a formal gesture of piety – as provided for, of course, in the rules of protocol.

Everyone who knelt in Artstetten on the morning of 4 July to hear the last rites, conducted by Prelate Dobner von Dobenau from the nearby pilgrimage church of Maria Taferl, felt grief or shock in differing degrees. But there were four particularly tragic figures in the chapel. Three of them, of course, were the dead couple's children. They had spent one last night at the Belvedere Palace before travelling down from Vienna with their aunt, Henriette Chotek, and here at Artstetten, as at Chlumetz, they were overwhelmed by the sight of familiar childhood surroundings suddenly made desolate by the absence of the father and mother around whom the closely-knit family had always revolved. The fourth pathetic figure was there to mourn not just the dead couple but also the homeland he had lost for good.

This was the youngest of Franz Ferdinand's equally ill-fated brothers, Karl Ferdinand, who in 1912 had been disowned, disinherited and stripped of all archducal rank, privilege and honours for marrying his Fraulein Czuber in defiance of the Emperor's orders. With the single (and, it must be added, enchanting) exception of Rottenstein Castle near Meran in the South Tyrol, all of the empire was banned to him. He seems, even after the brief span of two years, to have decided that life with his Bertha, the Prague University professor's daughter for whom he had defied the Emperor, was hardly worth all the sacrifice involved. At all events, the figure who had descended at Pöchlarn station that morning from the Munich express startled everyone as a gaunt shadow of his former self.

As plain 'Herr Burg' he was, strictly speaking, entitled to no deference. But no-one could bring himself to address him as

anything other than 'Imperial Highness'.[16] For that one day –
thanks to the intercession of his stepmother, Maria Theresa, and
his nephew, the Archduke Charles – the Emperor had allowed
him to set foot on the Austrian lands. When the service was over,
he reboarded his train for Munich, exile, and an early death –
killed, it seems, by sheer heartbreak.

An assassin's bullet was the lesser evil; the murdered brother
was the luckier of the pair. He and his Sophie were now carried
down to the crypt he had built to his own specification five years
before – 'a light airy place, where I can hear the birds singing' –
borne by officers of two of his former regiments, the 4th
Dragoons and the 7th Uhlans. Their coffins were eventually
encased in two handsome white marble sarcophagi of precisely
the same dimensions. Across the base stone on which they rest
side by side are carved the words, '*Iuncti Coniugio Fatis
Iunguntur Eisdem*,' 'Joined in marriage, united by the same fate.'
The simple legend, and the clean lines of the monuments
themselves, are in appropriate contrast to all the hyperbole and
stifling ornament of the Capuchin crypt.

*   *   *

One month to the day after that peaceful burial service held in
the Danube valley on Saturday 4 July 1914, the whole of Europe
was in flames. In the wake of the assassinations, Austria's inept
Foreign Minister, Count Berchtold – anticipating a repeat
performance, *fortissimo*, of his triumph over Serbia the year
before – despatched an ultimatum to Belgrade, which set the
disaster in train. It included demands for Austrian participation
in rooting out 'subversion' which were so humiliating as almost
to invite rejection. When its contents were shown, for example,
to Sir Edward Grey in London on the morning of 24 July, the
British Foreign Secretary could only comment that the note was
'the most formidable document I have ever seen addressed by
one state to another that was independent'.[17] After the Serbs, as
anticipated (and hoped for) by the 'hawks' in Vienna, failed to
accept the note in its totality, Austria broke off relations the
minute the forty-eight hour time-limit set for compliance was

reached. (European diplomacy had seen nothing to compare with it for speed. It was at 6 p.m. on 25 July that the ultimatum expired; by 6.30, the Austrian Minister in Belgrade, Baron Giesl, was already sitting in the train for Vienna with his entire staff.) The Austrian declaration of war followed on 28 July. This was not a wilful act to provoke a world conflict. On the contrary, it was a naïve attempt to deal summarily with Serbia while keeping the world at bay. Berchtold had made a hideous miscalculation in believing that Russia, the great protector of the Serbs, would keep her hands folded yet again.

Encouraged by strong declarations of support from his French ally, the Tsar, after some typical vacillations and half-measures, ordered general mobilization in Russia two days later, on 30 July. With that, Europe had reached the point of no return. Great powers could, as a political gesture, partly mobilize their armed forces and then, the objective achieved or abandoned, stand them down again without undue loss of face. But full mobilization was intended, and accepted, as a challenge tantamount to war. Austria-Hungary, her bluff called, was forced by the military code and political temper of the day to follow Russia's example. Germany and France, rival allies of these two rival powers now squaring up to each other in the Balkans, announced their own general mobilizations twenty-four hours later. The European Powers were trapped in those webs of alliances, dangled against each other, which they had spun over four decades. Despite a flurry of last-minute attempts from both camps to side-step disaster, mobilizations moved rapidly and relentlessly into hostilities. England, the only power in the two blocs not bound by written treaty, was the last to enter the ring with her declaration of war against Germany at midnight on 4 August. Her concern was not how, or even whether, Sarajevo should be avenged, but the defence of Belgian territory, violated by the German army in its march against France. The conflict had thus spread within six weeks across a matrix of formal pacts and secret understandings all the way from the mountains of Bosnia to the Channel ports of Flanders. The progression was as logical as it was ludicrous.

CHAPTER FOURTEEN

Youth Museum

SARAJEVO'S YOUNG BOSNIANS of today are a very different breed
from the comrades of Gavrilo Princip. They are not the hunted
but the vanguard of the hunters. Privileged because not of
bourgeois origin, their task is to preserve their own People's
Republic, and with it the whole Federation of Yugoslavia's
Communist states, from any relapse into imperialism. As if to
symbolize the change, the old Austrian Town Hall is now their
university library. The broad steps outside, which the Archduke
and his wife descended to make the last brief drive to their
deaths, are now dotted with students. They sprawl with their
books in the same June sunshine and look across the old Appel
Quay (now, after several renamings, called the Boulevard
Radicevica Vojvode Stepe) at the same Miljacka river, running
sluggishly, as it always did, in the midsummer heat.

Princip the assassin is now Princip the national hero, as he
himself predicted he would be. The Communists have marked
the spot where he fired his two bullets by sinking an impression
of his feet into a concrete paving slab. The footprints are set
wide apart, as though he were still steadying himself for the shots.
The old Latein Bridge opposite is now called the Princip Bridge
after him and the corner building where he stood, now the
Young Bosnia Museum, is, in fact, a shrine to his memory.

After a brief documentary display of Austrian 'oppression'
(which consists of nothing more sinister than a few routine
decrees and ordinances) there is a giant relief map of the murder
route taken by the Archduke through the city on 28 June 1914

and pictures of all the conspirators, together with a few earlier Bosnian heroes. But Princip, quite rightly, is the star. His mother's black apron and working tools are placed in one corner. Opposite, there are pictures of the wooden hut where he was born and a photograph of both parents – a splendid hawk-eyed, leather-faced old peasant couple, dolled out in their Sunday best.

Here too are pictures of Princip the prisoner. Though three of the conspirators, including Danilo Ilić, were hanged, the rest, either because their crime was judged less severe or simply because they were under-age, got away with prison terms. The latter condition was, of course, the one applied to Princip, who was sentenced, together with Grabez and Cabrinović, to twenty years hard labour 'with one foodless day a month and transfer to a dark cell with a wooden bed on every 28 June'. He died less than two years later of bone tuberculosis at the military prison of Theresienstadt, south of Vienna, having impressed even his captors with his stoic bearing. The death certificate, issued on 24 April 1916 in the middle of the war he had precipitated, is among the exhibits on the wall.

Groups of Yugoslav schoolchildren are regularly led in for a tour of the museum, which is a standard part of their indoctrination. The guide's commentary is restrained, even, at times, almost defensive in tone. Princip did not seek a world war, they are told: it was just that assassination had become the accepted method of political protest in his time. Even less had he wanted to kill a woman, for whom these idealistic freedom fighters of the nineteenth century had an almost mystical respect. The Archduke's wife had simply got in the way. It was regrettable; but these things do happen.

The Bosnian schoolchildren of today troop round the exhibits of Princip the assassin with the same polite earnestness displayed by the young Viennese before the exhibits of Franz Ferdinand, his victim. There is an even closer resemblance. Physically, they are almost indistinguishable from those Austrian children – the same untidy hair, the same jeans, the same T-shirts, sometimes even with the same motifs. To these young people, the museums are more like a Panoptikon than a shrine, and, in both cities, revolution seems a long way away. Few, even in the Bosnian groups, look fierce enough to live up to the terrible dictum of Bogdan Zerajić (also featured in the museum): 'He who wants to live, let him die. He who wants to die, let him live.'

In both museums, the older onlooker asks himself how much these youthful visitors realize the impact on their own lives of these exhibits in glass cases. The Tsarist empire may or may not have been doomed as such. But it is a moot point whether, for example, Bolshevism would have triumphed in Russia in 1917 had not Germany, as a short-sighted trick of war, enabled Lenin to leave his exile in Switzerland and cross the continent by sealed train to galvanize the revolution from St Petersburg. That revolution, happening when and how it did, was also one of the ultimate consequences of Gavrilo Princip's bullets. From it flowed, in the course of time, the victory of Communism in Yugoslavia after a later war, and the emergence of a neutral Austrian republic as the anaesthetized rump of the dismembered Habsburg Monarchy.

*   *   *

Though Franz Ferdinand may have had premonitions of his assassination, he could never have imagined what that deed would bring about in its train. The 'Great' War of 1914–18 is the only conflict in human history described by that one plain adjective. Even the conflagration which broke out twenty years later, to end after five years in the mushroom clouds of the atom-bomb, is known merely as the Second World War. The pre-eminence of the earlier conflict is grimly justified. For the first time, much of the globe was sucked into a battle which began in the heart of one of its continents. Afterwards, in every village of the old Europe, from the English Cotswolds to the Austrian Tyrol and from the Baltic coast down to Sicily, memorials were erected to mark the ten million it killed. Every city of the new world and the European dominions overseas erected similar monuments.

The political sea-change was more momentous even than this huge spillage of life. Three empires – those of the Romanovs, the Hohenzollerns and Franz Ferdinand's own – disappeared for ever from the map. Soviet Communism was born, a force which was eventually to bring nearly all of the old Dual Monarchy under its heel and to spread its tentacles throughout the world. So too was born out of that conflict the physical supremacy of America in the non-Communist world as those other empires which had emerged victorious in the war – the British, French, Dutch, Belgian and Portuguese – started out nonetheless on their own political decline. And with the vanishing of the old order, stability, which had been its hallmark, faded too. Like the Archduke's three orphaned children, the world was thrust into an age of insecurity and bewilderment.

It was in the wake of this upheaval that the Archduke came to be looked upon as a rock which, had it not been destroyed, might have held off the storm. Even that savage baiter of the Habsburgs, Karl Kraus, stepped a respectful pace back before Franz Ferdinand's image. In his satirical epic *The Last Days of Mankind*, the Archduke was described as 'the hope of all who still thought it possible to build an ordered political state on the marches of the great chaos'. Sir Fairfax Cartwright, the very perceptive British ambassador at Vienna through the five years (1908–13) of Franz Ferdinand's 'reign' at the Belvedere, felt that the Archduke, and he alone, might prove capable of settling his country's differences with Russia in the Balkans, just as England had settled hers with Russia in Asia. Moreover, to Cartwright, Franz Ferdinand was the one man who, as Emperor, could fill the role of 'the great Catholic sovereign of the world' in a revival of Austria's prestige and power alongside her overbearing German ally. In this way, the diplomat once philosophized in a long historical essay to Sir Edward Grey, the predominance of Protestant Prussia on the continent – established by the defeat of Austria in 1866 and France in 1871 – would at last be challenged, much to England's benefit.

Later generations were to compare the Archduke to a kingly de Gaulle, an authoritarian ruler who might have restored to his divided and lethargic subjects both unity and pride, simply by imparting to them something of his own burning sense of mission. Certainly, what mattered about Franz Ferdinand was not just that he was the most intelligent and forceful Archduke his dynasty had produced in the nineteenth century but that he was the only one who was convinced that it had a future in the twentieth. It was not so much what he wanted to do with the Dual Monarchy but the fact that he was determined to do anything at all which marked him out from the rest.

So it is fascinating to speculate what might have happened to the Dual Monarchy and to Europe had Franz Joseph succumbed to that serious illness in late April of 1914 and had the Archduke then succeeded him as Franz II of Austria-Hungary instead of meeting an assassin's bullet at a street-corner in Sarajevo two months later. Could he have modernized his empire in peace-time? Could he have helped prolong the European peace, which was itself an indispensable background for any such internal reform?

All we know is that he had identified the dangers, both at home and abroad, and that he possessed the resolution to tackle them. Any attempt in the domestic field to modify Dualism would, however, have struck at the basis on which the Monarchy had operated for the best part of half a century. Had he really been prepared to take the Hungarian bull by the horns, cut down the powers and privileges of Budapest by imperial decree and threaten the use of force to back his policy up, he might have prevailed for a while over Magyar resistance. But the empire might well have emerged more weakened by such an upheaval than by a continuation of the debilitating status quo, and the Hungarians – so much more vigorous and confident than their Austrian partners – would never have given up the fight with Vienna. It was not the self-centred Hungarian leadership which Franz Ferdinand had to fear (though Count Tisza, the Prime Minister he would have had to tackle as Emperor, was certainly a very formidable figure) so much as the spirit of the nation. Success at home was thus, at best, problematical.

What he might have achieved in foreign policy depends on

the non-existent answer to the riddle of whether the Great War was itself inevitable. Here again all we know is that Franz Ferdinand, even as heir to the throne, had a rare perception of the perils presented by those rival alliances which divided the continent and made even the pettiest of conflicts so difficult to localize. As sovereign, he would have been powerfully placed to bring about his life-long dream, the restoration of the Three Emperors' League, and thus rebuild a link of sorts between Austria and Russia. But whether such an old-fashioned dynastic bridge could have survived the poundings of the twentieth century – especially as it had to span the explosive Balkan battlefield of interests – is, again, a matter for doubt.

As for the Archduke's late conversion to England, it would surely have taken far more than a few more shooting-parties with King George V (himself utterly uninterested, unlike his father, in European politics) to alter the island-kingdom's informal but very binding military commitments to France. Franz Ferdinand had the right diagnosis as Archduke. As Emperor, he may well have come too late to effect the cure. As it was, four years after his murder, his own empire followed into the grave the one man who, just conceivably, might have saved it.

These ambiguities seem to flit across his death mask. Sophie's is serene, almost radiant, the face of a woman who had proven to herself, to her husband and to the world that their love had made all the agony worthwhile and had confounded the spite. The Archduke's features are also calm. Yet there is just the trace of an ironic smile in his frozen features, as if he suspected that his death would demonstrate just how right he had been in life.

Source Notes

CHAPTER TWO

1. Otto von Forst, *Ahnen-Tafel...
   Erzherzogs Franz Ferdinand von
   Oesterreich-Este* (Vienna, 1910).
2. Letter quoted in Theodor von
   Sosnowsky, *Erzherzog Franz
   Ferdinand* (Munich, 1928), p. 80.
3. The anecdote about the Duke of
   Modena's legacy was told to the
   author by the ex-Empress Zita on
   22 February 1976.
4. All in Briefe, Karton 5, Depot
   Hohenberg, Nachlass Franz
   Ferdinand, Staatsarchiv, Vienna
   (henceforth quoted as Nachlass FF).
5. Franz Ferdinand's letter quoted in
   Brigitte Harman, *Rudolf* (Vienna,
   1978), p. 426.
6. Nachlas FF, Briefe, Karton 5.
7. All in Nachlass FF, Briefe, Karton 5.

CHAPTER THREE

1. Nachlass FF, Archduke Albrecht,
   14 August 1889.
2. Franz Ferdinand to Baron Beck,
   quoted in Krug von Nidda, *Der
   Weg nach Sarajevo* (Vienna, 1964),
   p. 28.
3. Adam Mueller-Guttenbrunn, *Franz
   Ferdinand's Lebensroman* (Stuttgart,
   1919), p. 19.

4. Nachlass FF, Briefe, Archduke
   Albrecht, 28 July 1892.
5. Mueller-Guttenbrunn,
   Lebensroman, p. 50.
6. *Tagebuch meiner Reise um die Erde*
   Vol. I, p. 5, henceforth cited as
   Tagebuch.
7. R.A./I 88 (2): letter of Knollys to
   Ponsonby, 19 October 1892.
8. R.A. N/48/160/6.
9. R.A. I/88/5: telegram from Sir
   A. Paget to Lord Rosebery,
   1 November 1892.
10. R.A. N48/171: Lord Harris to the
    Queen, 20 January 1893.
11. *Tagebuch*, Vol. I, p. 268.
12. *Tagebuch*, Vol. II, p. 5.
13. Ibid., p. 421.
14. Ibid., p. 424.
15. Countess Sophie Nostitz to the
    author, 30 June 1982.
16. Former Empress Zita to the author.
17. His application quoted in Edmund
    von Glaise-Horstenau, *Franz
    Joseph's Weggefährte* (Leipzig,
    1930), p. 425.

CHAPTER FOUR

1. Albert von Margutti, *Vom Alten
   Kaiser* (Vienna, 1921), pp. 128 et
   seq.
2. Eisenmenger, *Erzherzog Franz
   Ferdinand*.

3. Nora Fugger, *Im Glanz der Kaiserzeit* (Vienna, 1930), pp. 323–4.
4. Unpublished memoirs of Count Sternberg, p. 284.
5. See, for example, the *Hofkalender* for 1915, pp. 106–8.
6. Mueller-Guttenbrunn, *Lebensroman*, pp. 16–17.
7. Ibid., p. 107.
8. For example, Archduchess Isabella from Pressburg to Franz Ferdinand, 12 September 1894 and 4 October 1895 (Nachlass FF, Briefe, Karton 3).
9. Nachlass FF, Briefe, Karton 3: Archduchess Isabella to Franz Ferdinand, 9 August 1885.
10. Nachlass FF, Briefe, Karton 3: Emperor Franz Joseph to Franz Ferdinand, 2 August 1895.
11. Eisenmenger, *Erzherzog Franz Ferdinand*, pp. 11–12.
12. Ibid., p. 18.
13. Sternberg memoirs, pp. 187–9.
14. Ibid., p. 206.
15. Nachlass FF, Briefe, Karton 1: Franz Ferdinand to Franz Joseph, Cairo, 17 March 1896.
16. Eisenmenger, *Erzherzog Franz Ferdinand*, p. 79.
17. Franz Ferdinand to Countess Fugger, 14 February 1897, Fugger, *Im Glanz der Kaiserzeit*, pp. 317–20
18. Nachlass FF, Briefe, Karton 1: Franz Joseph to Franz Ferdinand, 7 April 1897.

CHAPTER FIVE

1. Nachlass FF, Briefe, Karton 3: Archduchess Isabella to Franz Ferdinand, 11 August 1983.
2. Nachlass FF, Briefe, Karton 3: Archduke Frederick to Franz Ferdinand, 13 July 1899.
3. Ibid., 3 February 1907.
4. Paul Nikitsch-Boulles, *Vor dem Sturm* (Berlin, 1925), pp. 28–9.
5. Anecdote told by the Empress Zita to the author, 22 April 1968.
6. For example Gerd Höller, *Franz Ferdinand von Oesterreich-Este* (Vienna, 1982), p. 95. The sole source appears to be the well-informed but heavily embroidered *Lebensroman*, pp. 149–50.
7. All the above details provided by Countess Sophie Nostitz to author, 10 November 1982.
8. A well-informed but very highly coloured account is given in *Lebensroman*, pp. 146–54.
9. Nachlass FF, Briefe, Karton 1: Franz Joseph to Franz Ferdinand, 5 October 1899.
10. Nachlass FF, Briefe, Karton 5: Erzherzog Rainer to Franz Ferdinand, 2 May 1900.
11. Reminiscences of Bruno Richter, by courtesy of Countess Sophie Nostitz, 18 November 1982.
12. Nachlass FF, Briefe, Karton 12: Beck to Franz Ferdinand, 19 May 1900.
13. Nachlass FF, Karton 12: appendix to letters of Beck to Franz Ferdinand; 19 May 1900.
14. Mueller-Guttenbrunn, *Lebensroman*, p. 154.
15. Full description of the ceremony in the *Deutsche Zeitung*, the *Fremdenblatt* and other Vienna papers for 28 June 1900.
16. Reminiscences of Bruno Richter.
17. Descriptions of the wedding are given in contemporary newspapers preserved in the National Bibliothek of Vienna and at the Hohenberg Castle at Artstetten. The most detailed accounts are in the local journals such as the *Leitmeritzer Zeitung* of 3 July 1900.
18. *Teplitz-Schönauer Anzeiger*, 30 June 1900.
19. *Agramer Zeitung*, 2 July 1900.
20. *Teplitz-Schönauer Anzeiger*, 30 June 1900.

CHAPTER SIX

1. Franz Ferdinand to Archduchess Maria Theresa, 9 July 1900, quoted in Sosnowsky, *Erzherzog Franz Ferdinand*, pp. 35–6.
2. Empress Zita to the author, 10 April 1978.
3. Prince Gerhardt Hohenberg to the author, 30 June 1982.
4. A full account of this in Nikitsch, *Vor dem Sturm*, pp. 36–8.
5. Description by Regierungsrat Dr Teuber, reproduced in *Pressburger Presse*, 2 July 1900.
6. Nikitsch, *Vor dem Sturm*, pp. 180–90.
7. Countess Sophie Nostitz to the author, 28 March 1983.
8. Sosnowsky, *Erzherzog Franz Ferdinand*, pp. 37–44.
9. Countess Sophie Nostitz to the author, 30 June 1982.
10. *Die Grosse Politik* Vol. 34 (II) Von Tschirschky to Berlin No. 13000, 20 March 1913 (henceforth cited as *G.P.*).
11. Bruno Brehm, *Apis und Este* (Munich, 1931), pp. 142–6.
12. Brook-Shepherd, *Uncle of Europe* (London, 1975), p. 46.
13. Empress Zita to the author, 7 March 1977.
14. Eisenmenger, *Erzherzog Franz Ferdinand*, p. 145.
15. Jonathan Ruffier, *The Big Shots* (Debrett, London, 1977), p. 46.
16. Eisenmenger, *Erzherzog Franz Ferdinand*, p. 145.
17. Countess Sophie Nostitz to the author, 28 March 1983.
18. Empress Zita to the author, 22 February 1976.
19. Franz Conrad von Hötzendorf, *Aus meiner Dienstzeit* (Vienna 1921–5), Vol. I, p. 338.
20. Unpublished memoirs of Baron Morsey, pp. 26–7, 38.
21. Countess Sophie Nostitz to the author, 9 September 1982.
22. Empress Zita to the author, 7 March 1977.
23. Nikitsch, *Vor dem Sturm*, pp. 50–7 quotes the exchange of letters in full.
24. Nachlass FF, Briefe, Karton 16: telegram from Franz Janaczek to Franz Ferdinand, 14 January 1911.

CHAPTER SEVEN

1. For a brief illustrated essay on the Belvedere, see Gordon Brook-Shepherd in *Great Palaces* (London, 1964), pp. 223–9.
2. The former Empress Zita to the author, 22 February 1976.
3. 'Goldy' Mathé, née Montenuovo, to whom the author is indebted for the document.
4. Countess Sophie Nostitz to the author, 9 September 1982.
5. See page 75.
6. I am indebted to Prince Gerhard Hohenberg, a grandson of the Archduke's, for information on these points. See also Nikitsch, *Vor dem Sturm*, p. 33.
7. Countess Sophie Nostitz to the author, 30 June 1982.
8. Nikitsch, *Vor dem Sturm*, pp. 30–1.
9. Morsey, p. 10.
10. Empress Zita to the author, 7 March 1977.
11. Nachlass FF, Briefe, Karton 1: Franz Joseph, 6 April 1899.
12. Empress Zita to the author, 7 March 1977.
13. Document given in full in Leopold Chlumecky, *Erzherzog Franz Ferdinands Wirken und Wollen* (henceforth cited as *Wirken und Wollen*) (Berlin, 1929), pp. 355–62. For other details on Brosch and the Military Chancery see Sosnowsky, *Erzherzog Franz Ferdinand*, pp. 119–21, Nikitsch, *Vor dem*

Sturm, pp. 60–2 and Rudolf Kiszling, *Erzherzog Franz Ferdinand von 'Osterreich-Este'* (Vienna, 1953), pp. 165–7.

14. Printed in Chlumecky, *Wirken und Wollen*, pp. 37–8.

CHAPTER EIGHT

1. Franz Hubman, *K. und K. Familien-Album* (Vienna, 1971), p. 18.
2. Nachlass FF, Briefe, Karton 1: Franz Ferdinand to Franz Joseph, June 1907.
3. Franz Ferdinand to Beck, quoted in R. A. Kann, *Erzherzhog Franz Ferdinand Studien* (Vienna, 1976), pp. 114–5.
4. Quoted in Kann, op. cit. pp. 61–2.
5. Fugger, *Im Glanz der Kaizerzeit*, p. 302.
6. Empress Zita to the author, 8 March 1977.
7. Text in *Wiener Zeitung*, 9 April 1901.
8. Nachlass FF, Briefe, Karton 1: Franz Joseph to Franz Ferdinand, 20 April 1901.
9. Ibid., Franz Joseph to Franz Ferdinand, 18 April 1901.
10. Brosch Memorandum of 12 October 1913, reproduced in Chlumecky, *Wirken und Wollen*, pp. 354–65.
11. Conrad, *Aus Meiner Dienstzeit*, Vol. 1, pp. 33–6, describes this and other details of his appointment.
12. The whole story has been told, in a carefully disinfected style, by the lady herself. Gina von Hötzendorf *Mein Leben mit Conrad von Hötzendorf* (Leipzig, 1935). The story of the romance is covered in pp. 1–46.
13. Conrad, *Aus Meiner Dienstzeit*, Vol. 2, p. 94.
14. Empress Zita to the author, 18 February 1980.

15. For these and other details see A. E. Sokol, *Seemacht Oesterreich* (Vienna, 1972), pp. 102 et seq.
16. Kiszling, *Erzherzhog Franz Ferdinand von 'Osterreich-Este'* p. 104.
17. Edmund von Glaise-Horstenau, *Franz Joseph's Weggefährte* (Leipzig, 1930), p. 406.
18. Conrad, *Aus Meiner Dienstzeit*, Vol. I, pp. 564–5.
19. Nachlass FF, Briefe, Karton 6: draft to Emperor William, 8 August 1909.
20. Kiszling, *Erzherzhog Franz Ferdinand von 'Osterreich-Este'* p. 255.
21. Czernin's various memoranda are quoted in Kann, *Erzherzhog Franz Ferdinand Studien*, pp. 175 et seq.

CHAPTER NINE

1. See Brook-Shepherd, *Uncle of Europe*, pp. 153 et seq.
2. Margutti, *Vom alten Kaiser*, p. 75.
3. Royal Archives (henceforth R.A.), GV P609/4, report of Sir Maurice de Bunsen in Vienna.
4. Margutti, *Vom alten Kaiser*, p. 70.
5. Morsey, p. 43.
6. G.P. Vol. 26, No. 9550, Herr von Jagow to Chancellor Bülow, 10 June 1909.
7. G.P., Vol. 26, No. 11262, von Tschirschky in Vienna to Berlin, 23 March 1912.
8. G.P., Vol. 30, No. 11237, von Tschirschky in Vienna to Bethmann-Hollweg, 20 November 1911.
9. Conrad, *Aus meiner Dienstzeit*, Vol. III, p. 503.
10. Margutti, *Vom alten Kaiser*, p. 74.
11. Quoted in Kann, *Erzherzog Franz Ferdinand Studien*, p. 88.
12. Prince Bernard von Bülow, *Memoirs*, Vol. 1 (London, 1937), p. 397.

13. G.P., Vol. 30, No. 11085, Emperor William to Bethmann-Hollweg, 27 March 1912.
14. Bülow, *Memoirs*, Vol. II, pp. 613–14.
15. One of the best general accounts of the 1908 crisis and its solution remains Sydney Fay's *The Origins of the World War* (New York, 1928), Vol 1, pp. 368–406.
16. Bülow, *Memoirs*, Vol. II, pp. 325–6.
17. Chlumecky, *Wirken und Wollen*, p. 98.
18. Ibid., pp. 98–9.
19. See, for example, his own testimony in Conrad, *Aus meiner Dienstzeit*, Vol. I, p. 142.
20. Letter quoted in Kann, *Erzherzhog Franz Ferdinand Studien*, p. 79 (footnote).
21. See Nikitsch, *Vor dem Sturm*, p. 121.
22. Conrad, *Aus Meiner Dienstzeit*, Vol. I, p. 151.
23. Ibid., p. 158.
24. G.P., Vol. 26, No. 731.
25. G.P., Vol. 26, No. 9453, report of Count Brockdorff-Ranzau, 17 March 1909.
26. G.P., Vol. 26, No. 9087, Emperor William to Chancellor Bülow, 6 November 1908.
27. See Sir Edward Grey, *Twenty-five Years* (London, 1924), pp. 188–9.

CHAPTER TEN

1. Nikitsch, *Vor dem Sturm*, p. 129.
2. This and subsequent details of the visit have been taken largely from the *Neue Freie Presse* (henceforth cited as *N.F.P.*) of 10–15 July 1909. Nikitsch pp. 130–3 gives a sketchy personal account.
3. Nachlass FF, Briefe, Karton 1: Franz Joseph to Franz Ferdinand, 8 June 1905.
4. Nachlass FF, Briefe, Karton 6: Emperor William to Franz Ferdinand, 9 April 1909.
5. *N.F.P.* issues of 10–14 November give full details of the visit.
6. Nachlass FF, Briefe, Karton 17: Obersthofmeisterant to Franz Ferdinand, 13 March 1913.
7. Nachlass FF, Briefe, Karton 1: Franz Joseph to Franz Ferdinand, 31 July 1909.
8. Nachlass FF, Briefe, Karton 11: Colonel Bardolff to Franz Ferdinand, 22 December 1909.
9. Details in Nachlass FF, Nachtrag II.
10. Carl Bardolff, *Soldat im alten Oesterreich* (Jena, 1938), pp. 174 et seq.
11. Conrad, *Aus meiner Dienstzeit*, Vol. 2, pp. 373–5, describes the circumstances of his reappointment.
12. Ibid., pp. 379–81 and 410–12.
13. Ibid., p. 413.
14. G.P., Vol. 34, No. 12,788, private letter of Duke Albrecht to Prince Fürstenberg, copied by him to the German embassy in Vienna, 2 February 1913.
15. Conrad, *Aus meiner Deinstzeit*, Vol. 3, pp. 724 et seq. reproduces the full minutes of the Council meeting of 3 October.
16. See for example Chancellor Bethmann-Hollweg's warning letter to the Austrian envoy in Berlin, Baron Szögyenyi, of 6 July 1913 (reprinted in Fay, *The Origins of the World War*, Vol. 1, pp. 451–2).
17. Conrad, *Aus meiner Deinstzeit*, Vol. 3, p. 155.
18. G.P., Vol. 34 (I), No. 12,905, Kaganeck's report to Berlin, 26 February 1913.
19. For a detailed description of the episode see Conrad, *Aus meiner Deinstzeit*, Vol. 3, pp. 467–71.
20. King Edward's letter conveying the award is in Nachlass FF, Briefe, Karton 23: Edward VII to Franz

Ferdinand, 5 July 1902.

21. Wickham Steed, *Thirty Years*, Vol. I, pp. 235–6.
pp. 235–6.

22. R.A., G.V.: King's diary entry for 20 April 1904.

23. Nachlass FF, Briefe, Karton 23: King George V to Franz Ferdinand, 8 May 1910.

24. Mensdorff Diary, in Mensdorff MSS, Haus, Hof und Staatsarchiv, Vienna.

25. Mensdorff MSS, Nachlass, Briefe, Karton 1: (copy) to Franz Ferdinand, 14 May 1910.

26. Mensdorff MSS, diary entry for 12 May 1910.

27. Nachlass FF, Karton 2: report of Franz Ferdinand, 25 May 1910.

28. R.A., G.V.: diary entry for 23 May 1913.

29. Mensdorff MSS: letter No. 234 to Franz Ferdinand, 19 July 1913.

30. Ibid. Letter No. 238, Franz Ferdinand to Mensdorff, 23 July 1913.

31. Mensdorff diary entry for 18 November 1913, when already at Windsor.

32. Nikitsch, *Vor dem Sturm*, pp. 166–7.

33. R.A., G.V.: diary entries, 17–21 November 1913.

34. Ibid. Entry for 18 November 1913.

35. Mensdorff Diaries, entry for 24 November 1913.

36. The Duke of Portland, *Men, Women and Things* (London, 1937), p. 246.

37. Ibid., p. 247.

38. R.A., G.V.: Queen Mary to the Duchess Augusta of Mecklenburg-Strelitz, 20 November 1913.

39. Ibid.: Queen Mary to Duchess Augusta of Mecklenburg-Strelitz, 27 November 1913.

40. Unpublished memoirs of Baron Morsey, undated entry.

41. Empress Zita to the author, 22 February 1976.

CHAPTER ELEVEN

1. Countess Sophie Nostitz to the author.

2. Duke of Portland, *Men, Women and Things*, p. 331. There is no reference to this planned visit in the Royal Archives at Windsor, which suggests that the arrangement was only verbal.

3. Morsey, p. 33.

4. Morsey gives a sketchy account of these. A more detailed version is provided by Herr von Treutler of the German Foreign Office (who accompanied the Emperor) in G.P., Vol. 39, Nos. 15720 and 15721.

5. Vladimir Dedijer, *The Road to Sarajevo* (London, 1967), pp. 289–90. Dedijer, though one-sided in some of his judgements, gives a very detailed reconstruction of the plot. For a modern Austrian work, see Fritz Würthle, *Die Spur führt nach Belgrad* (Vienna, 1975). Fay, *The Origins of the World War* Vol. II, pp. 53–126, is still valuable though written more than half a century ago. The classic Austrian account of that same era is Dr Frederick Wiesner's writings in *Die Kriegsschuldfrage* (Berlin, 1926, 1927 and 1928). See also Sosnowsky, *Erzherzog Franz Ferdinand*, pp. 167–230.

6. Wiesner, *Die Kriegsschuldfrage*, September 1927. For biographical details on all the assassins, based largely on Austrian police records and their own testimonies, see Dedijer, *The Road to Sarajevo*, pp. 175 et seq.; Würthle, *Die Spur Fuhrt nach Belgrad*, pp. 59–78; and Höller, *Franz Ferdinand von Osterreich-Este*, pp. 207–22.

7. The complete text of the 'Black Hands' secret book of rules was first revealed by M. Bogicevic in the Paris periodical *Evolution*, 16–30 July 1927.

8. Dedijer, *The Road to Sarajevo*, p. 294
9. Franz Ferdinand, Military Chancery, No. 3911, 21 May 1914.
10. Conrad, *Aus meiner Dienstzeit*, Vol. III, p. 445.
11. J. A. Zibert, *Der Mord von Sarajevo* (Laibach, 1919), quoted in Höller, *Franz Ferdinand von Osterreich-Este*, p. 226.
12. Empress Zita to the author, 7 March 1977.
13. Dedijer, *The Road to Sarajevo*, pp. 297–300, gives a minute reconstruction of the journey.
14. Wickham Steed, 'The Pact of Konopischt', in Vol. 79 of *Nineteenth Century and After* (London, February 1916).
15. *N.F.P.*, 11 June 1914.
16. Morsey, p. 49.
17. G.P. Vol. 39, No. 15736. Report by von Treutler, 15 June 1914.
18. *N.F.P.*, issues of 12–15 June 1914, give exhaustive details of the occasion.
19. Empress Zita to the author, 7 March 1977. Her last statement is, in fact, not correct. The Archduchess Maria Theresa wrote her plea on 2 July 1916. William II wrote back – after consulting his Foreign Office – seven weeks later on 23 August, regretfully turning down the proposal on the grounds that this was a matter not for him alone to decide, but for all the states of the German empire. Neither they, he wrote, nor the German Parliament could be expected to sanction 'the removal of a part of the empire with the founding of a new (!) dynasty'. The exchange is given in full in Sosnowsky, *Erzherzog Franz Ferdinand*, pp. 43–4.
20. Morsey, p. 54.
21. Ibid., p. 58.
22. Baron von Eichhoff, quoted in Sosnowsky, *Erzherzog Franz Ferdinand*, p. 197 (footnote).
23. Gordon Brook-Shepherd, *The Last Habsburg* (London, 1968), pp. 26–7, quoting information given by the Empress Zita. (The desk, when opened by Archduke Charles six weeks later, was found to contain papers similar in content to the 'Regierungsprogramm' summarized in Appendix II.)
24. From the personal papers of his daughter, now Countess Sophie Nostitz, published here for the first time.

CHAPTER TWELVE

1. Morsey, p. 61.
2. Kiszling, *Erzherzog Franz Ferdinand von 'Osterreich-Este'* p. 293.
3. Morsey, p. 59.
4. Nikitsch, *Vor dem Sturm*, pp. 214–15.
5. Morsey, p. 64.
6. Höller, *Franz Ferdinand von Osterreich-Este*, pp. 278.
7. Dedijer, *The Road to Sarajevo*, pp. 312–14.
8. Morsey, p. 69.
9. Ibid., p. 7.
10. Formal statement made to the Court of Inquiry by Count Harrach on the day of the murder, and reproduced in Sosnowsky, *Erzherzog Franz Ferdinand*, pp. 219–20.

CHAPTER THIRTEEN

1. Margutti, *Vom altem Kaiser*, pp. 81–2.
2. See Irmgard Schiel, *Stephanie* (Stuttgart, 1979), p. 325.
3. Brook-Shepherd, *The Last Habsburg*, pp. 1–2.
4. *N.F.P.*, 29 June 1914.
5. Morsey, p. 77.

6. Countess Sophie Nostitz, letter to the author, 7 July 1982.

7. Brook-Shepherd, *The Last Habsburg*, pp. 2–3.

8. *N.F.P.*, 29 June 1914, report from Kiel.

9. Höller, *Franz Ferdinand von 'Osterreich-Este'*, p. 246.

10. Details of the journey were given by Major Höger in the *N.F.P.* of 4 July 1914 and in Morsey's diary.

11. Empress Zita to the author, 7 March 1977. This seems to dispose of allegations (see Sosnowsky, *Erzherzog Franz Ferdinand*, pp. 226–7) that anything was changed as a result of Archduke Charles's intervention.

12. R.A., G.V., p. 609: Sir Maurice de Bunsen to Lord Stamfordham, 3 July 1914.

13. Quoted in *N.F.P.*, 30 June 1914.

14. *Neuer Wiener Journal*, 9 July 1914.

15. Countess Sophie Nostitz to the author, 28 March 1983.

16. Nikitsch, *Vor dem Sturm*, pp. 19–20.

17. British Documents on the Origins of the War (London, 1926–30). Vol. XI, No. 91.

APPENDIX I

The following is a translation of the essential paragraphs of the Renunciation Oath as sworn by Archduke Franz Ferdinand on 28 June 1900. (See pp. 76–7.)

But before we proceed to tie the bonds of matrimony we feel ourselves obliged ... to declare that our marriage with Countess Sophie Chotek is not one between equals but is a morganatic union and is to be regarded as such now and for all time. As a consequence, neither our wife nor the children which, with God's blessing, may come from this marriage, nor any of their descendants can lay claim to those rights, honours, titles, coats-of-arms, privileges, etc. which would be accorded to wives of equal rank with their husbands and the children of such a union.

In particular do we recognize and declare with all emphasis that both the children of our own above-mentioned marriage and their descendants – not being members of the All-Highest Arch-House – have no claim to the throne ... and are thus excluded from the succession.

With these words, we pledge ourselves that this present declaration, of whose meaning and significance we are fully aware, is binding for all time for our wife, our children and the descendants of those children, and we further pledge that we will never attempt to retract our present declaration, nor to undertake anything which would aim at weakening or dissolving its binding force.

To confirm this present declaration, as drawn up in two copies, we have signed these deeds in our own hand and marked them with our archducal seal.

Given at Vienna, 28 June 1900.

APPENDIX II

Franz Ferdinand's Programme for Government

(Selected extracts only have been translated)

The informal and, at times, polemical style of the text shows that this was a rough outline of basic principles, as discussed between the Archduke and his advisers, rather than a finished blueprint. This was the document found by Franz Ferdinand's successor as heir to the throne, his nephew Charles, when he opened a locked desk at the Belvedere palace soon after the Sarajevo murders. (See p. 235.) The first full summary was made public in the Vienna *Reichspost* of 28 March 1926. The constant preoccupation with the Hungarian problem speaks for itself.

PROGRAMME FOR THE SUCCESSOR TO THE THRONE

(a) General Considerations

The succession must be carried out in a completely smooth fashion. There are plenty of voices, both at home and abroad, who believe that the Monarchy is only living on borrowed time and that everything will come apart on the death of the old Emperor. Revolution in Hungary, war with Italy and perhaps also against Serbia and Montenegro are expected as certainties. The purpose of the first governmental actions must, accordingly, be:

1. To assure foreign powers that our peaceful policy will be continued, while maintaining our well-established alliances, especially that with Germany.

2. To attempt, at least to begin with, to reach a peaceful understanding with Hungary so that the Monarchy's position abroad as a unified great power is not compromised ...

3. To convey the conviction, at home and abroad, that, from the first day, everything is being executed, according to plan, with a firm hand, calmly and decisively ... any impression of simply 'muddling through' must be avoided.

4. Policy should be expressed only in broad outline. It is absolutely essential to avoid publishing a government programme which only has to be revised soon afterwards.

5. Immediate statements must be made on the following questions:
   a. Foreign policy – peace pledge.
   b. Parliamentary suffrage in Hungary.
   c. Language disputes in Bohemia and Austria.
   d. Equal rights for all nations in Hungary.
   e. Equal rights for all religious faiths.
   f. Equal devotion of the crown towards all classes, whether high or low, rich or poor.
   g. Preservation of the unity of the empire.
   h. Maintenance of the unity of the armed forces.
   i. Maintenance of the 1867 Compromise with Hungary.
   j. Constitutional government.
   k. Clarification of Bosnia's relationship with the Monarchy.
   l. Revision of certain clauses of the 1867 Compromise insomuch as these are not consistent in Austria and Hungary.
   m. Assurances that the oath ceremony in Austria and the coronation ceremony in Hungary will be carried out once the constitution has been reformed.

(b) The Manifesto

... If possible, only one manifesto should be issued, to be published in all languages of the Monarchy ... As the manifesto needs countersigning, the Prime Minister of Hungary must be in agreement with the text. Should it not prove possible, because of Hungarian resistance, to issue one uniform manifesto then there is no alternative to produce three texts, as closely drafted as possible for

Austria

Hungary and

Bosnia-Herzegovina.

This, after all, would document, right from the start, the fact that Bosnia is just as much a component of the empire as Hungary ...

(c) Imperial Chancellor

The position of the head of the imperial house will be defined as virtually that of 'Imperial Chancellor' without immediately nominating him as such and thus provoking opposition in Hungary ...

(d) The position of Her Highness the Duchess of Hohenberg

The position of Her Highness as First Lady at the All-Highest Court must be settled on the first day:
[Sentence in bold type in the original.]

1. In order to prevent the royal house from being placed in an awkward situation (presence of foreign royalty at the funeral ceremonies).

2. Because surprise is the best method of shutting out completely irresponsible elements ...

3. In order to render impossible any Hungarian initiatives to make political capital by raising Her Highness to be Queen of Hungary ... The title and dignity of Duchess with the predicate of 'Highness' remain unchanged ...

(e) Position of Archduke Charles Franz Joseph as Heir

... Archduke Charles Franz Joseph remains heir to the throne until and unless a second and fully eligible marriage should produce children who would themselves have the right of succession ...

(f) Constitutional oath and Coronation oath

... The Emperor Franz Joseph was never called upon to swear an oath by the Austrian constitution, which he himself bestowed on his people ...

It is different in Hungary, where according to the law of 1791, the coronation ... and the swearing of the coronation oath have to take place within six months of succeeding to the throne ...

The basic principle must therefore be established: first reform of the Hungarian situation, then coronation. The various matters at issue should, if possible, be settled by constitutional means. If this proves impossible, then resort must be made to imperial decree.

(g) Extension of the coronation time-limit for Hungary

In order to dispose of the six months time limit, a law would be presented to the Imperial Parliament extending that limit for an indefinite period . . .

(h) Hungary and universal suffrage

The crown has only one effective weapon at its disposal against the stubborn Magyars – universal suffrage . . . This is already in force in all countries and thus cannot be excluded from Hungary . . .

The 19 million inhabitants of Hungary comprise, according to the 1910 census (which was certainly not drawn up unfavourably for the Magyars): 8.7 million Magyar (including 1 million unreliable Jews) and 10.3 million non Magyars, i.e. 2.8 million Rumanians; 2.1 million Slovaks; 2.2 million Germans; 1.1 million Serbs; 0.4 million Ruthenians; 1.7 million Coats. According therefore to the principle of universal suffrage, the 453 seats of the Hungarian Chamber of Deputies ought to be divided as between 206 Magyar and 247 non-Magyar members, whereas the present electoral system results in 40 Croat members plus 10 to 20 representatives of the other nationalities being opposed by about 400 Magyar deputies . . . It is they, the nationalities, who are, however, completely loyal to the imperial crown and want to have nothing to do either with a separation from Austria . . . or with any military concessions in favour of the Magyars . . .

. . . The introduction of universal suffrage in Hungary would therefore completely transform the political situation . . .

*　　*　　*

Other more detailed provisions in the programme go on to lay down new decrees regularizing the status of flags and coats of arms, always with the object of creating unified imperial symbols, to replace the confusion of the existing situation. In future, only the black-yellow flag (the house colours of the Habsburgs) and the imperial eagle are to be used to represent the Monarchy as a whole. With regard to the army, German is to be confirmed as the sole official language. The many concessions made over the years to the Hungarians – concerning both the use of their own language in the military field and the guaranteed posting of Hungarian officers to Hungarian regiments – will be annulled by order of the War Ministry.

After another section on coronation arrangements (and a coronation is foreseen in Vienna and Prague as well as in Budapest), the long document concludes with the text – this in its finalized form – of the proclamation which the Archduke would have made on succeeding to the throne:

MANIFESTO

To our People!

We Franz II
by the Grace of God, Emperor of Austria, Apostolic King of Hungary, King of Bohemia, Dalmatia, Croatia, Slavonia, Galicia, Lodomeria, Rama, Bosnia and Herzegovina, Kumania, King of Illyria, Jerusalem etc., Archduke of Austria-Este, Grandduke of Tuscany and Cracow, Duke of Lorraine, Salzburg, Styria, Carinthia and Bukowina, Prince of Siebenbürgen, Margrave of Moravia, Duke of Upper and Lower Silesia, Modena, Parma, Piacenza, Quastalla, Auschwitz, Zator, Tetschen, Friaul, Ragusa, Zara etc., Count of Habsburg, Tyrol, Kyburg, Gorizia and Gradiska, Prince of Trient and Brixen, Margrave of Upper and Lower Lausitz and Istria, Count of Hohenembs, Feldkirch, Bregenz, Samenberg etc., Lord of Trieste, Cattaro and the Windisch Mark, etc., etc.

It having pleased Almighty God to call from this life my august ancestor His Majesty Emperor and King Franz Joseph I after more than six decades of beneficent rule ...

We hereby solemnly proclaim before all peoples of the Monarchy Our accession to the throne, having been called upon by virtue of the Pragmatic Sanction to place the crown upon Our head ...

We desire to treat with equal love all the peoples of the Monarchy, all classes and all officially recognized religious faiths. High or low, poor or rich, all shall be held the same before Our throne ...

We wish to respect and protect with a strong hand the ancient laws and the established constitutional provisions which have emerged out of the historical development of the Monarchy. As our guarantee for this, we pledge ourselves to

290

the constitutional laws in Austria and Hungary, *inasmuch as complete uniformity can be established between them* ...
[Author's italics]

... We will stoutly preserve ... the unity of the empire on which the Monarchy's position as a Great Power depends. We will also resolutely ensure that the firm foundations of our army, which forms the surest guarantee of the peaceful policy ... we sincerely wish to continue, remains free from tendentious political influences ...

In conformity with our principles governing the equal rights of all peoples and classes, we shall strive to guarantee to every ethnic branch of the Monarchy its own national development, so long as this is perceived to be within the framework of the Monarchy; and to guarantee also to all classes and professions not yet so involved a share in the constitutional process through the promulgation of fair electoral laws.

We desire furthermore to strive with all our power to put an end at last to those linguistic disputes which, for decades, have hampered cultural and economic progress ...

True happiness can be built only upon a sense of piety; to preserve and deepen this shall be for us a matter of conscience ...

Given in our capital city and residence, Vienna, the ... in the year ...

Franz.

Bibliography

I. DOCUMENTS

The principal documents of interest are the Archduke's papers, collected under 'Nachlass Erzherzog Franz Ferdinand' in the Austrian State Archives and held under restricted access by the Hohenberg family. Less important references are scattered among various other collections of papers in the Vienna archives.

The only other contemporary royal archives consulted for this book, by gracious permission of Her Majesty The Queen, are those at Windsor, which contain much of interest on the Archduke, especially during the reigns of Queen Victoria and King George V.

The Archduke's daughter, Countess Sophie Nostitz, has provided the author with some unpublished contemporary reminiscences, notably those of Franz Ferdinand's secretary, Baron Alfred Morsey. She has also furnished several hitherto unpublished letters, telegrams and photographs. The diary of one of the Archduke's friends, Count Adalbert Sternberg, has been supplied by Count Karl Draskovich. Other documentary evidence, and some new picture material, has come from the permanent exhibition on the Archduke at the family castle of Artstetten.

The principal contemporary newspaper source used has been the *Neue Freie Presse*, back numbers of which are preserved at the National Library in Vienna together with other journals of the time.

There are references to the Archduke too numerous to mention in the German, French and British official documents on the origins of the Great War, all of which have been consulted.

2. CONTEMPORARY MEMOIRS

Auffenberg-Komarow, Moritz: *Aus Österreichs Höhe und Niederlage*, Munich 1921

Bülow, Prince Bernard von: *Memoirs*, London 1931

Bardolff, Carl: *Soldat im alten Österreich*, Jena 1938

Chlumecky, Leopold: *Erzherzog Franz Ferdinand's Wirken und Wollen*, Berlin 1929

Conrad v. Hötzendorf, Franz: *Aus meiner Dienstzeit*, Vienna 1921-5

Czernin, Ottokar: *Im Weltkrieg*, Berlin 1919

Eisenmenger, Victor: *Erzherzog Franz Ferdinand*, Vienna 1930

Franz Ferdinand, Erzherzog von Osterreich-Este: *Tagebuch Meiner Reise um die Welt 1892-3*, Vienna 1895-6

Fugger, Nora: *Im Glanz der Kaiserzeit*, Vienna 1980 (reprint)

Funder, Friedrich: *Vom Gestern ins Morgan*, Vienna 1952

Grey, Sir Edward: *Twenty-five Years*, London 1925

Margutti, Albert: *Vom alten Kaiser*, Vienna 1921

Müller-Guttenbrunn, Adam: *Franz Ferdinand's Lebensroman*, Stuttgart 1919

Nikitsch-Boulles, Paul: *Vor dem Sturm. Erinnerungen an Erzherzog- Thronfolger Franz Ferdinand*, Berlin 1925

Polzer-Holditz, Arthur: *Kaiser Karl*, Vienna 1980 (re-issued)

Redlich, Joseph: *Schicksalsjahre Oesterreichs 1908-19*, Vienna 1953-4

Steed, Henry Wickham, *Thirty Years*, London 1924

3. GENERAL LITERATURE (brief selection)

Aichelburg, Wladimir: *Erzherzog Franz Ferdinand und Artstetten*, Vienna 1983

Allmayer-Beck, Johann Christoph: *Ministerpräsident Baron Maximilian Wladimir Beck*, Vienna 1956

Brehm, Bruno: *Apis und Este*, Munich 1931

Bridge, F. R.: *Great Britain and Austria-Hungary 1906-14*, London 1972

Brook-Shepherd, Gordon: *The Last Habsburg*, London 1968
Brook-Shepherd, Gordon: *Uncle of Europe*, London 1974
Constant, Stephen: *Foxy Ferdinand*, London 1979
Corti, Egon Caesar: *Kaiser Franz Joseph*, Graz 1965
Dedijer, Vladimir: *The Road to Sarajevo*, London 1967
Dor, Milo: *Der Letzte Sonntag*, Vienna 1982
Franzel, Emil: *Franz Ferdinand d'Este*, Vienna 1964
Glaise-Horstenau, Edmund: *Die Katastrophe*, Leipzig 1929
Hamann, Brigitte: *Kronprinz Rudolf*, Vienna 1979
Hantsch, Hugo: *Die Geschichte Oesterreichs* 1618–1918, Graz 1950
Holler, Gerd: *Franz Ferdinand von Oesterreich-Este*, Vienna 1982
Hubman, Franz: *K. und K. Familienalbum*, Vienna 1971
Kann, Robert A.: *Erzherzog Franz Ferdinand Studien*, Vienna 1976
Kiszling, Rudolf: *Erzherzog Franz Ferdinand von Oesterreich-Este*, Vienna 1953
Krug von Nidda, Roland: *Der Weg Nach Sarajevo*, Vienna 1964
Macartney, C. A.: *The Habsburg Empire*, London 1968
Muret, Maurice: *L'Archiduc François-Ferdinand*, Paris 1932
Pauli, Hertha: *Das Geheimnis von Sarajevo*, Vienna 1966
Pappenheim, Dr Martin: *Gavrilo Princip's Bekenntnisse*, Vienna 1926
Popovici, Aurel: *Die Vereinigten Staaten von Gross-Oesterreich*, Leipzig 1906
Sokol, A. E.: *Die Seemacht Oesterreichs*, Vienna 1972
Sosnosky, Theodor: *Franz Ferdinand*, Munich 1929
Taylor, A. J. P.: *The Habsburg Monarchy*, London 1941
Trost, Ernst: *Das Blieb von Doppeladler*, Vienna 1966
Winder, Ludwig: *Der Thronfolger*, Zürich 1938
Würthle, Friedrich: *Die Spur führt nach Sarajevo*, Vienna 1975

Index

Index